# WHO STOLE THE NEWS?

WHY WE CAN'T
KEEP UP WITH
WHAT HAPPENS
IN THE WORLD
AND WHAT WE CAN
DO ABOUT IT

MORT ROSENBLUM

**John Wiley & Sons, Inc.**
New York • Chichester • Brisbane • Toronto • Singapore

For Jeannette and Grabowsky, on the *quai;*
For Goldsmith and the others, still up the road.

This text is printed on acid-free paper.

Copyright © 1993 by Mort Rosenblum
Published by John Wiley & Sons, Inc.

*Library of Congress Cataloging-in-Publication Data:*
Rosenblum, Mort.
    Who stole the news? : why we can't keep up with what
happens in the world and what we can do about it / by Mort Rosenblum.
      p.    cm.
    Includes index.
    ISBN 0-471-58522-X (acid-free paper)
    1. Foreign news—United States.   2. Associated Press.   I. Title.
PN4888.F69R62     1993
070.4'332—dc20                     93-15559

Printed in the United States of America

10  9  8  7  6  5  4  3  2  1

# CONTENTS

# PREFACE

This book is the result of talking for twenty-five years with nobody listening. At first, I thought it was me; I talked louder, then softer. Then I realized it was the company I keep. I'm a foreign correspondent. Being ignored never used to be a problem. We got paid to lead our glamorous lives and suffer our dengue fever in silence and send back our news from nowhere. When it mattered, we were there. In the meantime, our simple presence assuaged troubled consciences in the news business.

Now it is a problem. The world is going to hell out here, and still no one is listening. The more things go on this way, the greater the inevitable price.

This book began as an update of *Coups and Earthquakes,* an insider's spilling of the beans which I brought out in 1979. That was a "media book," as the marketers say, a blend of how-to and war stories to help readers make sense of how news is reported from abroad. But today there is too much more to say.

Fragments of the old book appear in this one, here and there. In part, my purpose is to offer a new and improved consumer's guide to following world news. Beyond that, this is meant as an international thriller about a crime which affects every one of us: Who stole the news?

To situate myself as a source, I am a special correspondent for The Associated Press, based in Paris. Except for time off to edit the *International Herald Tribune* and a year at the Council on Foreign Relations, I have worked for AP since 1965. This has given me a close look at the strengths and weaknesses of the news organization at the heart of it all. That is why AP figures prominently in this book.

I feel a certain duty to avoid biting a hand that has fed me for a quarter of a century. But that hand has kept me squarely fixed on the reporter's goal: to call things as I see them. I will be forgiven, I am sure, the odd toothmark.

I've tried to skirt generality, but "many," "most" and "some" are easily overlooked. In every category, exceptions make the rule. Where one organization is picked to make a point, it might have been another; no one is a specific target. This is to warn those tempted to read in more than I intended and to apologize to anyone who might feel tarred by too broad a brush.

My thanks go to countless colleagues and pals who helped me. Some are named, and some are cloaked in deep cover. I'm grateful to Lou Boccardi, president of AP, Bill Ahearn, executive editor, and Tom Kent, international editor, for keeping me challenged. To Charles Levine, Carole Hall and Carol Mann, for encouragement. To Bill Waller, for guidance. And to Jeannette, for everything.

M. R.

# Chapter 1

# Who Stole the News?

"Whenever you find hundreds of thousands of sane people trying to get out of a place and a little bunch of madmen struggling to get in," an old pro named H. R. Knickerbocker once cracked, "you know the latter are newspapermen."

That was when faraway news came home in dots and dashes. These days, flights to mayhem are packed solid. Knickerbocker's madmen are a multinational swarm of dual gender, which moves by mysterious radar to some stories and ignores others of greater moment. They are still the Press, but the term hardly applies anymore, not even to the newspaper people. Dispatches were once set in lead and pressed onto paper as though meant to last; now computers and cameras do it, offset and offhand. Correspondents in tight spots tape their car windows and roofs with a new message, clearer to assorted gunmen in the bushes: "TV."

In H. R.'s day, a bird was a pigeon. It carried only as much news as could fit into a tiny tin capsule. Today, a bird is a satellite which can show not only war as it happens but also the weathered grain of a correspondent's leather jacket. Yet, at the core, nothing has changed. People who need to know how the world is shaping their lives have two choices. They can depend on the government, in which case God help them. Or they must resort to Knickerbocker's madmen. This thought ought to terrify us all.

For all of its flash and promise, much of our coverage of news from beyond our borders is hardly better than it was in the days of Morse code. Television lets us watch the volcano erupt; it does not show the lava as it is overheating, while there is time to react. Newspapers, better equipped to probe deeply, too often scratch at the surface. Too many news executives believe that people want domestic, not foreign, news, as though there were any real difference between the two.

For years, the correspondents' rueful rule of thumb was that all anyone cared about was coups and earthquakes. Now even these don't necessarily qualify. Only major upheavals in prominent places need apply. "You can't even be Haiti," Cheryl Gould, senior producer of NBC's "Nightly News," remarked to me with a cheerless laugh. A Haitian dictator had fallen on a busy news day, and the coup was not important enough to make the cut. Days after the San Francisco earthquake of 1989 dominated the news, a tremor of similar proportions shattered Algiers. It was grist for those newspaper columns labeled "The World in Brief."

In 1979 I lamented in a book called *Coups and Earthquakes:* "Each person who reports foreign news is part of a process which is riddled with failings, beset by obstacles and tailored largely to wheedle attention from a public assumed to be apathetic and only mildly literate. This system is geared as much to amuse and divert as it is to inform, and it responds inadequately when suddenly called upon to explain something . . . complex and menacing."

This process, despite great strides forward, is still shot through with failings. The good news is that we reporters are now able to explain—and to show in full sound and fury—complex events as they happen. The bad news is that we seldom do it. Blame for this failure is shared all down the line, from purveyors to consumers, and everyone pays the price. Partly, the problem is simple inattention by people with a lot to do. But much of what goes wrong is the result of deliberate decisions; it is neither willful deceit nor conspiracy, yet it amounts to a theft of information that everyone badly needs.

By understanding how this process works, readers and viewers and listeners can make the best of it as it is. And they can stop it from going even more dreadfully wrong. This book is meant as a user's manual, a program to help you spot the players and follow the changing rules of the game. It can help you find the solid reporting and the background you need to keep up with the world. But more, it is a hard look at who is stealing the news.

Consider these basic paradoxes:

- Correspondents are better equipped now than they have ever been, steeped in background, driven to excel and supported by technology only dreamed about a decade ago. And yet few Americans are able to follow distant events which shape their lives. Most are shown generalities, simplicities and vast empty spaces, a parody of the real world beyond their borders.

- Many news executives believe that Americans do not really care about world news, that they block out news with no obvious impact on themselves. Their organizations scrimp on the space they devote to serious news, favoring impact over information and neglecting the subtle but vital undercurrents. They slash away at the corners, gambling that no one will notice. In doing this, they reinforce the ignorance they assume.

- The goal of news executives is to increase their ratings or circulations and to enhance their organizations' standing. If convinced that people wanted better coverage of the world, they would hurry to provide it. Surveys suggest that the demand is out there. If so, people had better speak up. This is easier than you think.

The danger here is obvious enough. Things go on abroad whether or not Americans pay attention. Foreigners started the last two world wars without us. They quietly eclipsed American industry to the point where the world's richest nation now has bread lines. Political brushfires escaped our notice, in Asia and Central America and the Middle East, until they raged out of control. In most cases, had Americans seen what was coming, they could have headed it off. Or at least ducked in time.

Long before American involvement in Vietnam grew into war, reporters warned that the ideologically committed and well-supplied guerrillas who had humiliated the French would do the same to us. Our allies were corrupt and disunited; it would be our war, not theirs. We lost, far more than militarily. And then, despite fresh warnings by some of the same reporters, we headed into yet another proxy war with Nicaragua. And so on. Japan did not awake one morning and torpedo the American auto industry. The Deutsche mark did not muscle aside the dollar overnight. We exported jobs in plain sight. The "economy," that domestic issue which dominated the 1992 presidential elections, went to hell overseas while we kept our eye on America.

Contrary to common wisdom, citizens can do a lot about events abroad. They can insist that their leaders shape policies that address the real world, keeping their economy competitive and their society humane. They can save millions of lives; eventually, perhaps, even their own. To do this, they need a complete and reliable running record of what is going on. And they are not getting it.

If anything, the nation's level of world awareness is dropping. Surveys show that two-thirds of Americans depend mainly on television for news, and more than a third read no newspaper at all. Whatever its value for immediacy and visual context, television can only cover part of reality. Relying on it alone is like trying to see the Mona Lisa at night with only the help of disco strobes.

During 1992, as World War II rekindled in Yugoslavia, as neo-Nazi zeal fired teenagers and as Charlemagne's dream of European unity began to take shape, NBC had only two "Nightly News" correspondents based on the continent of Europe, both in Moscow. It had no one in Japan. Around the world, CNN often beat the swarm when the madmen scrambled. But stories got priority based not on import but on whether they came with pictures. Crucial economic and political issues, hard to film, are not good TV. As Dan Rather of CBS put it, "You can't take a picture of an idea."

Newspapers have their own limitations. Most offer only pieces of the mosaic—generally on days when supermarket ads mean more pages—without an overall pattern to give them meaning. Nor do magazines fill in all the gaps.

These failings are often evident. On August 1, 1990, Saddam Hussein was to most Americans yet another faceless despot in a dishrag, at best a second-string news item. A day later, Iraq was big domestic news. When it was over, Walter Cronkite made a point: Had news executives used a fraction of the resources they spent on the war to report on what was about to cause it, war might have been averted. Hindsight taught us little. After America celebrated victory, the cameras moved on. Two years later, pilots were at the bombsights again, protecting Kuwait's unreconstructed autocratic sheikhs. At the beginning of 1993, Saddam still had his job, but George Bush did not.

Slow-moving trends, with a far more lasting impact on Americans' lives, can go all but unnoticed. Long before the Berlin Wall fell, people up close felt it tremble. Western Europe was ready, and North America was not. The irony is harrowing. At a time when jobs and buying power and even the climate depend on global decisions, when the world is changing shape violently and whole peoples are at risk, many news organizations are closing bureaus and slashing the budgets of correspondents who remain on watch. If the volcano blows, the theory goes, reporters can get there from home. That they will be unbriefed and probably untried and almost certainly too late does not seem to matter.

We are sometimes sabotaged by our own technology. When communications were precarious, correspondents told their editors what was news. With satellite phones, editors talk back. They see events unfold on screens above their desk and filter them through their own cultural prisms. Reality is distorted by assumption and accepted wisdom back home. It is also easier, now, to send back words and pictures. During crises, we run on at length, confusing as much as we inform. In the end, more is less.

With few correspondents who sit still long enough to hear the world turn, there is hardly anyone to set the agenda. Someone must decide what is important and what is only dramatic posturing which will disappear without a trace. If journalists don't do it, officials are happy to oblige. Before he retired as president of NBC News, Reuven Frank once grumbled, "News is whatever the goddamn government tells us it is." He ought to see it now.

America's world is shaped and defined in Washington. But governments lie; it is their nature. When leaders do not lie willfully to their people, they lie to themselves. Self-delusion runs so deep that even leaders lose sight of what is real. Images on television can reinforce misunderstanding. Satellites transmit messages direct from the Middle Ages. Nothing in a modern family's experience prepares it to be thrust into a Somali peasant's hut or a Serbian sniper's nest. But the vital context, wordy and complex, is the first to go.

Most editors, without their own agenda, follow Washington's. When Saddam was still a U.S. ally against Iran, Moammar Khadafy of Libya was monster of the month. Then, U.S. warplanes helped the French stop him from invading Chad, described as vital to

American interests. In August 1990, Libya dropped off the planet. While American troops hurried to protect Saudi Arabia, Khadafy's proxy rebels rolled unopposed into Chad. This was noted in a few paragraphs inside the *New York Times* and hardly anywhere else.

We journalists are seldom watchdogs. More often, we are hunting hounds, howling off after each fresh scent of meat. But unless someone draws the first blood, we mostly snap and snuffle. Administration officials have not missed this point. The press corps that brought you Watergate missed the Iran-*contra* scandal until a small Lebanese weekly broke the story and Attorney General Edwin Meese stepped forward to confirm it. But few details emerged. Ronald Reagan finished his term in glory, all major questions unanswered. Bush, who was either involved or badly out of touch, was elected as a shoo-in. In his final days, when new evidence surfaced in his own notes, Bush pardoned the main players. On the way out of the White House, his aides cleaned out the computers.

Before the 1988 election, Rather tried to pin Bush down on what he had known about the illegal arms sales. The candidate and vice president cried foul. The public objected. Washington reporters steered clear, and foreign correspondents went on to other things. When I asked Rather why his interview had created no resonance among his colleagues, he was pleased that anyone even remembered it. "Nothing puzzled me more at the time, and nothing puzzles me more to this day," he said.

Rather's account is chilling: "I intended to ask the question until we got an answer or established that we were not going to get an answer. I was not aware of how poised the Bush-Quayle campaign was to make such a big issue of this. They turned their phone banks loose on us before the interview was over. Hundreds of thousands of calls engulfed us, jammed our phone lines, everyone's phone lines. At least, I said to myself, other reporters will pick up on this story. The next day, nobody wanted to touch it. The politicians want you to be fearful and obedient, and that's what they got. It dropped like a stone."

A well-placed television friend told me that Rather had irked reporters at other networks by fixing ground rules for the interview and breaking them. Rather, rival reporters say, made a deal with Bush about what would be asked. He denies it. But how does this ground rules business even get to be an issue? We have sunk too deeply into the cushions of a modern Fourth Estate. When we first moved in, the roles were clearer: Politicians lied, and we caught them at it.

It goes beyond politics and the reporter. "Publish and be damned!" was once the industry's rallying cry. Now, often, it is "Don't offend." Stories are "lawyered" not only to avoid libel but also to ward off complaints from powerful people, interest groups or sensitive collectivities. Management seldom encourages editors to aim and fire at will; a loose cannon can puncture a tight ship. When prudence is demanded at the top, those below tend to err on the side of safety. The result can be a corporate cowardice that calls a spade a digging implement.

The system can work, but only when it is clear that enough people are interested. After the Gulf War ended, reporters still commanded an audience. The cameras moved on to southern Turkey, and people stayed tuned. Despite efforts in Washington to throw them off the scent, reporters revealed how Kurds who had risen against Saddam were left abandoned in snowbound mountain passes. To the shock of old hands who had tried for years to tell their story, the Kurds made headlines across the United States.

The United Nations was forced into unprecedented action, dropping a taboo on violating borders in favor of "humanitarian intervention." Turkey, fighting its own Kurdish insurgency, had to swallow its distaste and offer refuge. American troops scheduled to come home were diverted to help a people we had revved up and then tried to abandon. One of the world's more tragic human problems—a political time bomb in a pivotal place—seemed headed for sustained attention.

But then those big tents went up. The U.S. Cavalry had saved the day. It was time for something else. Forgotten again, the Kurds were caught between Iraq and a very hard place. The Turks yanked back the welcome mat. Bitter and frustrated, Kurdish zealots widened their war against Turkey, which was supposed to be the cornerstone of a restive region stretching all the way to China. Kurds would have to die, or kill, to get back on the air.

Within the flawed system, much of today's reporting is better than at any time in the past. Sensitive, solid pieces are dispatched at great risk from remote backwaters and marbled with context by editors at home. They come from familiar old capitals, from correspondents who might spend a month of nights worming into documents. They show up in newspapers and magazines, on television and on the radio. But you have to find them.

This is not so difficult. Simply look for what Vladimir Nabokov calls the shiver of truth. Some stories are compelling. These are what Arthur Lord of NBC describes as "Hey, Martha, take the meat loaf out of the oven and look at this." Others are less obvious, significant for their background on something which is bound to matter, sooner rather than later.

No one has time to watch every wrinkle on a map even Rand McNally can't keep straight. The trick is knowing what to look for, and where. To follow the world, you have to separate out substance from the razzle-dazzle of packaging. You should know who is reporting and how information makes its way to you. In sum, as with everything else, you've got to know the system.

Any news organization is a cottage industry made up of individuals with different cultural and political upbringings. Among the skilled and practiced correspondents, inept and sometimes even unprincipled contributors slip into the mix. There is no "media conspiracy"; inadvertent, inherent biases spoil any harmony. For these same reasons, there is no center line.

"Press" was a general enough term, but the word "media" is about as specific as "food." Each medium comes in varieties, and no single medium is enough. Television can place you in the thick of things. But the right word can be worth a thousand pictures. You need context and more than a few snatches of what people have to say, and yet a long printed dispatch can mislead more than it enlightens.

To understand world news, think about the individuals who bring it to you. Knickerbocker's madmen, even if they are women and work for television, are a colorful lot. Editors can be loonier still, gulping Maalox and turning fuchsia because their own correspondent missed something available from six other sources. And there are the editors' bosses, a mixed bag of real estate moguls, corporate clones and a few old hands who have risen through the ranks.

Also keep in mind that our news-gathering system is no public service. Forget the rhetoric: The news business sells a product that is blended and packaged, and the competition is cutthroat. When the product doesn't sell, its marketers tinker with the mix. Many news executives feel a special responsibility, but few can escape their quarterly reports. News from abroad is one ingredient, usually as optional as nuts in a Hershey bar.

This book's final purpose, then, is to show how readers and viewers can improve world coverage simply by demanding it. As cottage industries, news organizations are surprisingly easy to influence. A few sensible letters can convince most editors to experiment with the mix. Aroused consumers brought back Classic Coke. They ought to be able to keep us from ignorance in a perilous world.

The news business relies heavily on high technology, but there is nothing scientific about it. "Feel" is the oldest tool in journalism. Editors are guided by hunch, gut instinct and assumptions dating back to the Cave Bear.

"News," Corker explained to Boot in Evelyn Waugh's 1936 novel *Scoop,* "is what a chap who doesn't care much about anything wants to read." They were off to a war in Ishmaelia, foreign correspondents called up from jobs each knew was more important. Corker covered politics and scandal; Boot wrote "Lush Places," a column about ferny fens and crested grebes. That baseline has not varied anywhere, before or since.

News is the exceptional, something which threatens, benefits, outrages, enlightens, titillates or amuses. Preferably, it can carry a headline: "Madonna Joins Convent," "Killer Bees Eat Akron" or "Germany Invades Poland." But it also might be a slow pattern of details, like a deadly virus gradually spreading into a worldwide pandemic.

There is no shortage of news reports. Each day, we kill a buffalo to eat the tongue. An average newspaper's editors might sift through a million words of news daily, but they have room for only thousands. In television, hours of tape are edited into seconds. Decisions are not about what is fit to print, or broadcast. They are about what fits.

The closer news is to home, according to the baseline, the greater its import. A British press lord once tacked up a memo in his Fleet Street newsroom: "One Englishman is a story. Ten Frenchmen is a story. One hundred Germans is a story. And nothing ever happens in Chile." The old *Brooklyn Eagle* had it: "A dogfight in Brooklyn is bigger than a revolution in China." Editors might take note that neither the *Eagle* nor Fleet Street is still with us. But even those with a penchant for foreign news face an uphill fight. Where space is tight, news from far away loses on points. South Chicago conjures an image in American minds, and if a riot erupts, people know some of the reasons. Bosnia-Herzegovina is a lot of new syllables at the end of a hard day, and you could fill a fat book explaining why conflict there is so important.

This is a basic flaw in the system. If a story is important, it is complex. But if it gets too complicated, it invites the spike. A spike was once really a spike, a great nail on which discarded stories hung all night to weigh on the editor's conscience. Now it is an electronic delete key. One punch, and the story is off to Pluto. That was what happened to Bosnia-Herzegovina, until it was too late.

Logically, Sarajevo belonged on front pages from the first whiff of trouble. For centuries, the proud city-state sought to elude the empires it fell between, Ottomans and Austro-Hungarians. A Serb hothead shot an Austrian archduke there in 1914 and touched off World War I. With dry powder all over the Balkans, it would not take many sparks for history to repeat itself.

I went there for The Associated Press early in 1992 to see if sparks were coming. Clearly, they were. Bosnia-Herzegovina was a patchwork quilt in which the colors had run together, Croats, Serbs and Slavs from both ethnicities who had converted to Islam under the Turks. "If civil war starts here, it can't stop," explained one woman, a red-haired Muslim in a miniskirt. "We all live together. Mr. Bush does not have bombs smart enough to go along apartment corridors knocking on doors."

A deranged psychiatrist who was leading Bosnia's Serbs told me he would change all that, no matter what it took. At the time, no one had ever heard of Radovan Karadzic. His little office was cluttered with maps pocked by circles and arrows showing how he would purify Bosnia if only Serb leaders in Belgrade would help him out—and if outsiders did not meddle.

If trouble began, Muslim leaders warned me, Islamic states would weigh in, involving ancient peoples stretching from Turkey to Southeast Asia. The innocent would die in large numbers, and many more would lose everything they had built in life. Conflict would test the will of a newly linked Europe, a stronger United Nations and an America selling "a new world order."

Sarajevo, in short, was news.

When the killing started in April 1992, Bosnia-Herzegovina was still too many syllables. The Associated Press and Reuters were there, but as is often the case, they were mostly alone. Reporters and television crews came and went. When the siege grew intense, Sarajevo posed a dilemma. Yugoslav madness had killed thirty journalists in eight months, as many as had died in a decade in Central America. Was it worth a sniper bullet to report yet another world brief? Early in June, John Burns of the *New York Times* and Bob Rowley of the *Chicago Tribune* decided that it was. They loaded a trunkful of food and blustered past roadblocks. Then, careering down backstreets at 105 miles an hour, they drove into town and put Sarajevo on the front page.

"It was lunacy to go in then," said Rowley, an unlikely madman with a sparse mustache and a gentle manner, "but it was such a compelling human story it would have been greater lunacy not to. We had to go."

A hard core of reporters fought their way in. Television teams set up shop and stayed. By then, however, it was too late to do more than catalog the carnage. Hostility had deepened into irreconcilable hatred. The disturbed psychiatrist, as planned, was committing mass murder. And still Americans watched with half an eye. After thousands had died in months of siege, Bob Schieffer, a seasoned pro anchoring the CBS "Evening News," began, "In Bosnia, uh, Hairagovia . . ." Roone Arledge, ABC News president, insisted for weeks that anchors use a phrase to help viewers understand the besieged city's importance: "site of the 1984 Olympics."

By the time reports of death camps demanded attention in August, a million ethnically cleansed Bosnians were on the road, huddled in pitiful refugee camps or crowded into relatives' homes with their lives broken. Shelling was constant. Rape was systematic. The Bush administration pretended the events were too dangerous to meddle in but not as bad as they seemed and, in any case, nobody's fault. Only part of "the media" reflected reality, and not enough people noticed. A generation of Americans who had grown up with the promise "Never again" let it happen while they were watching. Or at least while they should have been watching.

Firm early action would have blunted the Serbs' advance. Shots across the bow of ships shelling Dubrovnik or a few blown bridges on the Drina River might have been enough. But after a year of slaughter, Americans were still debating with themselves and their allies. By then, the situation was so out of hand that hawks and doves had broadened their range to vultures and chickens. Anyone who did intervene could not revive the one hundred thousand dead, set right two million lives or temper the fresh hatreds that promised wider implications. The world's surviving superpower could only admit its impotence, swallow its shame and face history.

If World War III gets such short shrift, the outlook is bleak for German elections or Japanese fiscal policy, let alone trouble in South Ossetia or the Caprivi Strip. During the Sarajevo siege, millions quietly starved, unnoticed, in Somalia. When Somalia's turn finally came, the swarm descended. What little attention the system had to spare was poured into that story. In Sudan, Mozambique, Angola, Liberia and beyond, millions more starved, and their turn would not come at all.

Jeff Bartholet of *Newsweek*, one of the few reporters to keep after African misery, quoted a letter from a Christian missionary that had been smuggled out of Juba, in southern Sudan. "Lucky are the people in Yugoslavia and Somalia, for the world is with them," it said. "It may be a blessing to die or get killed in front of the camera because the world will know."

The reason for these discrepancies is "feel." Editors know when stories are important, but most are convinced that people simply don't care. That is, the prevailing belief is that Americans do not see the revelance to their own lives if entire populations suffer and die.

This need to define relevance is troubling to anyone prepared to think simply of news, without the qualifiers "domestic" and "foreign." During 1992, for example, the number of children who died worldwide for lack of simple attention—a little food, a measles shot—surpassed five million. Most were Africans. That is as if every four minutes, for an entire year, a school bus full of kids plunged over the north rim of the Grand Canyon. If that began to happen, in Arizona, someone would put up a railing. Why is Africa different?

Everyone knows the answer. Especially journalists. People have to see a connection to their own lives. Jack White, who spent four years in Africa for *Time* and was later the magazine's national editor, has gauged the apathy about anything that is not familiar. A cover on Yugoslavia in mid-1992, he noticed, was the worst-selling issue in a year. As an ABC senior producer for national affairs, he sees the same situation in television.

"People don't care about most foreign stuff," said White, who is black. His example was black Americans who were supposed to be interested in Africa. "When I came back, no one asked me anything. You start talking about Africa, and they change the subject. And they're naming their kids Jomo Kenyatta and all that."

Linda Mathews, White's ABC counterpart for foreign affairs, was hired from the *Los Angeles Times* for skills she had shown as a correspondent. She was happy to see Peter Jennings fight to ensure that "World News Tonight" covered world news. But, she said, if she handled only world news, she'd be underemployed. Fortunately, her colleagues regard as foreign anything west of the Rockies.

Jennings does his best with foreign coverage because he thinks a lot of people want it, and he knows they all need it. He spent twelve years reporting abroad, six of them in Beirut. "We're often told by people who pretend that they know something about television that Americans don't care about foreign news," he told me. "When I travel in downstate Illinois and see all those *Wall Street Journals* in farmers' mailboxes, I think about how much more connected to the modern world farmers in the Midwest are than the analysts of journalism or television." He offers more world news than his competitors, and his ratings are highest. Then again, Rather is close behind, with scant foreign coverage. And Jennings' warm-up act is Oprah Winfrey.

The trouble is that acting on feel carries a risk. Because competition for attention is so brutal, no editor can get ahead of the audience. If circulation or ratings don't keep up, the editor will be looking for another place to experiment. Temptation is strong to play it safe with the dubious-but-yet-to-be-disproved baseline: You're least likely to go wrong with a dogfight in Brooklyn.

In fact, editors have no reliable way to assess interest. Two years after the *Los Angeles Times* began its weekly "World Report" section, I asked Alvin Shuster, the foreign editor, what readers thought. He replied, "You know, the guy who massages my back . . ."

The masseur liked the section, as well he might. It ranged wide and moved in close, a mix of pieces edited by Dan Fisher, a fine correspondent who came in from the cold. Fisher knows his job is important, but he is an honest man. "Whoever is reading this section," he said, "it's not the young people. The young reader is an awfully real problem."

Newspaper readership is dipping as the video generation comes of age. In Los Angeles, you can watch it happen in any neighborhood. Once, delivery boys flipped papers onto every porch. Now trucks roll briskly down the street, and the old plop-plop-plop is a broken rhythm amid long spaces of silence.

The *Times'* media writer, David Shaw, analyzed what he said was a sharp decline in youthful interest all over the country. Surveys suggested that Americans between the ages of eighteen and thirty-three knew and cared less about public affairs than any generation in fifty years. "Most young people are not hostile toward newspapers, just apathetic toward them," he wrote. "Study after study has shown that they do not consider a daily paper either essential or relevant."

In 1985, the Times-Mirror Company hired Don Kellermann to apply what science he could to finding out how readers relate to their newspapers. From one of those lushly carpeted Washington suites, he takes a fresh look each week and charts the changes.

"If something does not directly affect their lives, people tune out, or at best they are indifferent," Kellermann said. "We are all flooded with too much information. People are intellectually and emotionally capable of absorbing only so much. They are not stupid. They are forced to make choices."

That point is made on the comics pages. In one Calvin and Hobbes strip, the spiky-haired little kid rails at his television set: "You call this NEWS?! THIS isn't informative! . . . This is a sound bite! This is entertainment! This is sensationalism!" In the last panel, he concludes: "Fortunately, that's all I have the patience for."

But something clearly is out of whack. Late in 1991, one of those Times-Mirror polls found that 92 percent of respondents agreed that "it is best for the future of our country to be active in world affairs." Americans realize that their family's well-being and their self-image as decent folk depend to some degree on events beyond their borders. That is, they are directly affected by world news.

Leo Bogart, a New York journalism professor, offers more evidence in the 1989 edition of his weighty *Press and Public.* Newspapers have shifted toward more soft local feature material, he says, but "most people turn to the newspaper primarily for news rather than entertainment." In his carefully researched survey, international news ranks second from the top in reader interest, only a shade behind hard news about the local community and above news of the President, Congress, and politics. Percentages of people who declared interest, by sex, by race and in every age group sampled, ranged between 60 and 70 percent.

The Gallup Organization asked people in 1990 to name the best thing about television. Thirty-four percent of respondents cited news from around the world. The next highest scores were tied at 7 percent: educational programs and entertainment value.

At the *Dallas Morning News*, editor and publisher Burl Osborne trusts his feel. A former Associated Press managing editor, he emphasizes serious foreign coverage because he knows it is important. His job, he argues, is to interest readers in distant events and show why they matter. The *News* has the fastest rising circulation in America; he must be doing something right.

A lot of editors agree that a steady diet of thoughtful dispatches from abroad, pegged to people, will create a heavy appetite for more. William German, executive editor of the *San Francisco Chronicle,* is a believer. "We're casting about with smoke and mirrors," he said of the industry at large. "If we stop giving them less, we wouldn't have these problems." But that is feel, and feel is mostly a lost luxury. Editors answer to executives who report to shareholders every three months. If the numbers are off, someone has to guess why. A hard eye is cast on the usual suspects. Foreign news, for instance.

A glance around the United States shows which view prevails. You can read some papers, even in large cities, for days and find only a few fragmented foreign stories. Network newscasts, from time to time, run a full twenty-one and a half minutes without mentioning a single foreign country. The CBS "Evening News" often mashes overseas stories into a segment of briefs illustrated by a turning globe. On one evening, the datelines were Chicago, Northern Maine and Outer Space.

Running for president, Pat Buchanan smirked when a reporter, a foreigner, asked him if the United States would still have a role in the world. "My friend, this campaign is not about the outside world," he replied. "It is about the U.S.A."

Accepting the Democratic nomination, Bill Clinton covered world affairs in 2 percent of his speech, a total of 141 words. George Bush, whose strength was that Americans thought he knew something about the world, did little more.

But there is the countercurrent. A. M. Rosenthal, Jr., a foreign correspondent before becoming the take-no-prisoners executive editor of the *New York Times,* recoiled at Buchanan's remark. He fumed in his column at "the insulting [pollsters'] line that Americans, who from the second decade of this century entered into the world with more responsibility, courage, generosity and understanding of national and personal interest than any people on earth, have suddenly become stupid and cowardly louts incapable of comprehending that their jobs, health and safety are tied to what happens in the rest of the world."

The point is not who is correctly reading the national mood. What matters is what we do next. Kellermann of Times-Mirror is right: People worry about making it through the night. If faraway events are important, it is often hard to see why. Schools do not whet curiosity about the world. News organizations have to kindle new interest and fan the flames. But too many are abdicating that responsibility in favor of a dubious and dangerous status quo.

Elie Wiesel, for one, is frightened at how little Americans learn about reality. Wiesel won a Nobel Peace Prize for showing how past and present are part of the future. He survived two death camps to see a different world take shape around him. During 1992, when others feared that Nazis might rise again in Germany, Wiesel worried about Bosnia and Somalia. The Holocaust, he knew, was not the excess of a fanatic party. It was a failing of the human condition, a collective memory lapse among people who should have known better.

When I asked him to characterize our flawed system of gathering news from abroad, his brow furrowed. He covered the full range, from economics to environment, and then came back to his main point. "We have failed to teach our children that man is not an animal."

The problem is not a lack of capacity. Dispatches from just about everywhere are tossed out for lack of perceived interest. Skilled correspondents hang around big bureaus shuffling through clippings, waiting for the call to get going. That undefined "audience" could broaden coverage simply by making itself heard. Until it does, however, let the consumer beware.

No one who wants an accurate reflection of the world can count on the headlines as an index to important events. No single source of information is enough. Certainly not television.

The advent of CNN has shaken the world. It is a vital briefing service, available around the clock. Nothing in print could match a live camera on Boris Yeltsin as he scrambled atop a Soviet tank to show that the dreaded Kremlin leaders had no more real power than the Wizard of Oz. But Yeltsin made nuclear policy off camera. Mostly, CNN is like the new radio I took to the Congo in 1967 when I went into the correspondent business. Each morning I'd switch it on. If I heard martial music, signaling a coup, I was up like a shot. If not, my world was safe until breakfast.

When Americans had the newspaper habit, there was room for everyone. Readers who cared could wallow in long gray columns about a worrisome war developing in Asia or reforms in the Soviet Empire. Others could skip to the school lunch menus. "If only 2 percent of our readers are interested in a story, we'll run it," a *New York Times* editor told me in 1975. A few editors still think that way, but they are headed for the tar pits of history. Television imposes a new imperative.

With broadcast news, a twinge of boredom can trigger the remote-control zapper. Ratings, i.e., survival, are at risk. Under television rules, the majority runs roughshod over any minority. Those citizens who want depth and subtleties about the world, however large a small slice they represent, are out of luck. The majority not only lacks interest in the world; it lacks interest in almost anything. During the 1992 Democratic Convention, the three main over-the-air networks had a combined share of 10 percent of all sets turned on at the time. The Fox network had 13 percent, with a film, *The Revenge of the Nerds, Part III*.

Faced with this situation, newspapers find it hard to press their comparative advantage. For some, the news hole has shrunk because advertising has wandered off in other directions. A few emulate television, distilling news into briefs and eating up space with graphics and splashy displays. *USA Today,* some reporters joke, is for people who find television too difficult.

As economic pressures grow, the best intentions are not enough. The *Fort Worth Star-Telegram,* looking for a national and foreign editor, hired James Peipert, a veteran AP correspondent. He pushes all the world items he can, but he knows the limits. Asked if he thought his readers got the world news they needed from his paper alone, Peipert squirmed a little, caught between loyalty and honesty. "A couple of years ago, I would have said unhesitatingly yes," he said. "Now I wonder."

At the *Atlanta Constitution,* editor Ron Martin believes that his readers want a thorough dose of world news, and in any case he is convinced they ought to have it. When the Soviet Union imploded, he sent a columnist, Colin Campbell, on a month of train rides. The copy, wry and incisive, ran for a week. Readers were brought close to that crucial story. But a pile of other foreign stories, crowded out, ended up on the floor.

If world news is an acquired taste, the optimists believe, exposure to it on CNN should increase the long-term demand. Martin's office is a block away from CNN Tower, and he likes his neighbor. "God bless CNN for being," he said. "They raise questions only we can answer."

But no one gets away from Nielsen. On his office wall, CNN's President, Tom Johnson, keeps what looks the dental chart of a tiger shark. When drama attracts the cameras, the audience shoots up. Then viewers switch off, bored with the Hollywood minutes, weather in the Solomons and garbanzo recipes that pad CNN's schedule.

As president of the AP, Louis D. Boccardi keeps track of who wants what sort of news. He finds that when dramatic television sharpens appetites, people turn to newspapers for the main course. "TV exposes more people to new places and thereby plants the seeds of some interest," he said. But he sees another side to it. "There is that unknowable number of people who having seen that ten-second clip from somewhere will feel that they know all they need to know about a place, and that's enough."

The madmen are out there. In fact, the raw numbers are up. Every so often, Professor Ralph Kliesch of Ohio University counts American correspondents abroad. This is an inexact science, but his figures are solid. In 1991, Kliesch reported good news. For the first time in twenty-one years, the total had risen.

Just after World War II, someone else's study estimated that twenty-five hundred full-time American reporters were working abroad for newspapers, magazines and radio. No TV. An Ohio University census, in 1969, found 929 full-time people working for U.S. news organizations abroad, including broadcast reporters. Three years later, the number dropped to 797. By 1975, there were only 676. Kliesch waited until 1990 to count again. He came up with 1,734. Of the total, 820 were Americans. In 1993, the total neared 2,000.

But Kliesch's numbers don't say much about working habits. At any particular time, as radar directs the swarm, many of those people are in the same place. For the first round of Middle East peace talks in 1991, five thousand journalists from around the world gathered in Madrid. Few got closer to the action than the television screens on which they could have watched proceedings at home.

Also, the census counted television producers, editors and camera crews based in large bureaus, a new phenomenon. When a network descends on a story, a single unit might account for 5 of the 1,734.

Strange imbalances emerge. The *Baltimore Sun,* financially hard-pressed in a restricted market, keeps a large foreign staff abroad. The prosperous Gannett chain, with eighty-two local papers, *USA Today* and broadcast outlets, has no overseas bureaus at all.

Nonetheless, the census reflects some hopeful trends. In 1975, correspondents were based in only fifty-seven countries. In 1990, eighty countries had at least one full-time journalist reporting to the United States; fifty-eight were covered by Americans. Even though a lot of these reporters are rarely home, this wider spread means that at least someone is watching the back corners of Eastern Europe, Latin America and Asia.

Smaller big papers, of the Detroit and Dallas size, are basing more reporters abroad. The *Chicago Tribune* has thirteen correspondents in eleven overseas bureaus, as many as the *Washington Post* had in 1978. The *Post* has gone over twenty. In the past decade, the *Los Angeles Times* has doubled its foreign staff to about thirty, the same as the *New York Times.*

All of these papers syndicate their reporters' dispatches, relaying them electronically to hundreds of newsrooms around the country. A glance at the small type under the bylines shows the range. The *Austin Statesman-American* has no foreign staff, but its readers may see stories from dozens of newspapers. One of seventeen Cox newspapers, it has access to the chain's seven foreign correspondents. But it also has the supplemental services of almost every major paper in the country. Nearly six hundred American papers receive *New York Times* dispatches, and six hundred papers, some of them the same ones, take the combined *Washington Post–Los Angeles Times* wire. The Knight-Ridder–*Chicago Tribune* service distributes stories from up to fifty correspondents to three hundred newspapers. Scripps-Howard, which is growing fast, goes to four hundred subscribers. There are others.

The newsmagazines also keep strong staffs abroad. Despite sweeping layoffs in 1991, *Time* started 1993 with thirty-eight reporters in twenty overseas bureaus. *Newsweek* had twenty-one in sixteen bureaus, with another two Miami reporters who were watching Latin America, as big a staff as it had ever fielded. *U.S. News & World*

*Report* had more than a dozen, with regular contributions from stringers.

If all three major American television networks each have cut back mostly to large hub bureaus and somewhere over a dozen far-flung fire-engine chasers, CNN is expanding quickly. By 1993, it had new bureaus dotted across Southeast Asia and in Latin America as well as in major world capitals.

Radio, badly hit by corporate cutbacks, is thin on the ground. But networks use regular stringers and print correspondents who fill in the blanks. National Public Radio has only half a dozen staff correspondents abroad on a tight budget, but with energy and flair they manage to cover a lot of ground.

Everyone's basic coverage is by the AP, the supermarket of news since Mark Kellogg cabled his last dispatch: "I go with Custer and will be at the death." Reporters in AP's eighty-eight bureaus overseas funnel news onto wires which reach nearly 10,000 newspapers and broadcasters around the world, including the 1,655 American papers which own it as a cooperative.

In an earlier time, humpbacked Model 15 printers spewed snakes of paper at the elbow of every editor. The steady clack, at sixty words a minute, was every newsroom's Muzak. Periodic alarm bells cut short conversations, and editors waited for what followed the terse slug, "BULLETIN." Then they dashed off cables to their correspondents, each beginning, "AP says . . ." and ending, ". . . proceed soonest." News now arrives by computer, and editors see only brief index lines unless they call up a particular story on a screen. Little else has changed.

The AP's foreign staff has a basic core of about a hundred New York–based reporters, nearly half women and mostly American, assigned to foreign bureaus. Each has paid dues in a domestic bureau and on the International Desk in New York, where stories are edited. Hundreds more are "locals"—nationals of countries they cover, Americans working cheaply or just about anything else. And there are "stringers," people with other jobs who cover for the AP from remote places or help bureaus during emergencies.

Although the AP prefers to assign correspondents via normal channels, through New York, its best people sometimes come up the other way. CNN's Peter Arnett started as an AP local hire, a New Zealander working in Southeast Asia, until he won a pair of Pulitzers in Vietnam. The bureau chief and news editor in New Delhi are Americans, but the depth of coverage comes also from Indians who know their society better than any foreigner could.

Twice a day, for morning and afternoon newspapers, the AP assembles a digest which highlights a dozen or so stories, either big news or features. Unless the world is in flames, all but two or three of these carry American datelines. On a typical twelve-hour cycle, the main A-Wire offers about sixty foreign-dated dispatches, totaling perhaps twenty-five thousand words. This represents about a third of the wordage supplied by bureaus. The rest goes only to overseas subscribers, or into the garbage can.

Until the 1990s, the AP had a major American rival. United Press International emerged in 1958 with the combined forces of the United Press and the International News Service. Scripps-Howard Newspapers owned it, making up an operating deficit that grew by the year. Like Avis battling Hertz, UPI people liked the image of trying harder. With fewer reporters on tighter expense accounts, UPI went after the AP in every arena. Occasionally, it scored knockouts. As a result, sizable newspapers had to take both agencies. UPI's preserve was small papers and radio stations which needed international news at rates lower than the AP's.

But underdog status was no advantage in a branch of journalism where depth and breadth of coverage outweigh performance on any single story. When a new breed of accountants sought out fat, they found duplicated news services. Editors who wanted an alternative could not justify the expense. This cut into UPI's operating capital, forcing it to close bureaus. Finally, UPI could no longer offer full service for subscribers trying to do without the AP. It seemed to be only a matter of time.

The Gulf War was perhaps UPI's last hurrah, a noble performance led by Leon Daniel, who was writing his agency to glory before most people had heard of Vietnam. Consummate wire animals, UPI reporters pounded away as though they were building on a reputation meant to last for centuries. But none of them dared to use a personal credit card. Tom Ferraro went to war with a $20.95 gas mask and a $200 advance.

In 1986, a Mexican publisher paid $41 million to acquire UPI in bankruptcy. The agency was sold again and then, once again, hung on a thread. While UPI was on the block, various people poked at it. When the television evangelist Pat Robertson made an offer, some professionals cringed. Bill Kovach, curator of Harvard University's Nieman Foundation and a former editor, put it: "The free press that motivated, enervated and energized our country is in real jeopardy. Everything's for sale."

Finally, UPI was bought for $3.95 million by the Middle Eastern Broadcast Center, a Saudi-owned Arabic-language cable network based in Britain. In 1993, its skeleton crew of reporters abroad was still trying to try harder, and sometimes it beat the competition. As in the good old days, it still pumped out the WIBs, "world in brief" shorts for the broadcast wire, which had become its mainstay. Mostly, UPI had slipped to the margins.

Reuters, meantime, has grown in the United States from a novelty also-ran agency to an important component of some serious newspapers. The British news agency, like the AP a cooperative at home, has been a stalwart of world coverage for more than a century. By 1993, its total of American subscribers was in the hundreds, counting broadcasters, and it had eighteen U.S. bureaus.

In a world that moves too quickly for diplomats and spies, these are important organizations. What they choose to report amounts to the virtual reality of a powerful nation. What they ignore, however, is often the real reality. By swarming to events, we correspondents miss the developments which are the basic factors of change. We were there when the Iron Curtain cracked, but few of us noticed how quickly it was rusting away. With each new crisis, we see a disturbing sameness to the pattern. After breakfast, a Margaret Tutwiler spends a few minutes learning how to pronounce some unfamiliar name. Moments after the State Department's noon briefing, we have a new monster of the month. Somalia is a story when the administration decides to make it one. Sudan is never a story.

We rush to keep up but always seem to be behind the curve. We criticized the Bush administration for denying us a look at the Panama invasion in 1990. But not enough of us went back to see the country in a mess, with the drug business booming, to hold U.S. officials responsible for the unpaid bills they had left behind. It should have been no surprise that Bush was booed off the stage on a visit in mid-1992. Washington never bothered to find out how many hundreds, or thousands, of civilians had been killed, let alone who had been compensated for the wreckage of Operation Just Cause.

Amid all the hand-wringing after the Gulf War, a sharp focus came from Robert Fisk in the London *Independent.* "Fiskie," as colleagues know him, delights as much in breaking icons as in breaking stories. Fearless, he is good at both. He never moved from Beirut, even after Muslim extremists kidnapped his friend, Terry Anderson.

Fisk believes that television has changed all the rules, forcing on print reporters the responsibility to take reality back from governments. "The need for pictures means that television will always submit to the demands of government," he wrote. That was why television executives accepted the pool system of coverage. The eventual outcome, he said, is a news-gathering system driven by programmers who sink to the lowest common denominator. By staying safely within the bounds of what they think people want, these gatekeepers do not let people see why they ought to want something more. This cycle leads to growing collective ignorance.

As a result of the system, most Americans misunderstood their government's purpose in the Gulf. They overestimated the military threat and missed the political undercurrents. On the battlefield, they read triumph as victory. In a broader sense, they read defeat as triumph. No one won or lost the Gulf War. Instead, the upheaval shaped a different reality. The winners would be those who could respond to it.

Fisk concluded his analysis: "The American journalist John Hersey—the reporter who first wrote of the horrors of Hiroshima—commented: 'Tube reporting of the Gulf war gave us a war of flags, yellow ribbons, parades, and great pride in our power. I'm not sure, however, that we were ever given the deep look into the real texture and meaning of the storm in the desert.' Newspapers ignore such warnings at their peril. So do foreign correspondents."

And so do the readers and viewers and listeners, the citizens who ultimately must pay the price.

Chapter 2

# West Malaria Revisited

To understand how correspondents operate, it is best to watch them in action. Some report the news faithfully. Some steal it. In *Coups and Earthquakes,* I concocted a rebellion in West Malaria, a shameless pilferage of Waugh's *Scoop,* to show the process reduced to absurdity. This time, there is no need for imagination. Somalia in 1992 was as absurd as real life ever gets. With a backdrop of famine and war, it was hardly funny. Yet many Somalis and those who came to chronicle their nightmare found graveyard humor preferable to any of the alternatives.

Except for the main character, this account is real.


Bertrand Bushjacket, flying from Nairobi to Mogadishu on the U.N. Children's Fund shuttle, expected what correspondents call a jug fuck. That is a gang bang, only not so mannerly: too many reporters on one story. Editors had overlooked Somalia for months, but the U.N. secretary general suddenly made it a story in July. He accused the West of ignoring African calamity in favor of "a rich man's war" in Bosnia. George Bush, facing election, sent fourteen Air Force transports to Kenya to do something, anything. The swarm would be there *en masse,* howling for information, phone lines and beds.

It was big news, by any measure. Rival clan leaders of Somalia's largest tribe had united against the president, a durable despot from a minority tribe who ruled by exploiting ethnic rivalries. They won a vicious war, murdering whole villages and plundering farms. In 1991, outsiders could have brokered peace, had anyone cared. Without the Cold War, Somalia was no longer "strategically located." Not enough kids had begun to die in any one place to attract the cameras. Left to themselves, the warlords fought one another, all but leveling Mogadishu and devastating a country crippled by drought. By August 1992, four million people were starving. A story.

But Bertrand found few colleagues in town, except for the Germans. It seems that two new private German channels, both rich, were scrambling for ratings. One splashed Somalia, and the other followed. The two state-owned networks were not to be left behind. Altogether, two dozen Teutonic TV types made up half the press corps in Mogadishu. There were also crews from France, Japan and Iceland. The Americans were in Mombasa, Kenya, filming U.S. air crews waiting for orders to fly. Few big papers were around, but there was a guy from the Japanese edition of *Playboy*.

Bertrand met a reporter, an old Africa hand, who explained the dearth of newspaper people. "Look, the good hacks who are interested in this story have been writing it since April, when no one cared," he said. "Now that it's a big deal, editors want them to do it all again, and they figure they've done it. And some are scared shitless of this place and only come in for the day. The Brits were all here last week, but they've gone. Now it's Germans. Jesus, who knows what's next?" It was easy enough to see who had already been in. The young thugs' weapons were plastered in decals with TV logos.

As usual, the agencies were there, the AP and Reuters, each with its logo on a huge flag over the fender of a rented jeep. A few magazine people worked quietly at the edges. There was also the usual ragtag cluster of freelancers, mainly photographers, hoping to sell something to pay their way home.

It was a classic paradox. The story was that millions were starving needlessly and, because outsiders were doing the wrong thing, many of them would die. Words were needed to explain this complex process. But busy people half a world away would not sit still for the words unless there were also pictures. And only the best snappers looked for pictures that helped explain the process. Most figured that the story, once noticed, could only tug heartstrings for so long. They had to move fast.

"Yo, Bushjacket, you wanna get some stick action?" one photographer asked. Bertrand looked blank. "You know, skinny kids. A refugee center. I need to make some pictures, and it's safer to have someone else along."

Even reduced, the press corps was enough to choke the place. Mogadishu's hotels were roofless relics of better times. The city had no electricity or water, and marauding gangs picked clean any foreigner bereft of firepower. Instead, there was UNICEF. The U.N. Children's Fund had taken on the job of baby-sitting the press, and its guest villa was crammed with cots and bedrolls. The International Red Cross and other voluntary agencies also housed journalists, who ate up their supplies, stole their vehicles and griped about the service.

At UNICEF, Bertrand found an English logistics officer who was rapidly losing his mind. "I thought I'd come here for a while, but I only have thirty dollars," a Danish freeloader was telling him. "What can you suggest?" He suggested CARE's grain warehouse. The Englishman was on his way out of town. A Somali worker he had fired came back with a Kalashnikov and stitched lead across the wall just above his head. He got the message. Before leaving, however, he found Bertrand a room.

At the guest compound, a friendly U.N. driver announced, "You must get Somalia press paper, quick."

"Why?" Bertrand asked. "There's no government."

"Because they shoot you without."

"Oh," Bertrand replied, climbing back into the van for a ride to the United Somali Congress headquarters.

The Ministry of Information was a single table, unencumbered by so much as a paper clip, in a tiny, bare room. Behind it, an old man in a knitted wool cap extracted a sheet of paper from a drawer and said, "Fill this." The application form asked only for name and organization.

"Do you need a letter? A press card? Pictures? Passport photocopy?" Bertrand asked. No novice, he had them all.

"Ten dollars," the man said. It was a bargain. Until that morning, credentials had cost fifteen dollars for each day in Somalia. That approached looting, reporters pointed out, and United Somali Congress officials were worried about their image.

With elaborate calligraphy, the old man wrote out a receipt, and he breathed on a dry rubber stamp to sanctify it. Pocketing the bill, he bowed slightly. "Welcome to Somalia," he said.

Next Bertrand looked for a "fill." Beside the expense account, no correspondents' institution is more hallowed than the fill, a briefing from colleagues who got in first. It is a time-saver, a fast way to find out which sources can be trusted, which roads lead to what stories and how to find a satellite phone. In places like Somalia, it is also a lifesaver. Avoiding fatal encounters is best not left to trial and error. Unfortunately, no one had much to suggest.

With limited experience in hiring teenage killers, Bertrand settled for a Toyota pickup driven by a young madman in a pink shirt, goggle sunglasses and a Rocky the Flying Squirrel helmet. The shotgun rider was his thirteen-year-old brother, Mahat. At Mogadishu Port, a free-fire zone, Mahat seemed professional enough, although his Czech submachine gun weighed more than he did. But, as the Toyota sped away, he announced that he had forgotten his shoes. Mahat's preferred means of communication was a high-pitched giggle, and his brother's English vocabulary was limited to "hundred dollar."

Next Bertrand found Ali, a mild-mannered father of three in a Jeep Cherokee that looked suspiciously as if it had been looted when the American embassy was evacuated in panic. His guards were lackadaisical and somewhat undersized. But when Bertrand and his photographer friend, Rocco, disagreed on how to spell diarrhea, Ali cut in to correct them both. His numerous skills did not include how also to prevent it, but war is hell.

Like aid workers, reporters depended heavily on their hired wheels, known as "technicals." They ranged from battered little Japanese sedans to monster all-terrain trucks bristling with gun barrels, a cross between Mad Max and *Mad* magazine. Guards were also known as technicals. When journalists filled the seats, the technicals clung to the top.

"We nearly lost a tech last week," an American reporter remarked, with a rueful chuckle. "The driver thought the goons up ahead were going to open up a roadblock, and he didn't slow down. They didn't open it. He slammed on the brakes, and this poor guy came flying over the hood. He dusted himself off, picked up his AK and climbed back on."

Rocco the photographer found that his overenthusiastic techs came in handy. He went into the desert to find nomad camel herders, who are seldom fond of camera lenses. The driver roared up to one group of nomads, and his technicals piled out with their guns leveled. Everyone lined up for the picture. Or else.

Between road trips and cadging the occasional plane ride, Bertrand got a close look at calamity. People near death are distressingly easy to talk to. They are too numb to question motives and too weak to resist. Overpowering human stories write themselves; the reporter only has to stand back out of the way. The problem was finding a way to get dispatches back to the desk.

No matter what reporters know, or what lengths they have gone to in order to find it out, without communications they might as well be home. Normal channels were out of the question, so Bertrand studied his options. Television crews with satellite telephones seldom share them. One news agency had a sat phone, at twenty-eight dollars a minute, but it wasn't working. Médecins sans Frontières, the French doctors, ran their phone for only six hours a day to save generator fuel. In the afternoons, they needed it. In the mornings, the people who gave permission were asleep.

That left, yet again, UNICEF. By waiting in line, charming the operator, paying fifteen dollars a minute and praying for no sunspots, Bertrand sent faxes to his paper. Once, he wrote an important, urgent dispatch and found that the UNICEF phone was down. By calling in favors, releasing his last bottle of scotch and pleading, he turned up another U.N. phone. Hours later, he was able to call his editor to see if the fax had arrived.

"No, it's not here, and we need it immediately," the editor said. "Can you dictate it?"

"Look, I'm lucky to get sixty seconds on this line. Are you sure it's lost?"

"Yes. We need it fast."

Bertrand waited four more hours for the phone to clear. He passed up a trip to the port and a handful of interviews. Finally, after watching his story roll through the machine and into the vapors, he called his editor to verify receipt.

"Oh yeah, we found that just after you hung up," the editor said, miffed that he was being disturbed on deadline. "The copyboy had put it on Henry's desk."

The phone shortage worked both ways. Bertrand had trouble filing, but his editors could not load him up with suggestions. The last one, relayed in Nairobi, was an assignment he decided to ignore. "I want you to identify one bag of food and follow it, step-by-step, until it gets to where it's supposed to go," the editor said. You mean, Bertrand thought, until some dickheads machine-gun everyone within thirty feet of it.

One night, Bertrand returned to find P. T. Barnum's circus encamped in the UNICEF villa. A CBS television crew had arrived with 2.65 metric tons of equipment, a load that cost fifty thousand dollars in overweight, one way. It was a joint shared-cost expedition with a private German network, RTL Plus. Mosquito net tents and silver crates occupied all but a few square feet of the spacious livingroom.

This was a mixed blessing. CBS had a satellite phone on which Bertrand could call his girlfriend. The cameraman was a kindly Brit he had met in Saudi Arabia who could get his touchy printer to work. But they would broadcast live to New York, running their clamorous generator until 4 A.M. Worse, they would pursue stories with the single-minded vigor of Labrador retrievers after a wounded duck. Within days, their antics would get to be the baseline for Somalis' idea of foreign journalists.

The CBS correspondent, a strapping blond doctor with a bone-breaking handshake, cruised Mogadishu's mean streets on his roller blades. Someone in the group, the word went around, was wearing a T-shirt emblazoned with a naked woman, unsettling the Muslim inhabitants. At first, relief workers rejoiced that live broadcasts might focus some needed attention on two million Somalis about to starve to death. But the mood shifted quickly. At Baidoa, a desperate crossroads town in the worst-hit region, the crews tumbled unannounced into a crowded hospital, jostling patients with tripods. In one ward, they tried to heighten the drama by placing on a table a bucket of amputated limbs. Then they asked a nurse to disconnect a patient's intravenous drip and reenact his arrival at the emergency ward.

As they worked among hungry patients, crews passed around cookies among themselves. A correspondent sipped a Slim-Fast milk shake. Later, an American doctor shook his head in disbelief. "It was amazing to watch people's faces when this truck rolled up, and all these guys started unloading millions of dollars worth of fancy equipment," he told Bertrand later. "You could just see them thinking, 'Finally, after all this suffering, we are saved.' Then they watched the same guys load up every bit of stuff and drive away. They just kept watching, like they couldn't believe it."

Later, when reporters checked eyewitness accounts with the CBS crew, the producer denied any excesses. The correspondent blamed them on the Germans. It didn't matter; everybody paid. And they would keep on paying. Long afterward, I tracked down others who had been at the hospital to doublecheck Bertrand's details. An American medic, reached by phone in Maryland, told me, "I've been misquoted and jerked around by reporters so many times I don't talk to anyone." I explained my purpose. "You're still a reporter, aren't you?" he insisted. Begrudgingly, he confirmed some facts before abruptly hanging up. He had said, "They talk to me for an hour and then take one sentence that makes me look like an asshole." He took care of that himself, but I got his point. A nurse, more helpful, said the crew had focused only on American aid workers, ignoring Somali doctors who were risking their lives, at no pay, to help their own people. Before the crew left, someone handed out a toy: a Sesame Street Cookie Monster, the furry beast who demands insistently that someone feed him dessert.

American television reports, if melodramatic, stuck roughly to the facts. One German correspondent, however, decided that reality was not enough. In the town of Hoddur, north of Baidoa, tribal elders had acted quickly to ward off famine. Their region was spared the worst of clan warfare. A police force kept order, and feeding centers saved lives. Nonetheless, the correspondent announced into the camera, "Here is hell." Tanks are in the streets, he said, showing hulks from some forgotten battle. He found men gathering sand and said they were digging graves.

There was the other extreme. As Bertrand pored over maps to figure out how to travel twelve hours over the desert in bandit country with no gas, his editor messaged that CNN had produced moving footage from the very spot he was trying to reach. A Canadian reporter took off one morning and reappeared five days later with hair-raising tales from remote corners no one in his right mind would have gone to alone.

Night after night, BBC took the story further, broadcasting reports from news agencies and its own correspondents. Bertrand felt a twinge he recognized. He was there and almost everyone else was not; he had better start coming up with some decent copy. As the AP's George Esper once taped to his typewriter in Saigon, "You're only as good as your last biggie." Bertrand set out to learn something.

The best sources, reasonably enough, are the people who make news. But they tend to be the hardest to reach. If they don't avoid reporters as a dangerous nuisance, they are likely to be overwhelmed with requests for their time. In Somalia, the guys to see were the two enemy warlords who had torn the place apart.

The leader in North Mogadishu, a glad-handing hotelier who called himself president of Somalia, was easy to see. You only had to get there. That involved telling UNICEF well in advance that you wanted to cross the Green Line. A radio operator asked various militia chieftains to try not to shoot you in the neutral zone. One vehicle took you to the last roadblock. You sprinted across to the first checkpoint on the other side, where another vehicle was waiting. The problem was usually the vice versa, coming back. Someone always forgot to send a vehicle, or not to shoot.

Occasionally, you could find a South Mogadishu driver crazy enough to cross the Green Line. One Japanese reporter brought his own "technical" from the south. His teenage killer bodyguard dozed off, and someone grabbed his gun. The reporter lost his whole army, along with his cameras, passport, money and the pens in his shirt pocket. It could have been worse.

Bertrand and some friends eventually reached the president. His white-washed office, hung with tapestries and a great seal, looked like a standard-issue seat of power. Ending some long pronouncement, he concluded, "and I can assure you that I am in complete control of . . ." A deafening KA-WHOOM punctuated his sentence as the room disappeared in a fog of shattered plaster. The president, Bertrand and everyone else dove for cover under the furniture as chunks dropped from the ceiling. In a corner, an aide rasped, "Don't worry. It's outgoing." Right.

Beyond comic drama, not much came out of the interview. The president approved of U.N. peacekeeping troops and reasonable dialogue, which meant few Somalis took him seriously. If the interview was good color, the world learned little from it.

In the south, the leader was better value, journalism-wise. He was a balding general with a demonic stare, full of dire warnings that the United Nations had better not endanger Somali sovereignty by trying to save lives. But he was preoccupied with stamping out diehard followers of the deposed president and a cast of rival clansmen who envied his power. He dug in near Bardera, far beyond Baidoa. To get there, Bertrand would have had to go back to Kenya and hitch an uncertain ride on a relief flight.

Normally, the alternative is lower ranking officials with time to spare. They tend to know more about day-to-day business than their bosses, and many will reveal sensational stuff off the record. Once these officials trust a reporter, they become the time-honored "usually reliable sources" who can confirm stories or set the reporter on the trail to something significant.

Somalia, however, offered few such reliable sources. Neither leader placed much trust in his lieutenants, and both lived somewhat removed from reality. The self-declared national government in North Mogadishu had a minister of tourism. Bertrand made the rounds of Somali contacts, but he resisted attributing anything to "off-the-wall sources, prone to lying, who have no clue about what their general is really thinking."

Normal places offered up the good old standby "Western diplomats," meaning U.S. embassy officers. But the last of those had scrambled into a helicopter eighteen months earlier. The only diplomat in town was an excitable Egyptian. That left foreign relief workers and, of course, the United Nations. These were good enough as sources, since the main story was what was being done to get food past looters to victims.

The facts were plain. With minimal security, the port could handle three thousand tons of food daily, which could be sent by armed convoys to feeding centers in the worst hit areas. Both warlords agreed to allow five hundred Pakistanis to patrol the port, and U.S. transports were waiting to fly them to Mogadishu. But U.N. bureaucracy delayed the deployment for nearly two months. Once they got there, they managed to protect only the airport. Meantime, Washington focused on its airlift, which would take weeks to deliver three thousand tons—and then only to a few airstrips far from many of the most desperate settlements.

After a few days, Bertrand found himself in a familiar bind. To write a story, he needed to identify his sources. But no one wanted to criticize. Voluntary agencies risked their supply of U.S.-donated food. U.N. officials risked their jobs.

People expecting to be quoted by name said things like "Every contribution is valuable" and "Yes, we are late, but now we are here and must look ahead and do everything we can." When assured of anonymity, they translated that into plain English: "The American airlift is a gigantic waste; Bush is running for president" and "If the Americans or Europeans or U.N. headquarters had paid any attention at all to Somalia, this whole thing could have been avoided."

Public relations won out over journalism. For two weeks, the airlift shuttled food to northern Kenya, easily reached by paved road. Deliveries into Somalia began with a thirty-five-ton load to the secure and relatively well-off town of Belet Wein. In fact, U.S. Air Force C-130s simply substituted for chartered C-130s that had been shuttling in, paid for by the International Red Cross; no new food was added. But three dozen journalists were on the first flights, one for every ton of food.

After a week, the airlift flew fifty tons to Baidoa, no more than five trucks could carry on the three-hour run up a blacktop highway. Unnoticed by anyone but German television, the German Air Force did better with fewer aircraft, half the size of C-130s, because pilots were not afraid to get their wheels dirty on remote strips where aid was most needed. Nonetheless, a *New York Times* editorial praised the U.S. operation and depicted Bush as the savior of Somalia.

Bertrand was hardly surprised. An American aid worker once cracked in Bangladesh, "There's as much ego and greed involved in trying to save the world as there is in owning Trump Towers." That applies to governments, voluntary agencies and individuals. But there is no lack of genuine sacrifice by people who want no reward at all. If reporters need not assess motives, they ought to expose flimflam so donations end up in the right place. Too often, the best press goes to people with press offices.

Bertrand mentioned the supply lines to a television guy, a thoughtful stringer hired to help steer the talent up African creeks. It was too bad, he lamented, that reporters could not correct the misconceptions. The TV guy shook his head. "Yeah," he said. "That's a print story."

Bertrand's best source was the Algerian diplomat sent as special envoy of the U.N. secretary general. He explained, on the record, how foot-dragging, lack of courage, poor information and botched negotiation had created a crisis where one need not have existed. He spoke bluntly in hopes of shaking the United Nations out of its torpor and provoking action. It worked; he was fired.

As time went on, more reporters showed up. They began reaching villages lost in the desert, finding pockets of victims whose life slowly ebbed as they waited for the relief effort to find them. Miraculously, no newspeople were lost. In fact, it was hard to miss the

irony. The U.S. military, which had required reporters in Saudi Arabia to show them pushups and a long-distance run to prove they
had the right stuff, stayed clear of the merest whiff of danger. Sec-
tors of Somalia in dire need were off limits because someone might
take a potshot at a giant transport. Correspondents did fine, including one pair working on a segment for "60 Minutes." One was eight
months pregnant. The other was confined to a wheelchair.

Late one night, deep into a bottle of someone's bribery scotch,
Bertrand and his pals ran out of gossip, war stories and sexual lies.
A light wind ruffled the frangipani, picking up a heady scent. A
sturdy green gate kept the random crazies at bay. Everyone was
remembering why he or she had gone into reporting, and the conversation shifted to a loftier plane.

"With all the nonsense that goes on, how do people make sense
out of any of this?" asked a British news agency person. "I mean,
my stuff is pretty good, but yours?"

"Just think of trying to follow this only by television," Bertrand
replied. "It took TV to get Ethiopia into the papers in '84. People got
worked up, and something was done. This time, no one is singing
'We Are the World,' and the Somalis are screwed."

Together, they traced why the story had taken eight months
to break. Until December, no one went near a savagely dangerous
story in a remote place. Then Jane Perlez, Nairobi correspondent of
the *New York Times,* flew in with the Red Cross. She stayed only a
few hours but got the first dateline. Stung, Keith Richburg of the
*Washington Post* went in for a day, crossing the Green Line to interview both warlords. A Reuters reporter set up the trip, so the AP
was not invited. An AP man went later.

For months, news agency bureau chiefs decided that since Somalia was getting so little play, it was not worth risking anyone's
life. One, asked by his desk if he wanted to go, messaged: "I
wouldn't send my ex-wife to Somalia."

After a tenuous cease-fire in March, reporters made periodic
raids on Somalia, sometimes for days at a time. But the story still
caused little stir. The *New York Times,* after that December trip, did
not return until July. Finally, in August, Richburg of the *Post* decided
that people didn't care about Somalia because they didn't know what
was happening. He stayed five days and traveled around. His copy,
splashed on page one, galvanized an election-year White House into
action. The *Los Angeles Times* correspondent was nudged to go in

for his first trip. The AP came back in to stay, the only permanent operation.

It all depended on the editor or, even more, the reporter. *Newsweek* was in Somalia early and often. *Time* did a cover on "The Agony of Africa" in early September which barely mentioned Somalia. The Somalis it quoted were from refugee camps in Kenya. To show the East Africa correspondent at work for the publisher's page, she was photographed by a tent at Nairobi Game Park. That is equivalent to camping in Central Park, which is also prohibited and a lot more dangerous.

The networks finally noticed a story they had left to CNN, but they focused mainly on the airlift. A range of newspapers showed up, with varying results. One U.S. reporter got caught in crossfire near Bardera. His report, spread over two pages, explored his ordeal under fire. It said little about Somalis.

"But a lot of really good copy has been written, if anyone actually read it," concluded Bertrand's Canadian pal. "Some guys took the trouble to get the facts right and show what was happening before it was too late." He was one of them but did not say so. Also, he added, there was some good television. "I guess people have to know how to understand what we do."

"Yeah," someone said from deep in a lounge chair that had miraculously escaped looters. "Somebody ought to write a book."


During the fall of 1992, the calamity worsened, but hardly any newspeople came to Somalia. Only the agencies stuck around. Then, on Thanksgiving Day, the swarm's radar blipped bigtime. President Bush, leaving office, decided to act: He would commit thirty thousand troops to protect food deliveries. The parachute journalists mobilized fast. Within days, Dan Rather, Tom Brokaw and Ted Koppel were broadcasting live from Mogadishu. Hundreds of correspondents, photographers and technicians rushed in, bringing everything from satellite uplinks to camembert. Kenya Airways diverted a flight to Cyprus to pick up a CNN crew who paid an extra $50,000. Drivers who charged $50 a day in August got $350 from the networks. Everyone was in a hurry to picture those skinny kids: "stick action."

Bertrand, back home for turkey, was amazed. Everyone, everywhere, suddenly knew Somalis were starving. "Warlord" was a household word. In Washington, the usual pack of pundits explained the ins and outs of politics in a country few could have found on a map the week before.

The same Somali experts were shaken out of the Rolodexes, each giving a personal slant on the multifaceted crisis as though it was an objective overview. One daytime television talk-show hostess, whose specialty is following crucial subjects, sounded as if she had just heard of the place. "Are there any hospitals or emergency centers?" she asked a guest. Every reporter in Somalia since early spring had focused on the hospitals and emergency centers.

In Somalia, newcomers seized on the symbols. A favorite was *khat*. Somalis, like Yemenis, worship the leafy plant. They chew it into a slimy green lump twixt teeth and cheek. It is mildly mind-bending, bringing on a hazy state that can range from sullen to silly. It can, on occasion, add itchiness to a trigger finger. *Khat* reaches so deeply into the culture that millionaire distributors have their own airport. Supply lines never faltered during the worst of the revolution. Steady as a metronome, planeloads arrived from Kenya. Within hours, bundles reached remote markets where secondary items like food were in short supply.

Newcomers wrote of "drug-crazed warriors," with the obvious results. Somali violence was easier to understand; it was a narcotics problem. Bertrand watched one television anchorperson badger the Kenyan ambassador to the United States. Why wouldn't his country ban *khat* shipments? The diplomat groped for a polite answer. He did not attempt the real answer: *Khat* is legal, less pernicious than beer and part of a culture. You might as well try to put a limit on the speed of light.

Dutybound, Bertrand checked in with his desk. Within hours, he was headed back to Somalia. This time, the story was every old hand's worst nightmare. ABC alone sent sixty-seven people. TV crews came from stations in every major city in America, filming themselves in action for duPont Award nominations. Everywhere Bertrand turned, an eager sort thrust out a hand and boomed, "Hi, I'm Brad/Cindy/Nguyen from KXYZ in Glitz City. Can you drink the water here?" It is best, Bertrand always advised, not even to breathe the air. The press corps numbered somewhere near five hundred.

As reporters streamed through Nairobi toward Mogadishu, a UNICEF press officer pleaded for takers on a rare trip to southern Sudan, where the threat to life was nearly as great as that in Somalia and the prospects for help were far dimmer. UNICEF would fly people in and out quickly, long enough for them to see the calamity but briefly enough to let them file and move on. Only CNN went. Farther south, the worst drought this century, coming after sixteen years of civil war, had pushed three million people toward starvation in Mozambique. But the story was Somalia.

In Mogadishu, abandoned villas miraculously fell together, with the incentive of many thousands of dollars, and Mediatown came to life. A wrecked hotel reopened, still wrecked, and crammed a hundred journalists into its fifty-eight rooms. Many of the rooms were offices, and people slept in the halls. Everyone, including the courtyard guests, got the same bill, one hundred dollars a night. Crudely mimeographed, it read: "Sahafi [Journalist] Hotel. Comfort, Luxury, for Business or Discrete Weekends. London, Tokyo, Mogadishu." The comfort part was stretching it, particularly when a hundred diarrhea-plagued journalists discovered the lack of running water.

The Marines landed in pitch dark, faces smeared black and green to deaden any glint of light that might give them away. They used all those cool war-game hand signals, leaping from one position to another with weapons ready. We know all this because they were lit up like Macy's at Christmas by camera crews who had gathered to wait for them at the Frankie Avalon Beach Party. Ringed by reporters in funny bush clothes, the Marines looked like a nightclub act. When the Navy Seals slipped ashore, the only resistance was a knot of reporters who insisted on interviews.

At one point, furious Seals drew a bead on one persistent obstacle. "I am a German journalist," the obstacle declared. "What are you going to do, shoot me?" One guy nearly did.

The Pentagon, which had timed the assault for prime time back home and announced the details days ahead of time, pretended to be angry at the coverage. As usual, those pesky journalists were endangering American lives.

The scene was similar when, more than a week later, a convoy finally made it to Baidoa. Marines waited for first light so photographers could catch the Texas-sized American flag flying over the lead tanklet. CNN cameras followed the convoy, live. Journalists' pickups and jeeps weaved among the military vehicles as they moved through town. Marines smashed a few of them and ran another off the road. At one point, a spooky looking guy in a sedan waved a black passport and thundered, "American Embassy. Slow down." Reporters chuckled and sped up.

As a photo opportunity, Marines quickly escorted food to a local orphanage. A horde of snappers crowded inside to watch kids receive the largesse. Several of them tromped on tiny bare feet, ignoring colleagues' admonishments to be more careful.

Amidst it all, some superb reporting got done. Reporters drew lessons from what had happened in Somalia and, with deft and moving descriptions, explained what Operation Restore Hope was up against. One of the best correspondents, a veteran of South Asia, the Middle East and Africa, sat down next to Bertrand to watch the Baidoa media circus. "You know," he said, shaking his head, "I have never been so embarrassed to be a journalist."

More newspaper space and air time were devoted to Somalia in the first days of Operation Restore Hope than during the entire previous year, in which at least three hundred thousand people had starved to death. In the first weeks, news organizations spent more than twenty million dollars, as much as the largest relief agency, CARE, spent all year in Somalia. Better late than not at all, Bertrand reasoned. Whatever else, some people would get fed. Then he left.

Predictably, interest waned before the Americans finished their mission. Few reporters saw them bog down, easy prey for taunting kids. Warlords, not disarmed, waded in with new vigor. Thieves got so brutal that even the redoubtable International Medical Corps went home to Los Angeles. Despite the help they brought, Americans had shaken a hornet's nest and left the swarm to an ineffectual United Nations. In the end, the humanitarian group Africa Rights reported, Restore Hope did as much harm as good.

Soon American forces were back again, this time with guns blazing. President Clinton ordered air strikes to punish one faction for an attack on U.N. troops. He declared success, and most Americans took him at his word. People back home had had their rush from Bush's cavalry charge and then went back to ignoring Bosnia. Had they continued to follow Somalia, they might have seen how they could do better the next time, in the next place. But Somalia was old news. Here was a chilling example of that crack by Reuven Frank, at NBC: "News is whatever the goddamn government says it is."

Chapter 3

# Know Your
# Dirty Bird

As an Italian photographer watched the American-German television team swoop into Baidoa hospital in Somalia, bumping into patients and chasing nurses out of their way, he tried to think of the English word for *avvoltoi,* which is vultures. He came up with "dirty birds," thus coining a nickname for all journalists. Ours is a hard business, and in action we are not a pretty sight.

When Saddam Hussein's "human shields" reached safety at the Amman airport, for instance, the freed women and children found a scene as terrifying as anything they had faced in Iraq. Entering the terminal, they were blinded suddenly by a thousand points of light and hammered with questions shouted in five languages. The surprise party from hell.

Peering at the dozens of Greeks, Egyptians and others trying to escape them, reporters yelled at one another, "Was anyone on board? You see anyone?" They meant people who mattered, Americans or Britons or even French. When all else failed, they settled for Arab wives of white people. No one intended any ethnic slurs. They just knew what they were after and had no time to mess around with niceties.

It was perfectly predictable. Alone on a story, reporters can take the time to empathize with their sources, speaking gently and compassionately to learn the human motivations behind the events at hand. But this is a luxury. Too often, like dirty birds, we must snatch our quarry from the talons of competitors.

Among news gatherers, there is no such thing as extenuating circumstances. When distant citizens open the paper or flip the switch, you are there, or you are not. Correspondents have not forgotten the *New York Times* guy who had sneaked off to Lebanon with a girlfriend, in 1952, a day before King Farouk was overthrown in Cairo. His editor tracked him down and cabled: "OPPOSITION REPORTING FAROUK RESIGNED. WHAT ARE YOUR PLANS?"

In the old days, a correspondent's major obstacle was the gnawing temptation to be a normal human being. In the age of the swarm, that's the least of it. Competition, always intense, can be brutal. Television crews fight for angles. Sometimes, two dozen lenses poke toward the same tiny face. Photographers edge in among the tripods. And reporters hover at the back, straining to hear the odd word and hoping for simultaneous battery failure.

That is part of it. Sometimes, fierce foes band together like childhood chums, sharing their last liters of Evian and letting one another call their wives on whichever satellite phone happens to be working. They pool sources and pass along tips, and the lion lies down with the lamb. This happens during those frequent situations when everyone's life might depend on it.

There are nobler professions, and harder ones which take a lot more brains, but few demand as much from the soul and stomach lining as reporting from faraway places. When the call comes in the middle of the night, a fireman only has to put on his pants and extinguish the flames. A correspondent must tell a million people who struck the match and why.

We dinosaurs who remember the old way often grumble at how the business is changing. Once it was what Bill Claiborne of the *Washington Post* called a 9-to-5 job. A double. "You'd get out about 9 A.M. and gather news all day and come back at 5," he said. "There'd be a lot of drinking and eating, and you'd sit down to write at 9. By the time you punched your copy and got a telex line, it would be 5 A.M. It was like that, day after day." Now, Claiborne says with some scorn, you see correspondents carrying briefcases.

Trenchcoats are going the way of spats and gaiters. If you're a sophisticated Eurohack, you wear a topcoat, cashmere if you can afford it. For runners and gunners, it is a vest covered with pockets which makes you look like a grouse hunter. The status symbol is now a new Toshiba and not a passport that looks like a paperback edition of *War and Peace*.

Leon Daniel of UPI still looks like an extra in a Ben Hecht remake. From Knoxville, he worked his way to UPI's Vietnam bureau in 1966. Nearly sixty, he outhumped the kids in the Gulf War. Now he clings to the vine for all the old reasons. "I just like to knock on doors that nobody gets to and talk to people, smell the cabbage cooking," he said. "None of us got into this racket for the money. We just like the work."

The Leon Daniel types are thinning out fast. When Terry Anderson emerged from seven years as a hostage in Lebanon, he looked around and left journalism. "I don't see that kind of passion we all shared that is so vital to coverage," he said. "I don't think reporters really care that much any more. That's a real killer."

But briefcase-carriers might argue this point. A big story still brings out the instincts. Diverse types fall together in a recognizable subclan. Something happens. Nonsmokers light up and teetotalers clutch the whacked-off end of a plastic water bottle that serves as a highball glass in a pinch. Television producers speak to newspaper freelancers. Women who file sex discrimination complaints back home tell rank jokes to the boys.

And, whoever the players and whatever the new tools, the job is always the same. One morning in Athens, a passing tourist noticed Martha Teichner of CBS hovering by a hotel elevator on the chance that it eventually it might disgorge Yasser Arafat. She and her crew had been there, doorstepping Arafat, for five hours. Gee, the man said sympathetically, sounds like a rough job.

"This is great," Teichner replied. "No one's shooting at us. It's not snowing, or raining. There's no sun beating down. We've got food. A phone. We don't have to drive six hours to file. This is paradise."

There has never been much of a mold for correspondents, and now there is none at all. Take Teichner, for example. She went into journalism because she got fired as a waitress when the Band-Aid on her finger showed up in someone's salad. Teichner got to be one of the best by a simple process: She gave up everything else in her life. With no spouse or unfinished afghans, she is always packed and ready.

One-fourth of American journalists overseas are now women,

but Teichner broke in when male editors back home still had to be shown that women were tough enough for the job. I met her in 1982. Arafat had sailed into Athens, having fled Lebanon, and only sound men with boom mikes had picked up what he said at the dock. As she and I sprinted for our cars, she ran the tape for me, and I took notes at a dead run. Suddenly, a wall of Greek security goons blocked our way. They meant to delay reporters long enough for Arafat to elude us all. Teichner did not pause. She selected one poor bastard and slugged him in the shoulder. Stunned, he unlinked arms with the guy next to him. We followed Arafat.

Next, we were in Bucharest the day after Nicolae Ceausescu fell. Teichner gaily recounted how she and her crew had played dodgeball with 9-mm bullets on their way to feed tape at the besieged television studio. Then, in Ljubljana, she told me where to buy raspberries, change Deutsche marks and learn something about Slovenia.

In Dhahran, we talked seriously about this business. Teichner had argued hard for a combat pool slot, and she got a nasty one, right up front where the poison gas was supposed to be. She was sensible enough to be scared silly. She went, of course, and produced her usual good stuff, which would have been shared by all networks had the buffoon U.S. Army minders ever managed to get it back to the pool editors.

According to the literature, physical agility is a requisite of the job. That does not explain John Hockenberry, a former National Public Radio correspondent who switched to television news. He has been confined to a wheelchair since an accident at sixteen. Hockenberry does it like everyone else. When reporters stuck in Jordan discussed ways to get across the closed border into Saudi Arabia, he offered, "Why don't we go across the desert disguised as Bedouins?" In a wheelchair? someone asked. "Oh, right," he said. Sometimes, his colleagues say, he forgets.

If generalities are harder to apply today, a few linger on. Correspondents share two traits, figures Colin Smith of the London *Observer:* a certain rat-like cunning and a modest literary ability. Boy Scouts might always Be prepared. Among correspondents, the watchword is Be neurotic.

Above all, good correspondents are cursed with febrile curiosity. Most read avidly as children and took frequent trips while growing up. They are driven to make something of themselves and usually poor enough to want to travel on someone else's money.

They cultivate the self-image of independence but spend their lives at the end of a yo-yo string. Any will admit to outrageous mistakes. Do not, however, lightly accuse a correspondent of willful distortion, especially if he or she is bigger than you.

With few exceptions, foreign correspondents see themselves as professionals bound to a rigid code of ethics. Separated from the barroom banter, they take their work seriously. A lot of them, down deep, feel a certain mission. Being human, each must fight against inherent biases. But telling a lie, for people of this persuasion, amounts to murder most foul. The few who do it and survive are marked as pariahs in the pack.

What correspondents have most in common is the challenges they face. As it was a generation ago, the main danger is getting something wrong. Back then, a careless news agency reporter could misinform a billion people. Depending on how long it took to correct the error, fortunes could be lost or armies could scramble to war alert. Now, with live television, this danger is even more acute. The network reporter who announced that Iraq had gassed Israel sent most of a planet into needless panic.

Until the mid-1980s, journalists mostly stood by and watched the news unfold. In Seoul, television reporters joked about "the Teargas Festival." It was routine. Korea University students assembled on one side. Police, lightly armed, lined up on the other. At a time all participants seemed to know, spontaneous riots broke out. Students yelled ugly taunts at American reporters but apologized later. Cops excused themselves for all the gas.

On a morning in March 1985, however, there was a chilling sense of a new danger. Terry Anderson and Don Mell, AP people in Beirut, drove home after tennis. Islamic fanatics bundled Anderson into a Mercedes and kept him for seven years. Suddenly, reporters realized they were part of the stories they covered. An increasingly crazed world had gotten downright risky.

Between 1954 and 1972, forty-six correspondents and photographers died in Vietnam, and others lost in Cambodia were never found. In El Salvador, thirty journalists died in less than a decade. And then Yugoslavs killed nearly that many in less than a year. Journalists were no longer simple casualties, unlucky victims in the wrong place at the wrong time. They were targeted by combatants wanting to make a point or vent their spleen. By the end of 1992, reporters who covered Serbs and Bosnians were getting such virulent hate mail that some took security precautions.

A group in France, Reporters sans Frontières (Reporters without Borders), makes a yearly stab at tallying casualties. During 1991, they counted sixty-five journalists killed, an increase of thirty-three from 1990. The Committee to Protect Journalists, in New York, has similar totals, along with breakdowns on who was gunned down on purpose and who died of bad luck. No one even attempts to keep track of the wounded. In 1982, the dead numbered nine. A year later, there were fourteen; one was Dial Torgerson of the *Los Angeles Times*, ambushed while driving along the Honduras-Nicaragua border. Then the casualties rose quickly.

Numbers tell only part of the story. Michael Goldsmith, for one, did not make the statistics. A gentleman of English manners but indeterminate nationality, he collected a lot of hard knocks in forty-five years with the AP. My first posting, in 1967, was to replace Mike in the Congo (now Zaire). He had been expelled for the fifth time by officials who resented his penchant for writing what he saw. As a point of professional honor, Mike routinely flouted a first rule: Do not send a nasty story about Country A until you are safely in Country B.

In 1977, I took over the AP's Paris bureau, and my first job was to get Mike out of a stinking African prison. He had written a dispatch about Emperor Bokassa I's coronation in the (former) Central African Republic, and he telexed it to Johannesburg. The line was bad, and return messages came back garbled. Bokassa's thugs assumed it was code from South African agents. He was taken to the emperor, who opened his forehead with a whack from an ebony cane. A month passed before Mike was freed.

Twelve years later, Goldsmith was back in Africa, in Liberia, to cover a free-for-all massacre that passed for civil war. He was nearly seventy, trying to decide if he could live on a meager pension and whether he could give up the life. Then a group of soldiers left him no choice. Unprovoked, they pummeled his guts repeatedly with rifle butts. Mike stayed on the job. It was only later, back home again in the hospital with heart trouble, that he died of internal bleeding. Doctors weren't clear about what went wrong, but his colleagues knew.

Paul Taylor, freshly arrived in South Africa for the *Washington Post*, wrote: "On my sixth day as a foreign correspondent, somebody tried to kill me." He did not take it personally. He was driving in a township with local reporters, one white and one black, in hopes of learning how to cover his star-crossed beat. Taylor escaped with a bullet in the shoulder.

These days, journalists get it from both sides. In Thailand, during 1992, riot police thrashed thirty reporters and photographers with batons, seriously injuring some. They did not want witnesses to their crowd control. One trooper screamed at a British photographer: "We got one of you last night. You're next!" He was referring, apparently, to still unconfirmed reports that a foreign journalist had been killed. Later, Hindu mobs in India attacked reporters and camera crews covering their assault on the Ayodhya mosque. Several were bloodied by rocks and clubs.

In a booklet written for reporters headed overseas, the AP quotes a veteran smoke-eater, Ed Blanche, who is Middle East news editor: "Survival is the name of the game. . . . Taking chances is one thing. You have to get up close. But dead correspondents don't write stories."

Of course, that's not necessarily true. Tony Clifton of *Newsweek* remembers how Al Rockoff, a photographer in Cambodia, was hit in the chest with shell fragments. A passing medic found him by the side of the road, clinically dead, and restarted his heart. Rockoff recovered fast and was soon headed back into action. "Be careful," someone yelled. "You could get killed." He replied, "It wouldn't be the first time."

Clifton tells the story in the context of how the business has changed. In the Overseas Press Club *Dateline,* he recalls how he offered this prize bit of lore to a young reporter anxious for advice. When he got to the punchline, the kid said, "Oh, right," and they went back to his question of whether to spend a few years abroad before returning home to do real journalism.

Correspondents joke a lot about the danger, and none of them thinks it is funny. Courage, skill and the best kind of love for the story are not enough to shield them from it. Sharon Herbaugh, AP bureau chief in Pakistan, was smitten by the crazed beauty of Afghanistan. Periodically, in the house newsletter, she recounted with offhand humor yet another perilous journey. One ten-hour trip took five days while she was held by renegades, shelled and shot at. She suffered only "coward's elbow," caused by diving to the ground at the sound of passing mortar, rockets or bullets. She explained why Afghans called their capital Jhannum, meaning "hell." But someone else wrote about her last trip, in April 1993. At 39, she died in one of those badly maintained, overloaded helicopters on a ride she would have never dreamed of refusing.

But danger is only part of the job, often a very small part. More commonly, there is the routine trip to the office which ends three months later after flights to half a dozen countries. News has a way of changing reporters' plans at short notice. Two unwritten rules of the craft survive from the early days. You don't say no. And you always pretend you're having a good time.

Frequently, you don't have to pretend. Once while telling war stories at a university, I noticed a young woman studying me as if I were a pickled newt on a biology slab. "That doesn't sound interesting," she finally said. "It sounds sick." Probably. But she wasn't with us dancing on Red Square the night that communism died.

The Goldsmiths and Herbaughs set the tone. They get on the damned plane, hop on the truck, bang on the door and don't leave until they get answers. They have what you can't learn in school or an office: a novelist's feel for people, a stateman's sense of politics and a streetfighter's instinct to go for the gut.

Among the pros who get their stories the hard way, there is a new sort of reporter who feels neither the mission nor the traditions. One friend of mine, a wizened monument who works for *Time,* was troubled when young colleagues declined to cover the siege of Sarajevo on the ground that they had wives and children. "They are sensible to stay away," he said. "But then why are they in this business? It is our job to go. If we're not going to do it, someone else should take our place." Mocking himself but letting fly from the heart, he concluded as a character in *Scoop* might have done: "It is a breed without honor, sir."

Yet some gung-ho veterans have been at it for thirty years, and they still miss the point. Others, hardly out a few months, catch on by instinct. In a new age of cost-cutting, reporters are often sent from home to cover a foreign story with neither background nor experience. This invites shallowness but hardly assures it. Nothing tangible defines a good correspondent. The best ones, however, can recognize one another at a glance.

On the night train to Vienna from Bucharest, John Kifner of the *New York Times* got suitably loaded with Alison Smale of the AP. They had done a week of revolution and were headed to their respective homes for New Year's Eve. North of Budapest, a newsmagazine reporter they knew padded by to the bathroom. He was wearing slippers and a robe and was carrying his toothbrush in a glass. Soon, he padded back, nodding as he passed. Kifner giggled. "That man," he said, "will be an editor in a year."

This is where the consumer must beware. In every case, the quality and depth of reporting depend upon the individual who is doing it. All those columns marching across a newspaper page suggest a certain uniformity. Television is the same, despite the trend to promote star talent. One face follows another on the screen, each explaining complex events in the same authoritative tones. But if there was ever a field of endeavor where all persons are not created equal, it is reporting from abroad.

Like the correspondents themselves, readers and viewers must take nothing at surface value and, instead, look for that "usually reliable source." With some attention and practice, anyone can learn to pick up telltale signs that suggest solid reporting—or trigger alarms. This is important at any time, but it is crucial during such crises as the Gulf War.

CNN's great triumph was not in having someone in Baghdad; it was in having Peter Arnett. Despite the restrictions, Arnett conveyed more with his eyebrows and nuances than Pentagon briefers got across with a rack of charts. The difference was that he was trying to reflect reality, not anyone's particular version of reality, and was skilled enough to do it under any circumstance. Once his anchor asked on the air about reports that civilian casualties blamed on American bombs had been caused by anti-aircraft fire falling back to earth. Arnett barely masked a sneer. "Those things," he said, "don't dig craters twenty feet deep."

Arnett's manner suggested confidence, even to those who had never seen him before. He knew the names and the story, without stumbling over pronunciation or groping for some all-purpose cliché to pass for political analysis. When he could be, he was rich in detail, background and military explanation. When Iraqi censors wanted it otherwise or when he could not see something for himself, he said so. Good print reporters operate in the same manner, and their work can be recognized just as easily.

The surest way to know whom to trust is to watch the bylines. This is not nearly as difficult as it sounds. Most editors depend upon a hard core of regulars who appear again and again. Kifner was one example. He came up as a local reporter and excelled on the New

York police beat. Looking for a challenge, he applied the same skills overseas. His was among the best copy from Lebanon, Iran and then Poland. After a while, he went back to cover page one news in New York, but he kept his war bag packed. Whenever something big broke, he was off again.

Kif's approach is to focus on people. Officials make the moves, but the impact falls on the same sort of ordinary working stiffs who are the real news back home. His ear for irony is sharp, and his bullshit detector works. Kifner usually gets it. He understands the workings beneath a story, enabling him to explain not only what happened but also why it matters.

It helps, of course, that he looks like an inoffensive gnome with an impish grin. In 1982, when the Syrian Army shelled the ancient city of Hama, Kifner got through roadblocks that others could not penetrate with valid passes. "I used my schmuck tourist mode," he explained, grinning. When he shifts to madman buzzsaw mode, it is too late to stop him. It took courage to try either tactic. Earlier, the Reuters bureau chief was shot in Beirut; the bullet just missed his spine. Syrians had spread the word that they did not like his copy.

Kifner, who favors what he calls the juvenile delinquent element of foreign reporting, mocks colleagues who take themselves too seriously and spoil the fun. But he also gets serious. In 1982, a small Middle East war began when the *New York Times* man in Jerusalem profiled an Israeli press officer, a zealot from New York, who impugned the courage and balance of reporters based in Lebanon. Kifner, enraged, wrote about what it was like in Beirut: "To work here as a journalist is to carry fear with you as faithfully as your notebook. . . . Unlike journalists in Israel, who can receive government press releases over a special telephone line which rings simultaneously in all correspondents' homes or offices, journalists covering the Arab world operate in an alien and frequently hostile environment."

But this was Kif. With tongue slipping cheekwards, he ended with a slice of life to make to his point. The Jerusalem story had singled out a badly covered incident. Kifner explained why coverage was difficult:

> During a period of intensive Israeli air raids last spring, journalists got a report at about midnight that Israelis were landing near Damour, just south of Beirut. Five of them crowded into an old car driven by this correspondent and went down the coastal road to investigate,

a venture many of their peers regarded as ill-advised. The car was stopped by a group of guerrillas, bristling with guns and grenades. . . . The guerrillas, who were somewhat excitable, having been bombed and strafed earlier in the day, took the journalists to their headquarters.

The reporters had put on coats and ties for a party at Kifner's, leaving press cards at home in their work clothes.

After several hours, what had been a fairly cordial atmosphere turned suspicious when the guerrillas discovered a bulletproof vest belonging to this correspondent in the trunk of the car. For some reason, this greatly upset them. The five correspondents were locked in tiny isolation cells, stripped and searched and interrogated to determine if they were Israeli spies. They were held for about 20 hours. Meanwhile their colleagues began a frantic search, located them, produced the missing identification papers and negotiated their release. When it was established that the five were indeed journalists and not spies, they were released with ceremonies more time-consuming than they would have preferred. The incident was regarded as something of an embarrassment to all concerned.

Kifner's byline is now rare. Unexpected treachery struck him down, and he spends his time training others. "My computer attacked me for writing too fast," he said, with the old grin. "After everything I survived, my own machine got me." It was the new occupational hazard, carpal tunnel syndrome. Too much banging at computer keys can cause severe wrist pain, leading to paralysis. Like gout, it is funnier to talk about than to endure.

Flash and dash are not the determinate factors. Michael Dobbs, in Moscow for the *Washington Post,* always looks as if someone dropped the world on his shoulders just as he was heading home for dinner. Behind his furrowed brow, however, lurks a brain pan which contains more data than an average university library on a stretch of Europe from the Balkans to the Baltic. When he decides to crack a joke, he can do it in Russian, Polish, Serbo-Croatian, German, Italian or French.

There are plenty of others, some of whom populate later pages. Over time, readers and viewers can pick up a stable of favorites, who get to be like old friends or family. It is a surprisingly small group, especially in television. Each network has a handful of regulars who manage to beam themselves huge distances in no time at all.

The process quickly gets easier as it goes along. Anyone interested in South Africa would have noticed John Burns of the *New York Times*. He went to the Soviet Union, replaced by Alan Cowell, someone else worth following. Burns fans might have missed him when he left Moscow, but they had Bill Keller, a master of the craft. And then Keller turned up in South Africa. About then, Bosnia and the Balkans were big news. Among the bylines to watch were John Burns and Alan Cowell.

Some of the most rewarding bylines to follow are in small papers. With syndication, you don't have to be in Philadelphia to read dispatches from the *Inquirer*'s first-rate team of eight correspondents. Some of the best work from the Gulf War was by Randall Richard, a special writer with the *Providence Journal*. When most reporters fixated on what was being hit, Richard found the shooters. A pilot who went to war with Led Zeppelin blasting in his head told him: "I gotta say, I love it."

News agency dispatches can be a problem. Although they are usually signed on the wire, papers often remove the byline. And, because of the editing process, the dispatch might not read the way the correspondent filed it. But a particularly noteworthy AP story might carry a byline in hundreds of newspapers. After a while, the same name comes back again and again from different parts of the world. Eventually, the name may appear regularly in a newspaper which poaches him, or her.

Even when the names are strange or there are no bylines at all, there are ways to test whether a dispatch is solid. The first step is to understand how reporters gather news and how their editors decide what to do with it. Although each medium operates differently, the broad guidelines are the same.

Coups and earthquakes, like plane crashes or killer storms, are straightforward stories. When they are dramatic, editors love them. They take bold headlines and produce gripping footage. There are death tolls, eyewitness accounts, causes, effects, winners, losers, lessons to draw for the next time. But for reporters, these generally take more work than skill to cover. If they are tragic for those who suffer, their long-term impact is usually minimal.

Sudden political upheaval is big news, but it is tricky to handle. Even the best reporters can do no more than scamper along behind events. Instant analysis tends to be proved wrong; at the least, it ages quickly. These stories can be fascinating to watch in action, but sense is made of them only when the dust settles.

The most important news is often the least obvious. A story in this "also-ran" category comes in fragments: one day, a long feature on an inside page; another, a few paragraphs stuck in the world briefs. This is a paradox of the system. Reporters spot crucial trends taking shape at the normal pace of human events—slowly—but editors have trouble packaging them.

These also-ran stories signal when societies are turning corners, forming new attitudes which their leaders will have to take into account. Most people noticed revolution in Eastern Europe when Tom Brokaw popped up in front of the collapsing Berlin Wall, grinning widely because he was there and his competition was not. But anyone who had followed the months of uproar in Leipzig knew change was only a matter of time.

News briefs catalog squabbles over oil policies and border disputes, such as an Iraqi dictator telling a Kuwaiti emir to hand over his keys. By the time these stories climb up the front page, it is too late to react to them.

The best correspondents find ways to convey the importance of news about to happen. When it happens, they look for vantage points that are well clear of inevitable flock of dirty birds. Rarely, however, do their insights muscle ahead of breaking stories. Always, readers and viewers must look beyond the headlines.

During the few days when the Soviet Union suddenly fell apart, there was no missing the news at hand. Hard-liners tried a coup, and they failed. Mikhail Gorbachev came back to power and found that he had none. The story was Moscow. After Boris Yeltsin raised the Russian flag over the Kremlin, however, the main lines were clearly drawn. Headlines stayed focused on political process, the old who's-on-first routine. But the bigger story was elsewhere. Names and positions would change a dozen times. What mattered was the people and their republics. How would they respond? What did they face? What were they ready to swallow?

The *Los Angeles Times* sent reporters to every part of the dissolving country, and Mark Fineman went to Central Asia. In Tajikistan, he found the main square roiling with whiskery old men in medieval robes, hard-eyed youths in black beards and Tajik yuppies in fat ties, all demanding that die-hard Communists give up the ghost. Rahman Nabiyev, a cartoon caricature of a party hack who had been cashiered years before for corruption and drunkeness, was clinging to power with a Communist-dominated legislature.

In the chaotic present, Fineman saw the future. He wrote a colorful piece that started on page one and wandered through the paper, showing how far old assumptions could be from reality. Islam had thrived under repression, and ancient ties forged centuries earlier along the old Silk Road would outweigh any fragile compromise conceived in Moscow. The Russians would be going home. Iran and Turkey, and then China, would struggle for influence.

On his way out of Central Asia, Fineman rode the train from Bishkek, in Kyrgyzstan, to Tashkent, in Uzbekistan, described by its conductor as the worst train in the world. The story was rich in humor, small details and anecdotes. But no one could miss its point. Windows were broken because Kyrgyz peasants threw rocks at the Uzbeks in the cars. They weren't replaced because the glass factory was paralyzed since no one would deliver silicon. While long-distance "thumbsuckers" were making pronouncements on the future of the former Soviet Union, Fineman brought readers into the heart of it.

As vital as they are, also-ran stories command no assured place in line. A plane crash in Chile might pass quickly into the statistics, but it cannot wait a few days until the paper has a larger news hole. An adjustment by Germany's Bundesbank must be reported when it happens, along with the usual analyses about the momentary ups and downs of national cash flows. Though probably more important in the long run than either story, an also-ran may never see print.

In the case of Tajikistan, *Los Angeles Times* readers had up-close coverage, if they looked past the main headlines. I was there for the AP, and some of the agency's subscribers made space for my dispatches. A *Washington Post* reporter came late and left. Few others bothered; each had other also-rans to cover. Within a year, many thousands died in a widening civil war which endangered the region and Russia itself. Fineman fans were not surprised.

The *New York Times* is the closest thing the United States has to a national newspaper of record, a publication which keeps track of the twists and turns of also-ran stories. After the early Tajikistan turmoil ebbed, the *Times* announced new elections in a tiny item at the bottom of an inside-page column; it said voting in four days would be crucial to the future of Central Asia. But the paper did not report the results. The first item was less to inform than to plug a hole on the page. Had there been a hole on election day, readers might have known the winner.

Bernard Gwertzman, the *Times'* foreign editor, chuckled when his attention was drawn to this slip. Nothing is perfect, least of all a news organization. More than a simple error, however, this reflected what Gwertzman called a change in the *Times'* traditional role. Rather than trying to log each major event in every country, the paper now prefers periodic long dispatches which sum up developments in a broader context. "We're not that interested in who wins these little elections," he said, and he wasn't talking about Tajikistan. His Rome correspondent had just tried, with little success, to sell him a general election in Italy. "We can't get that serious about Italian elections." When corruption later made Italy a story, it got in the paper.

As State Department correspondent, Gwertzman wrote at length about every ripple in the status quo. Now, he said, foreign affairs can no longer be seen in fragments. "Once, if Labor won in Britain, that meant a weaker NATO, which affected a bipolar power balance. Things are different now. Straight political reporting is in jeopardy." He had just handled a dispatch full of names from some second-rank place. "It's a parody," he said. "You keep thinking of that Marx Brothers film, *Duck Soup.*"

Other big papers also use periodic broad dispatches, a logical practice. Few important news stories have a beginning or end. Reporters seldom "cover" a foreign story, as we like to say. Mostly, we look in on it from time to time. Long dispatches with plenty of context are easier to understand, but they also impose a burden. When it comes time for, say, Turkey, readers have to absorb the latest developments and retain the flavor so they can make sense of later news briefs.

All of this means that readers had better not skip a day. Some time after Fineman left Tajikistan, for example, a *New York Times* correspondent nosed around the same territory to bring his paper up to date. Instead of demonstrations as the "peg" on which to hang a story, there was shooting. Then the reporter went home, and only serious bloodshed would get Dushanbe back into the paper.

Television handles also-ran stories in much the same way, but in the extreme. When cameras move in, along with a script that is sharply written by someone who understands the story, the message strikes home.

If the subject were Tajikistan, distant viewers would form mental images that would last for years, context for the otherwise incomprehensible briefs to follow. Except that the subject is seldom

Tajikistan. Air time is too tight, and crews too thinly distributed. Restive Tajiks would have to discomfit Americans in a major way before they made the grade.

Newspapers can be stacked up in the corner to be perused when time allows; television offers one shot. If you're home and tuned to the right channel and not getting a beer when the story airs, you're covered. If you miss it, there will be a long wait. Tajikistan might have its turn. But then for months, maybe years, afterward, producers will be advising correspondents from Turkey to China: "We've *done* angry Muslims in Asia."

With television, a correspondent's credibility is as important as it is with newspapers, but it is harder to rely on old favorites. Several problems arise. Famous does not necessarily mean best. Those most frequently on the air are those most on the move, leaving them little time to dig into the nuances of stories they cover. If something happens in France big enough to attract a Sam Donaldson, for example, viewers have a comforting sense of the familiar. ABC's Jim Bitterman has smaller eyebrows and earns less, but he lives in France; he is more likely to know what's lurking beyond the range of the camera.

Television correspondents suffer from a new style. To save money, networks routinely show someone else's footage with their own narration from a distant studio. A correspondent who would much prefer to be there in person must put words to pictures from some unknown crew. When a report from Sarajevo ends, say, "Barry Peterson, CBS News, London," the viewer's real source of information was whoever wrote the original script. It might have been a first-rate British reporter with experience on the ground. Or maybe not. It wasn't Barry Peterson.

CNN overcomes some of television's systemic drawbacks. Also-ran stories are repeated frequently. A solid staff of regional experts watches for trends that amount to news. Some roving heavy hitters need little time in town to begin making sense of things. But CNN has produced some howlers, skewed reports from hit-and-run teams who simply missed the point. Nothing is perfect.

Newsmagazines fall in between newspapers and television. With the luxury of time and space, a perceptive weekly reporter can sketch a broad-bush portrait with colorful fine strokes that bring it to life. It might be set among powerful photos, maps and graphics. Altogether, this is a compelling package. Provided, of course, that it reflects reality.

The newsmagazines' strength is also their weakness. Each article survives a decathlon of tests, from the correspondent's first query of interest to the last desperate phone call to persuade editors that a revolution in China is, in fact, more important than a dogfight in Brooklyn. For better or worse, what emerges from this process may be significantly different from what goes into it.

In the scramble for audience, weeklies press the advantage they have over other media. More than simply summarizing recent events, they can show why also-ran stories are important to the world. All of them have the flexibility to draw conclusions from the facts at hand. These themes, in bold, black type between glossy covers, take on the weighty feel of authority. But all of them depend heavily on their correspondent on the spot, who is just another dirty bird. Some are excellent, and some are not.


To every reporter, nothing is more important than sources. These cover a vast range, and you should scour every report for clues. Except in eyewitness accounts or news analyses, the reporter steps out of the way and lets others tell the story. Accuracy depends upon whom the reporter consulted; balance hinges on which sources comment and how their thoughts are packaged. The goal is objectivity, but we are talking about human beings. Honest intent often has to suffice.

This is tricky stuff. A skilled reporter can go to the right sources, name them carefully, quote them accurately, and still be wrong. People can be misinformed, or they may lie. Situations change. In any case, things may not be what they seem.

When possible, reporters identify their sources and say why they were included. For simple events or announcements, these are obvious choices: official spokespersons, police chiefs, party leaders, or anyone else who might call a press conference. When it comes to revealing hidden facts, exposing wrongdoing or reading a collective mood, it gets a little murkier.

A careful reporter consults a lot of people and then quotes a few of them to make a point. These may be the only ones willing to be cited by name. If there is a denial to be made, someone has to express it. Stories on trends need the obligatory wise voice, a professor or intellectual or somesuch. Example and detail add weight. People lie on the record. But in the end, if a story full of named sources feels solid, it probably is.

The trouble comes when sources cannot be identified. Often, what people say for quotation is the exact opposite of what they reveal when assured of anonymity. No one wants to lose a job, or a life, by refuting the official line. Yet people in sensitive positions are troubled by consciences or thwarted by frustration. Without a Deep Throat, we would have had no Watergate exposé. But how can you be sure a Deep Throat is telling the truth?

Whatever the medium, readers must learn to follow the codes. How a reporter identifies quotes or attributes information is crucial to evaluating the overall message. In some cases, the editors offer clues according to their own style. For example, when *Newsweek* uses a "top byline" instead of the usual signature at the end of an article, it means the reporter, not a desk editor, wrote it. These pieces are closer to interpretive columns than news dispatches. They help readers make sense of complex situations that defy the old "he-said, she-said" formula. The catch is that the writer must understand the subject.

When newspapers label a story "news analysis," sources are less important. As in an editorial, the writers can draw their own conclusions. But editorials can state opinions. In an analysis, the writer is bound to conclude only what the hard facts suggest. On television, the term "commentary" works the same way.

Like the reporter, the consumer must look for the good old "usually reliable source," and then find a second source for confirmation. Professional newspeople use two devices when informing themselves: suspended belief and triangulation. They absorb any one account with some skepticism; this is suspended belief. It is not so much the messenger who is in doubt as the message itself. Facts and impressions are then tested against another account—and then a third; this is triangulation. If the first source is a newspaper article, look for others, and then watch for television footage to add a visual backdrop. If television is the first source, check the papers for what was left out. At the end of the week, a magazine might fill in the blanks. Where discrepancies remain, keep looking.

As time allows, columnists, general magazine articles and television specials can go into the mix. Weightier backdrops, like the journal *Foreign Affairs,* lectures and private conversations, help in evaluating daily coverage. Once you begin to look at news in this way, you build a basis for evaluation. Some stories make no sense right off the bat. Others ring true. The more you know about the setting, the more interesting the main event. This is the way people get hooked on keeping up with the world.

Over time, you will notice glaring errors and omissions when you read or watch your regular sources of information. Tell the editors. At the very least, they will know you noticed.

Beyond suspended belief and triangulation, consumers have few means to check up on reporters who ask them to take things on trust. That is why it helps to know the system.

The way a correspondent works depends on the medium and the story. Agency reporters, the packhorses of the profession, raise the most dust. They are responsible for all the news in their territory, around the clock and holidays included, and they are expected to report it faster than the competition. Their time is eaten away by queries about the mayor of Pigeonplop visiting the Sphinx. They sell their service to local papers and send off temperatures for the world weather roundup. They entertain traveling publishers, cover football for South Korea, fix teleprinters, write radio spots and argue with the landlord over a backed-up toilet. In Bogotá, a bureau chief once helped a publisher repair barbed wire fences at his ranch.

In Rome, an AP desk person starts each day by sending the lira rates, the weather, and financial items; sifting through the bureau's photo output and messages; reading fifteen papers, several magazines and two local newswires; and editing stories from six satellite bureaus. Then maybe there is time to write the news. And there is always that possible phone call. Terry Leonard had two hours' warning before heading to Baghdad to cover a war. Another call came at 1 A.M. for him to fly to Bulgaria and drive all night and the next day to Sarajevo. Then, home in Rome only long enough to do an expense account, he was gone again. Over two years, he was out of town for nine months.

When major news breaks, agencies rush off a first dispatch and then follow each development, writing new leads with every turn of events. Somewhere, always, a newspaper is on deadline. If the coup at hand is the twelfth since Catherine the Feeble, agency reporters must say so. They must find the Red Cross worker who keeps casualty figures and then compare the death toll to that of Hurricane Irving of 1903. Information is gathered fast, by phone if the phone is working, and little time can be spared for leisurely chats with the local pundits.

Agency reporters send their dispatches to editors back home, who add background and inserts on related developments. Sometimes a reporter's story is hurried to the wire without a comma changed. Other times, a long dispatch is written on the desk from a range of material, and only the byline is his. During the Gulf War, when up to fifteen reporters worked out of a suite at the Dhahran International Hotel, New York would call twice a day with the same question: "Who gets the byline this cycle?" Reporters took turns, whether or not they had contributed anything that day.

Newspaper correspondents do it differently. Usually, they write once a day, sticking to the main story. Before starting, they "download." By punching a few computer commands, they gather in everything the news agency people have written. They brew some coffee or order a beer. Then, reviewing their own notes, they sit down to find a better angle. If this sounds a lot easier, it usually is. Then again, if often isn't.

In major cities, the agency usually has a local bureau, or at least a regular stringer. Someone can chase down press credentials, order out for tadpole kebabs, find the foreign minister in his favorite bar or convince the telephone operator to free a line. Even if the agency correspondent parachuted in, local staff people have been there since birth. Newspaper people routinely drop in to the agency bureau for grounding. What they get depends, in the long run, on what they share in return.

Newspaper correspondents, known as "specials," know that their editors can always use the agency version. If that happens more than rarely, they know, someone is going to start calculating their cost. If phone lines are working or they have their own satellite, filing their dispatches is simple routine. As often as not, however, reaching their desks is a nightmare race against time. Agencies are always in a hurry, but they have no set-in-stone deadlines. Newspapers do. A special dispatch that comes in fifteen minutes late may be out of the paper.

Newsmagazine reporters have even more time to cruise, early in the week. When it gets to be filing time, steam exudes from their pores. On one breaking story, I watched a mild-mannered colleague battle a newspaper reporter for the only phone around, frantic to get the last-minute deadline. "But you're a weekly," the other guy said. "Yes," came a reply that was accompanied by a sharp straight-arm to the chest, "and it's Saturday morning."

When news happens in some remote backwater, these diverse methods tend to merge. Everyone scrambles for bits of news and some way to file it. In the extreme, newspaper specials count on their desks to put together the pieces in the same way as agencies. And on investigative stories or background features, a news agency reporter may take the time to work like a special, with a single, polished piece written at leisure, complete with the coffee or beer. In this business, there is no routine.

Television crews have a different set of problems. In another time, networks kept bureaus around the world. Each had editing facilities, background clips and fixers who could fake a yellow fever stamp in two minutes flat. Freed of routine coverage, correspondents could watch trends that meant something, pursuing angles until they had something solid. When it was time to move, three people hit the road, with camera and sound gear.

Today, the other side of fancy technology is having to get it from place to place. When an earthquake struck Iran in 1990, Chris Dickey of *Newsweek* did not wait for a visa. He whipped off his Hermès tie, wriggled into someone else's white coat and flew in with the French doctors. Try that with a portable television studio and a satellite earth station.

Today, television crews race out of big cities lugging along a mountain of silver crates. They might spend hours negotiating satellite feed time at local television studios. Time is lost on establishing shots to give some context to the story. Then they have to write, edit and feed. All of this, plane ride included, must be squeezed in between breakfast and bedtime. Scant time is left for the only flexible part of the process: reporting.

A lot can go wrong. What astounds insiders, however, is how much goes right when correspondents are good at their work. One medium complements another, and the result can help people understand their world. As reporters looked for angles at the Rio de Janeiro Earth Summit in 1992, for example, Tom Kamm of the *Wall Street Journal* hopped over to Curitiba for a story that began: "Working from a log cabin surrounded by woods, Mayor Jaime Lerner is trying to invent the city of the future." Curitiba's 1.6 million residents recycle their trash. A bicycle beltway reduces traffic. Old buses are converted to mobile schools for the poor. A tramway car houses a child-care center at a pedestrian mall. Kamm's piece gave Americans a dozen ideas for saving their own cities, and it countered some outworn myths about Brazil.

CBS dispatched a crew to show what Kamm could only put into words. It ran long on the "Evening News." Cameras showed how people sold their trash for vegetables grown on garbage heaps and how pollution-free buses were rigged to carry bikes. Mayor Lerner explained how he had designed the schemes because he was short of money and how the enthusiastic inhabitants had made them work. Steeped in context and color, the piece showed even the owl-killers in the First World what environmental concern might accomplish.

Thus alerted, anyone who cared could find magazine articles which looked more closely not only at Curitiba but also at other cities which had attacked problems that defy old solutions.

Triangulation takes you beyond a world in brief. Suspended belief helps you get an accurate picture. Careful perusal keeps you in touch with the also-ran stories before they burst into headlines so that you can follow big news when it breaks. Subsequent chapters offer some specific guidance in making sense of each medium. Others look at some types of reporting which bring special rules into play.

Like keeping fit, following world news takes regular sessions of sustained effort. The more people pick up the habit, the more reporters' work will get through the gate. If editors and news executives sense a growing interest, most will be happy to oblige. Meantime, looking for the good stuff is a fascinating pastime. It helps to know your devoted dirty bird.

Chapter 4

# The Boys
# on the
# Boeing

Holding forth on the subject of grand old-timers one evening in Kuwait, I made some slur about "the kids" of the profession. Tony Horwitz raised a finger, amused, and replied, "Hey, I'll speak for the kids." He didn't have to bother. Barely broken in on the *Wall Street Journal* when the Gulf War started, Horwitz wrote us all into the ground. Then he beat us all to Kuwait.

Good reporters at work these days transcend all ages and styles. Horwitz is a cum laude product of the Hey-This-Is-Fun school, a new breed of correspondent who takes little seriously but the mission, which he never mentions. He sees reporting for what it is, a running account of the extremes of the human condition. Even when covering the abstract affairs of nations, he writes about people. He would put it less grandly: "I hate press conferences." If some young reporters steal news by not caring much about it, the Horwitz types snatch some of it back.

A glance at Tony suggests his approach to life. With curly blond hair and a rosy glow, he looks like a health club version of a Renaissance cherub. When microbes or machine guns blacken his day, he can look serious. His eyes, however, are always smiling.

Reared in Washington, D.C., Horwitz went abroad by falling in love with a homesick Australian reporter and following her home. He worked for the Sydney *Morning Herald,* grabbing up the shark attack and outback murder assignments. When his wife, Geraldine Brooks, was named *Wall Street Journal* correspondent in Cairo, he went along as spouse-stringer. He hustled up what part-time newspaper work he could, working hard for nearly nothing. Then the *Journal* took him on staff.

As a *Journal* Middle East specialist (Brooks was the other), Horwitz covered the war step-by-step. He was the first to hang out on the Jordan border to get to know the Third World workers who were flooding out of Kuwait, across the Iraqi desert.

Through the eyes of ruined Egyptian entrepreneurs and Nepalese nannies, his readers saw beyond the geopolitics. Any reporter could see pitiful clumps of refugee families camped on Amman streetcorners. Only Horwitz found the modern-day version of an old camel market where you could buy a slightly soiled Mercedes-Benz for $1,500, if you didn't mind Kuwaiti plates.

Then he took a turn in Iraq. Though scared like everyone else, he did not dwell on the muted personal heroics that marked some others' copy. In a series of deft strokes, he brought to life a Saddam Hussein who loomed above the facile caricature assigned to him. His readers saw a cunning, charming brute, rooted deep in the past with an eye on the future, whose power base rested unshakably on fear and awe. Every blow he took enhanced his standing, at home and among Arab leaders who wanted to hate him. Reading Horwitz, you understood what George Bush did not: This man will win by losing, and that is his plan.

Beyond the big picture, Horwitz looked for snapshots of pathos and irony to convey the mood. As it happened, he had a leg up on correspondents who rushed out their doors with photocopied bits of Baedeker. His first book, which had just appeared on the market, was entitled *Baghdad without a Map*.

When the air war started, Horwitz hurried to Saudi Arabia. He declined to join all the reporters waiting around Riyadh to be lied to by American briefers. A Washington-based colleague wanted him to sit in Dhahran where, Tony knew, he would drown in pool copy. Instead of pacing hotel carpets and bitching about the Pentagon, Horwitz went to cover the war.

He hitched a ride to Hafr-al-Baten and stayed one jump ahead of American MPs. One U.S. colonel ordered, "Get the hell off my battlefield." Hey, Tony figured, this is fun. He found the Egyptians and stayed with them until the ground war started. Thinking logically, he realized the coalition forces would hold back and let Kuwaiti troops spearhead a triumphant homecoming. So he jumped to the Kuwaitis.

Sure enough, he was up there at the head of the parade, kissing the babies and scribbling notes as fast as he could write. The first guy he met said: "Come stay at my house. I have a generator and a freezer full of T-bone steaks." The second said, "I have a satellite fax." Score one for the kids.

When others followed anticlimax up the road, Tony stayed to let readers know what the fighting had been about. He summed it up in a dispatch that began, "The emir of Kuwait, Jaber al-Sabah, returned home yesterday, 15 days after the liberation of his land, and 10 days after his furniture." Whatever world leaders might tell their people back home, it was the same old Kuwait.

From Saudi Arabia, he quoted one smug prince who boasted about the "white slaves" who had fended off danger. The other Gulf states, he wrote, had emerged as "pimples on the backside of Saudi Arabia."

Later, he made his seventh trip to Iraq to write the aftermath, catching the mood in a sentence: "Postwar Iraq has the trapped, anguished air of a ruined marriage that one partner refuses to end." The hot item in Baghdad was a pirate video of U.S. warplanes making their hits. He found that many Iraqis had stopped watching television, no longer able to bear Saddam's face. Some risked capital punishment, telling "hanging jokes" about Saddam's vanity, mother and manhood. He let a foreign ambassador sum it up: "It's as if the Gulf War never happened. We've got the same old Saddam—arrogant, ambitious and inflexible."

With the *Journal,* Horwitz has the luxury of taking a chance on a different angle. The paper does not cover every turn of foreign events; instead, it looks for an odd twist that offers new insight. That's his speciality. Sent to Bosnia, Horwitz wrote the horror but also captured the absurd futility of war in the Balkans. He avoided the Muslim part of Sarajevo, where he felt a brave but one-eyed press corps was covering only part of the story. Serbian monstrosities reached all over Bosnia. And few reporters covered the Serbs themselves.

In character, Tony took a bus into battle. From Pale, he wrote: "The 6:15 A.M. bus from Belgrade to the Bosnian front is standing room only. 'There is still some space, but I do not recommend it,' the driver says, as travelers cram the aisle. Two days before, Bosnian guerrillas ambushed the road, killing nine Serbs. 'If people must run for it,' the driver adds, 'it is not so good to have others standing in the way.' "

His characters tell the story. A Serbian irregular in World War I hat and round John Lennon sunglasses explains his success with Belgrade women: "I tell all girls, 'Tomorrow perhaps I am dead,' he says with a grin." There is a moneychanger in an L.A. Lakers cap. A soldier snoozes, his grenade rolling onto the floor. "At one artillery post, soldiers—most of them urban folk from Sarajevo—struggle to roast a sheep that died of a heart attack during the morning's artillery exchange."

An elderly businessman eyes the armed youths anxiously. "There are no answers in this war because we do not even know the questions," he tells Tony. "Why are we fighting? How can we win? No one asks such things. Only, they want to kill."

The killers' chief has the last word. Horwitz describes the man's armored battlewagon, painted with shark teeth: " 'The Muslims run away in fear when they see it,' the commander claims. More likely they double over in laughter." When the officer invites him back to invest when it's all over, he writes:

"A future of peace and profits seems far away, but the commander, in contrast to almost everyone else in this blood-spattered republic, thinks there is still hope for putting Bosnia together again. 'It is easy to forget about fighting,' he says, draining his slivovitz, 'if you have a good conscience about what you have done in the war.' "

In Sarajevo, Horwitz camped in a Serbian sniper post to check out the mysterious killers who held the city in terror:

> The view from front-line posts—visited at random and without military escort—isn't always so intimidating. Here, the self-styled army of the Serbian Republic of Bosnia-Herzegovina seems at times a loose corps of ill-equipped, ill-trained and even underfed troops enduring what looks like a wretched camping trip. At one post, the latest recruit is a young female secretary and the newest arms shipment is a pair of Tommy guns, straight out of a James Cagney gangster film. Serbian irregulars—whose numbers are roughly equal to the army's 35,000 men— are even more ragtag, appearing more like bikers than fighters, with ponytails, running shoes and black patches bearing skull and crossbones stuck on their mix-and-match fatigues.
>
> Beneath a thick crust of bravado, often stoked with plum brandy, many Serb army units appear driven not by dreams of a greater Serbia, but by fear of a foe they regard as a fanatical and better armed than themselves—dubious notions fostered daily by Serbian propaganda.

One gap-toothed and bearded thirty-year-old told Horwitz: "I don't fight for ideology, or religion, or nationalism. I fight because I want to be back down there with my books and CD player and my Gitanes [cigarettes]." The soldier was particularly anxious to visit what was left of the library and check out a writer he had heard about and one of the man's better titles: "*For Who Is It the Bell Tolls?*"

All of this made for good reading. But it was even better reporting. As pressure grew around the world to rescue Sarajevo, to send in an outside force to break the siege and stop the same sort of "ethnic cleansing" that Hitler practiced in World War II, the Pentagon argued that the risk was too great. The Serbs were invincible. Tony Horwitz, and his readers, knew better.

Yet another Hey-This-Is-Fun correspondent, an aging kid who was also part of a man-woman team, covered the other side. Like Horwitz, Blaine Harden of the *Washington Post* has a goofy grin surgically attached to his face, but those Sarajevo snipers sometimes managed to dim its light. Harden was terrified of the story, as he told his editors, and he went back seven times to cover it.

Readers first noticed Harden in 1985 when dispatches from Africa suddenly grew richer in new sorts of personages. Along with the tyrants and hungry children, there were thinkers and planners, loony artists, and BMW-borne lawyers in red suspenders. He pierced myths with sharp humor and moving drama, revealing a continent of clichés as simply the outer edge of the human condition. He and his partner, Mary Battiata, described not only Africans but also the visiting tribes of deluded outsiders who fly in to put things right.

Harden grew up in Moses Lake, Washington, and edited the paper at Gonzaga University. He wanted to do a junior year in Florence. But he was the first kid in his family to go beyond high school, and his parents felt that college was already enough. Then, at the journalism school in Syracuse, he ran into a man who started a lot of careers: Howard Simons, then managing editor of the *Washington Post*. Simons gave him an A-plus and a job. He worked his way through *Post* farm teams, finally covering Fairfax County and then working on the Sunday magazine.

In 1983, he was passed over as Texas correspondent and quit but, as he put it, came crawling back. At the time, Jim Hoagland was foreign editor, with a soft spot for his first assignment abroad: Africa. He hired Harden and sent him to Nairobi. After time out to do a book, Blaine transferred to Poland in mid-1989, and began covering countries that collapsed the day he arrived.

Even in the blood-spattered streets of Bucharest, Blaine managed to find zany human touches. Once, working together, we were stopped by insurgents at a roadblock. Blaine had gotten in by flying to Sofia, Bulgaria, and driving all night at a hundred miles an hour. His dinner, four apples, rolled around in the trunk. A guard peered at the fruit, suspecting disguised hand grenades. To find out, he laid one on the ground and, with the heel of his boot, he smashed it to applesauce. Fortunately enough for him, it was an apple. Blaine giggled for an hour.

But Yugoslavia got to him. Deep into the siege of Bosnia, Harden wrote of a teacher of Islam who had buried his wife, his three daughters and his only granddaughter, one after the other, in his tomato patch between a pear tree and a cherry tree on a Sarajevo hillside. All were killed by random Serbian shelling. In its first five months, Harden wrote, the siege had killed at least 1,954 and wounded 25,000 others. "But the tragedy of war does not touch the dead; rather, it curses the survivors whose connections to love and family and home have been abruptly broken. . . . [In Sarajevo] broken connections are the rule, not the exception. Perhaps no one was cursed more than Ismet Spahic."

Of the six members of Spahic's immediate family, only fifteen-year-old Amina survived, a piece of mortar lodged deep in her buttocks. Each dawn, he started his day with morning prayers at the makeshift graveyard beside his house. "I really had beautiful children," he told Harden. "If I did not believe in God, I would dig my own grave and lie down with them." It began in June when his wife, who could not adjust to the war, died of a heart attack in the street. By September, the rest were gone. Reading the details, we see a message emerging. These are not aliens in some distant galaxy. These are humans, and not far away. At the time, Americans seemed captivated by a little book on Provence. Bosnia, if the roads are clear, is only a day's drive past Aix.

Spahic concluded: "This is not war; it is genocide. The evil is too great to stay in Bosnia, and I believe it will spill back into Serbia, afflicting the people who started all this. The pain that I have was also assisted by the West. They have been watching how the Serbs are killing us. They can see that these crimes cannot be stopped by a tin of macaroni, but only by power." Then he excused himself. He had to go to a funeral.

"It was so depressing, the lack of any effect of the reporting," Blaine told me later. "I've never been so sickened by a story. It was appeasement in our time. So shameful. People will look back and this will be a black mark for the West. It already is. Maybe there are 130,000 people dead." He could not understand why Americans did not connect with the story. "Maybe it's the connotation of the word 'Muslim.' It all seems so complicated. It's no more complicated than armed robbery."

Blaine Harden and Tony Horwitz met for the first time in Split, on the Adriatic, and they compared notes. Harden had seen the Serbian leaders as monsters. Horwitz, who had watched their atrocities, saw some of the reasons behind them. The Croats, he felt, got an unbelievably easy ride because so many correspondents had gravitated to the main story. Any reader who followed either's work was well-informed. Those who read both had a deep understanding of the whole picture.

Sarajevo was a dilemma for editors. Alvin Shuster, foreign editor of the *Los Angeles Times,* decided to let the story go uncovered. He did not want to endanger his people. News agencies and stories from the edges would have to do. The *New York Times* man, John Burns, went to Sarajevo in June and decided not to leave. The *Times* let Burns make the choices. Harden talked with Michael Getler, his foreign editor, who wanted him to go but also wanted him to come back. He went for the reasons most correspondents usually go. It was the story.

"The worst was the depression and the confusion," he said. "You are so afraid, living in a helmet and flak jacket. At night, you lie in bed and listen to shells, knowing that any one could pick you out. Then you have to go back and do it again." When he last left, the airport was closed. He and AP photographer Jerome Delay drove to Croatia, crouched on the front seat of their car, which they nonetheless drove at a hundred miles an hour.

In 1993, Harden took time out to go home to write a book about the Columbia River. It was a safe bet that he would have fun.

Burns of the *Times,* a citizen of Britain and Canada who exemplifies the Cultural Chameleon school, had commanded his colleagues' respect for half a generation. Witty and friendly, Burns draws a picture with sweeping strokes and brings it alive with deft dabs of color. He has always pushed the limits. In China, he was jailed as a spy for trying to trace the steps of Edgar Snow, the American journalist who first profiled the Communist leaders. He rode a motorcycle through countryside the Chinese had declared closed. Burns covered South Africa, the Soviet Union and a lot in between. In each place, he saw things through the eyes of the people he was writing about.

In Rhodesia, where black rebels fought the war that gave them Zimbabwe, Burns reported from both sides. But he also spent a night on guard duty with black soldiers in the Rhodesian Army, showing how nothing complex is ever only black or white.

After 1990, Burns spent most of his time in Iraq. Then, assigned to a restful tour in Canada, pulling out of brutal treatment for stomach cancer, he felt the call. Leaving his wife at home with their three kids in school, Burns volunteered to help in Yugoslavia. He went to Belgrade and headed for Sarajevo. His editors argued and then gave up.

By staying so long, and commanding the respect of his sources, Burns reflected not only the daily horrors of the siege but also the broader picture. His copy made crystal clear what the Serbs had in mind, and how they were going about it.

In late November, he spent seven hours with Borislav Herak, a twenty-one-year-old Serb who had left his job pushing a handcart in a textile factory to take part in wholesale extermination. Herak was charged with twenty-nine "ethnic cleansing" killings, genocide, systematic rape and looting. Burns' story ran below Herak's photo, his wide forehead, fleshy lips and eerie eyes accentuated by a wide-angle lens. It began:

> What Borislav Herak remembers most vividly about the sunny morning in late June when he and two companions gunned down ten members of a Muslim family is the small girl, about 10, who tried to hide behind her grandmother as the three Serbian nationalist soldiers opened fire from about 10 paces.
>
> "We told them not to be afraid, we wouldn't do anything to them, they should just stand in front of the wall," said Mr. Herak, 21. "But it was taken for granted among us that they should be killed. So when somebody said, 'Shoot,' I swung around and pulled the trigger, three times, on automatic fire. I remember the little girl with the red dress hiding behind the granny."

Herak had taken a wrong turn into a Bosnian roadblock. Faced with a firing squad, he agreed to open up to a reporter who was patient enough to draw out the details. Burns related how Herak and the others had kept teenage girls in a motel and raped them to death and how he had helped Serbs throw Muslims, still alive, into steel furnaces. Serbian irregulars, Burns reported, were trained to kill by wrestling pigs to the ground and then slitting their throats.

The account offered insight into a conflict that was often reported on the surface. Herak loved his sister, who was married to a Muslim. Months earlier, he had no animosity toward Muslims, who, he told Burns, had always treated him well. But Serb propaganda said that Bosnia was to be made into an Islamic state and that youngsters would have to wear Muslim dress.

"We were told that Ahatovci must be a cleansed Serbian territory, that it was a strategic place between Ilidza and Rajlovac, and that all the Muslims there must be killed," Herak said. "We were told that no one must escape, and that all the houses must be burned, so that if anybody did survive, they would have nowhere left to return to. It was an order, and I simply did what I was told."

Then Burns drew the conclusion:

"Although Mr. Herak's experiences were limited to a 10-mile stretch of territory just north of Sarajevo, his account offered new insights into the ways that tens of thousands of civilians have died, most of them in towns and villages where there have been no independent witnesses."

Burns' Pulitzer Prize for 1992 was probably the most predicted award in the history of American journalism.


Correspondents come in all types. The business has gotten too diverse, too full of people who parachute from home or who spend a few years abroad before going home to serious journalism. But correspondents know who their heroes are.

The Medieval Monks, rare as California condors, work at the other extreme from the Hey-This-Is-Fun school. Their fingers foul up computer keyboards, not meant to be hammered woodpecker fashion at breakneck speed. However light they travel, they are encumbered by the weight of a world they expect someday to put right. Impatient with fools, Medieval Monks are seldom loved by editors, whom they tend to lump in that category. Their writing can be awkward, and they may skip over frills which lighten up a somber subject. But they are the power tools of the profession.

When the Kurds were suddenly a story, after the Gulf War, Jon Randal's telephone rang without letup. Everyone wanted to harvest his brain. Randal, of course, was so deep into Kurd country that not even his *Washington Post* editors knew where to start looking for him. After four decades on the road, he moves faster than any kid. When he gets where he is going, few can match him.

Randal, over sixty, looks somewhere between forty-five and ageless. Colleagues swear he has not spoken a complete sentence since high school. Instead, he launches into a thought, and his turbocharged neurons propel him into a dozen others. He is a warm and generous companion. "He can't give you the shirt off his back because he gave it to the last friend," one old pal put it. Yet he is capable of searing the eyebrows off of anyone, friend or foe, for no apparent reason.

The archetypal Medieval Monk, Randal has watched the world take its present form, and he remembers exactly how it happened. To him, vague concepts like European unity, Islamic resurgence, and the balance of power amount to organic reality. He knows the characters and their assorted human frailties. He is smart enough not to try predicting the future. When he writes about the past and present, he is not guessing.

Randal has met a lot of people, and he remembers most of them. He reports from the inside, consulting Arab ministers who are old cronies, getting blasted with the U.S. ambassador he knew as a scared trainee, waking up generals who are pleased to hear from him. One colleague remembers Randal sitting down at a Palestinian leader's desk, throwing his feet up and lecturing the man on policy blunders. He wrote the book on Lebanon, literally. Turning the tables on most of us, he intimidates the French.

Each night, Randal types up his notes in a personal shorthand with James Joyce logic and strange anagrams and symbols to jog his eight-track memory. Important people get arcane nicknames based on word associations. In interviews, he sometimes refers to people by his own code names and can't figure out the blank looks that produces.

Randal spent a Harvard year in France and stayed to work on a farm. A woman was involved. Dabbling in journalism, he realized he could see the world on an expense account. He started with Agence France-Presse and then covered the Algerian War for United Press. He worked for the *New York Herald Tribune*'s Paris edition and *Time*. In 1966, he joined the *New York Times*. Later, he moved to the *Post*. Somewhere along the way he heard the call. Nothing biblical or dramatic or even definable, it was more like an addiction. Down deep, at some level accessible only on a long, unwelcome plane ride, he knows that what he does can make a difference in the world he works so hard to watch.

He is always on the move. No sooner has he arrived in one place than he cables his desk about where to go next, usually ending his message with "I kiss your feet" or a fervent wish for the long life of his editor's camel. Always, he gets close to the story. When Ayatollah Ruhollah Khomeini returned to Iran in 1979, Randal knew huge crowds would throng the Martyrs' Cemetery. The night before, he took a sleeping bag and camped out in the graveyard. A helicopter carrying the ayatollah was mobbed by so many people that its rotor nearly slashed through the faithful, and he added one of those Randal lines that are meant to be excised: "It was nearly a case of the Shiite hitting the fan."

Randal's editors joke that he writes French grammar in English. Someone stuck up on the bulletin board a line from one of his dispatches: "It did not go unnoticed that . . ." But he has his flights of literary inspiration. When the Shah of Iran was deposed, his intro was from the first lines of Percy Bysshe Shelley's poem "Ozymandias": "Look on my works, ye mighty, and despair!"

The Kamms combine a Medieval Monk and a Hey-This-Is-Fun in the same family. Henry Kamm, in pretend retirement from the *New York Times,* lives in Geneva with a bag packed. If he ever passes on, his editors suspect, they'll have to install a telex at graveside for his dispatches from beyond. In forty-four years on the paper, he has been everywhere else, from the Balkans to Borneo. Once, a Kamm story goes, he spent a month on a family vacation in Normandy. Then he flew somewhere, checked into a hotel, unzipped his typewriter and sighed, "It's good to be home." When I asked him about it, he laughed. "I don't remember the circumstances," he said, "but it sounds right." The life is hard on some families, but Henry started a dynasty.

His son Tom's first job was as a copy boy at the *International Herald Tribune,* where the editor often sent him to get takeout noodles. "Do it," Henry advised when Tom grumbled. Not long afterward, Tom was covering South America for the *Wall Street Journal.* When a Brookings Institution survey asked all foreign correspondents to name who they thought was the best in the business, Tom answered, "My father."

As scientists argued over the ozone layer, Tom Kamm flew to Punta Arenas, Chile, to write how the figurative "end of the world" was adding a more ominous meaning. People were getting mysterious Hawaiian sunburns. Trees were sick; horses got spots. At one farm, Kamm wrote, "sheep were so blinded by conjunctivitis they crashed into each other like bumper cars." It was, someone said, as if "a sorcerer has cast a spell."

Dick Blystone of CNN is an Avuncular Charmer, by now a familiar face in livingrooms. When he appears, people know what to expect. Some "talent," as television correspondents are collectively known, seeks every occasion to get on screen. Bly's goal is not glory but excellence. He came to the untried Cable News Network in its earliest days, already a respected agency man. Courageous, resourceful and among the finer writers in the business, he is past having to prove himself.

When the Gulf War loomed, Bly raced to Jordan. Then he went to Baghdad. As the January 15 war deadline approached, CNN asked if he wanted to stay. Bly did. But he had promised his wife, Hella, that after a six-week Gulf stint, he would be gone this time no more than three weeks. For twenty-five years Hella had put up with every sacrifice, and Bly respected her wishes.

Blystone was replaced by Arnett, his old Vietnam AP colleague, who for weeks running had the world's greatest story. Overnight, Arnett joined history's most celebrated reporters. Then there was a lull when correspondents might have rotated. "I could have been home in two weeks, anyway," Bly said, with only a trace of wistfulness, when asked about the timing.

From Baghdad, after time at home, Blystone went to Israel. When the Scuds started, he was in the streets in chemical gear. On another channel, someone panicked and announced that Iraq had gassed Tel Aviv. But a flip of the remote brought Blystone, the Avuncular Charmer, reporting only what he knew for sure. He wore no props for the camera, always removing his mask. When Larry King asked if he was afraid, he answered, "It's a big world, Larry, and a small missile."

My first brush with Bly was in 1972 when I went to Vietnam to help out, from my base in Singapore. I was in Hue, working up the guts to go on some harebrained South Vietnamese helicopter mission behind enemy lines. I was having no luck in the guts department but had decided to go anyway. Suddenly, Blystone appeared. He was almost immobile with diarrhea, but he insisted on going, and not for the glory. It was his bureau and his responsibility. I argued, hard. He won.

For a craftsman of the written word, he took naturally to television. Bly made no attempt to talk down. He just organized more tightly and looked for stronger images. When the Iron Curtain began to fall, he and a crew worked their way along it, picking places to stop and hang out. Bly stood back out of the way and let the people talk. Underwritten, underspoken, his narrative filled in the rest. Few television viewers could have learned more had they been there themselves.

Among the Wonder Women, there is Alison Smale, the AP's bureau chief in Vienna, who was the first person through the collapsed Berlin Wall. She suspected that Checkpoint Charlie was about to open. When it did, she went through with the German woman she was interviewing. Since then she has stayed ahead on almost every story in Eastern Europe and Yugoslavia. As with other Wonder Women, with Smale the Woman part is incidental. And she would also argue about Wonder. But few women, and certainly no men, could produce a flow of smooth copy while carrying a baby and maintaining a home life with a wild-whimmed Russian Jewish composer.

Smale ran into some AP correspondents as a kid backpacking around Spain. They bitched about the life and recommended she do something else. To her, it sounded great. Soon she was a UPI intern in Bonn, and shortly after, she was bureau chief for Germany. The AP got tired of getting beaten, so it hired her. Within a year she got to Moscow, where she added Russian to her German and French. Then she was made bureau chief in Vienna, in charge of Eastern Europe and most of the Balkans.

Like the best of wire animals, she is an all-around hand. As an editor, she gets top work out of correspondents who like her and want her approval. For features, she has a deft, light touch. She can weave a dozen loose ends of a breaking story into a single running dispatch, rich in history and color.

When Czechoslovakia threw off communism, Smale wrote, "The revolt moved with such dignity and speed it was almost as if everyone knew their part in advance, and [Vaclav] Havel had written it as a real-life drama." And she knew all the main players. Later, when Jiri Dienstbier, the new foreign minister, stood solemnly for a photo at the Budapest ceremony to dissolve the Warsaw Pact, he winked when he saw Alison. The message was, Who would believe it? Dienstbier, like Havel himself and the rest of his cabinet, were Smale's old drinking buddies in Prague when they were dissidents in between jail terms.

When Yugoslavia began to break apart, Smale spotted it early. She went to Glina, a little town in Croatia, near the Serbian border, just after Serbs had attacked the local police post. They were enraged at Croatia's declaration of independence. Not many people realized it, but the raid was a spark that helped ignite all that would follow:

> In the hours before the attack, rival bands of armed men had swept into the woods, setting up their own checkpoints and pointed aged guns—some of World War II vintage—at anyone seeking to pass through. Five reporters eventually negotiated a dozen makeshift roadblocks to enter the Croatian end of Glina. There they found villagers willing to talk about the repressed fear and desire for revenge now feeding the Yugoslav conflict.
>
> At stake are the issues of everyday life in the rural Balkans; which ethnic group will control the police, courts, schools, and hospitals and thus wield power over the small towns and villages that make up rural life. For years, Croats of the Glina region say, those privileges belonged to a dominant ethnic Serbian majority in the area. "We always hated each other," said a Croat, who refused to give his name out of fear for the safety of his brother, a policeman in Glina.

She gave more background and then fit the microcosm into a larger picture. In Zagreb, she quoted a Croatian leader who dismissed the incident as a clash between security forces and insisted, "This is absolutely not civil war." Smale knew better. She added a last line: "But in towns such as Glina, the battle lines were drawn months ago."

Smale followed the Bosnia siege, but she describes herself as a different sort of war correspondent. "I'm not very good at saying here is this weapon or that weapon," she said. "I would rather explain that here is a Serb peasant and, yes, he is a brute, but he really sincerely believes that he is defending his village. He is protecting a lifestyle rooted in something we have long forgotten. It's not that he is right, but he thinks he is right. That helps explain the complexity of the situation."

Mark Fineman of the *Los Angeles Times* excels in two schools. In the Just-One-More-Question-Sir department, he combines a scattershot, low-key Lieutenant Columbo approach with the dental drill technique of an SS storm trooper. Then, smoking like a forest fire and consuming coffee by the liter, he shifts to Deadline Poet mode. The result is a rambling dispatch, full of humanity and detail, that conveys the news in a broad context.

At a packed U.N. briefing in Mogadishu, Somalia, Fineman perked up at a brief remark in someone's long statement. The city's water was being turned on again. Others simply reported the fact. Fineman, smelling a better story, made his way through deadly roadblocks to the pumping station. He found the aging leader of a tiny clan who had fought eleven battles over two years to hold the waterworks. It cost him two sons, but his was the only installation in Mogadishu which escaped destruction.

When U.N. engineers arrived, the clan leader wanted four hundred dollars for his spoils. No, he was told; the United Nations does not pay extortion. With Somali inflation, his figure soon rose to four thousand dollars. For months on end, he kept the valves closed. Mogadishu residents went without water, hostages to the stalemate. Finally, a compromise was reached: The United Nations hired his men to run the waterworks. Focusing on the microcosm, Fineman said everything there was to say about Somalia.

Friends rejoice when Fineman shows up on a story. Handsome in a rough sort of way, ready for any challenge, he is a jolt of good energy. In a business that is losing its flavor, he is a teller of jokes, a hugger of shoulders and a sharer of good whiskey. This, he happily admits, is the result of Bill Claiborne's Behavior Modification Program. Claiborne was in New Delhi for the *Washington Post* when Fineman arrived on his first posting abroad, with the *Philadelphia Inquirer*. Having risen fast from the Chicago streets, Fineman was a major fan of his own work.

"He was the biggest jerk I ever met," Claiborne said, when pressed by Fineman to tell the story. Actually, he used another word. "But he had this knack for finding a story. He'd walk into a village and see things no one else would. He was good to travel with. And I kind of liked him. So I launched this program. Every time he acted like an asshole, I told him. I made him miserable."

Now Fineman has crossed the line to lovable eccentric; he laughs at the early days. "Do you have to put this in a book?" he asked. "Well, I guess you can't argue with the truth."


Back when lines were more clearly drawn, one editor profiled a perfect composite. In *Coups and Earthquakes,* it came out like this:

The Bionic Correspondent has no ego, libido, mother, career drive, cultural snobbery, fallen arches or fear of flying. He persuades officials to answer their telephones and comment forthrightly. He speaks Urdu and Lingala in a gentle manner which charms shy villagers and melts the hearts of tyrants. He sends his uncensored dispatches to a desk which cherishes his every comma and adds only a few trenchant words from elsewhere to broaden his dimensions. And, just to keep his focus sharp, he returns home every so often to mingle among Harvard dons and Virginia ham curers.

Ed Cody has a mother and a libido and speaks gently only in Arabic, French and Spanish. Bionic Correspondents aren't supposed to have black Porsche Turbos. Cody came back for a stint as the *Washington Post*'s assistant foreign editor, where some among a new breed of editors pronounce him slightly strong-willed. ("Am I supposed to be weak-willed?" he asked.) Otherwise, he's a flesh-and-blood version of the mythical model.

Cody never looks as if he is working. He smiles a lot. He reads at a desk cleared of papers. He tells stories in amusing detail. He eats dinner, ordering with elaborate care and enjoying every molecule. Sometimes he talks to people, but only a suspicious mind would think that might be an interview. Back at the hotel, he fiddles with the phone, affixing clips and wires from his little black kit to hook up his computer. And then, the next morning, you realize he has impaled every reporter in town.

Like a lot of correspondents, Cody grew up in a small place and dreamed of bigger places. He was raised with Umpqua Indians in the Oregon timberland town of Grand Ronde; his father kept the books for a logging company. Like Harden, he went to Gonzaga University in Spokane. An honors program put him on a fast track; he did a junior year in Florence and stayed. He enrolled in law school in Paris, supporting himself by working in an ad agency.

Cody decided to try journalism. After studying at Columbia in New York, he bought a copy of J. W. Cash's *Mind of the South* and went to the *Charlotte Observer*. A year later, the AP hired him after a visiting executive spotted his potential. "You're learning to type fast," the man pronounced. Cody spent an obligatory stretch on the AP's foreign desk and then moved to New Delhi. The Lebanon War flared, and he transferred to Beirut.

In Paris, edging toward executive status as the AP's assistant bureau chief, Cody switched to the *Post*. He was a reporter.

Cody's specialty is putting together logic with logistics to produce a story when no one else can. He works out the basics and then lets fortune fall into place. One night in Paris, word came that a Pan Am jumbo jet had crashed mysteriously over a little town in Scotland. It was 8:20, and the last flight to Britain had gone at 8. It took a few minutes to find a willing charter operator. It took longer to convince his foreign editor to cough up six thousand dollars from a tight budget. Within hours, Cody was landing in Glasgow.

Only two cabs were left in the lot, and instinct pointed him to the one on the left. He explained how he had to reach Lockerbie in spite of police roadblocks that had sealed off the area. "You're in luck," the cabbie said. "I'm from Lockerbie." After a long, fast ride and a few sharp turns in blackness, they were in the middle of town. They split up and met later. The driver had collected as many quotes and telling details as Cody. Then he found a friend who opened his pub so Cody could call Washington. As usual, Cody scooped the pack.

Into the 1990s, Cody worries whether these old skills will live on much longer. "It's the subject of amusement," he said, puzzled at how young journalists can miss the excitement of making the system work, no matter what. "If you get through, they figure it just happens," he said. "If not, so what?"

When the USS *Vincennes* shot down an Iranian airliner in the Gulf, Cody did it again. He found the captain of a merchant ship who, he reasoned, would be able to help him file. The captain patched a call through Dubai, and Cody dictated his story minutes before deadline, the only dispatch from the scene that night. "They thought it was amusing," Cody said, shaking his head.

Once, when we were being rebuffed in yet another place we could not spell, Cody laughed. He had put up with censors, desk editors, outraged readers and everything in between. "You know, the ultimate humiliation in this business," he said, "is that there is no ultimate humiliation."

For newcomers, Cody is an enticing model. He is a no-frills version of the All-American Boy in khaki pants and oxford blue shirts that live forever. His blond hair is cut short. Sensible reading glasses hang from a cord around his neck. He laughs easily and speaks softly, with none of the hard edge that people picture when typecasting foreign correspondents. But on closer inspection, you realize it may not be so easy to be Cody. It's in the eyes. At full bore or at rest, they always seem to be seeing through things, Bionic style.

Along with the good ones, there are a lot of the other kind. The I'm-Good-and-I'll-Prove-It types are a pain in the ass. Competitive on the smallest details, they milk colleagues for information but seldom share. Their drive is not for the story but the byline or the air time. They avoid dull but important subjects and shun tedious legwork if it promises no glory. Their conversation is rich in accounts of small victories.

The Stenographers are obsessed with getting the details right, but they often miss the point. Reporting is a series of briefings, press releases and tape-recorded minor interviews that are carefully transcribed at the expense of time better spent probing into substance. Stenographers excel at relating events that happen on the surface, but they seldom get across what those events really mean.

There are Happy Hypers, Shortcutters, Pontificators and Plodders. There are the Obsessed, who report by addiction, escaping unhappy lives or making lives unhappy by racing off blindly at every bell. Readers do not always suffer. A reporter's motives or manner need not affect the final result. But caution is advised. Shoddy reporters not only get things wrong but also leave things out. It is easy for people to be skeptical about what they read. It is harder to read what is not there.

Some of the most important names in the business are hardly ever seen in print. For every famous correspondent, there is a handful of "locals" and stringers who slog away in the shadows. Like chefs' assistants, they do the shopping, cleaning, cutting and stirring. When it is over, they clean up the mess. In many cases, the story would be better served if the correspondent missed the plane and left it to the unsung hired help.

By the time war in El Salvador drew in the big-timers, much of the country was a no-rules killing field. A wrong turn could be fatal. Lives depended on knowing when to stop and when to stand on the gas. The story was hopelessly complex, with secret alliances, arms supplies, diplomatic deals and political poker. To understand it, reporters had to get past the high walls, figuratively and literally, that shielded family compounds.

Local reporters, who held the keys to El Salvador, faced a double risk. Anyone might run into bad luck on the road. But outsiders could file their stories and move on before any offended death squad could fix sights on them. They had a certain leeway as uninitiated foreigners. But Salvadoran journalists had no such luxuries. People expected them to take sides. If they crossed someone, even inadvertently, their kids were easy to find.

The AP relied on some sterling locals, including Any Cabrera, who stayed put while New York–based correspondents came and went. One morning, an American newsmagazine reporter, looking for a countryman to take for coffee, stuck his head into the AP office at the Camino Real Hotel. "Anyone here?" he called. Glancing around at three Salvadorans banging away at machines, he answered his own question. "Nope. No one."

Under the star system of reporting, even full-fledged players get short shrift if one prejudice or another disqualifies them. After the Gulf War, a CNN producer boasted in a book that his people were the only TV journalists in Baghdad except for some Jordanians. That kissed off Michel Haj, Middle East chief for Worldwide Television News, a tested professional who thinks quickly in half a dozen languages and is equipped, alas, with only a passport from Jordan.

In fact, CNN's main point of light in Baghdad, Arnett, rose to glory as an unsung local for The Associated Press. Most of these little-known stringers work for news agencies. Each agency has its share, but I know those at the AP best.

Ondrej Hejma is a Czech rock star. His instrument is a guitar, but when it comes to news, he does a pretty mean keyboard. Until the revolution, he led a quiet double life as singer-songwriter for Žlutý Pes (Yellow Dog) and the AP's Czechoslovakian correspondent. Prague produced few headlines. Mainly, reporters dug at the edges and carefully wrote stories under the harsh gaze of the Communist Party's Central Committee. But the mood was changing. Hard-liners didn't know what to make of a guy with a cheery mustache, a bald spot and long hair falling over his gold earring. Like most East European stringers, Hejma was hired for his language skills. A friend of his translated for Japanese reporters who shared an office with the AP. Although Ondrej's specialty is Chinese, his English is perfect. The AP hired him, and a year later he replaced the correspondent, who retired.

Hejma learned reporting fast. Late in 1989, with the Berlin Wall open, Czechoslovakia needed only a spark. A young woman provided it. She told reporters that state police officers had beaten to death a student named Martin Smid. People rallied, and a patch of Prague sidewalk where it had happened was an instant shrine. Reuters carried the story; AFP said three youths had been killed. Other reporters wrote it as fact. AP editors pushed Hejma hard for a matching story. He was late, and the agency looked bad. But he insisted on seeing some evidence. With his wife, a doctor, he scoured the hospitals and morgues. No body. After two days, others had to report that Martin Smid was not as dead as all that. It was a phony story which nonetheless triggered a revolution. Thanks to Hejma, the AP didn't fall for it.

Ajay Singh was a tea planter in India, but Darjeeling leaves grew a little too slowly for his tastes. Earlier, he had studied some veterinary medicine and biology and classics and who knows what else. Singh, tall and dashing but self-effacing, is a cultured man. When Rajiv Gandhi was assassinated in 1991, he was the new guy in the bureau, assigned to roam around Delhi with me as a colleague and translator. We were checking the mood of the street. In such instances, the Big Foot is supposed to call the shots. I just sat back and let Ajay follow his instincts. Our story was political and social and big news. But Ajay took me to a bird hospital run by an ascetic sect, the Jains. He thought we'd find something interesting; as usual, he was right.

The assassination had shaken India, a nation so vast that Churchill once called it a geographical term. All over New Delhi, the swarm was finding people to comment on how everyone had been affected by the event, how no corner of India had been untouched by the sudden turn of events. But in the heart of Old Delhi, Ajay found us a man who could not have cared less. He was preoccupied with giving a pigeon an intravenous drip.

Yet another unsung champion of the business, Ali Ibrahim Mursal, worked for the AP less than five months. I hired him as my driver in Mogadishu in August 1992. Ali was a smooth translator and wise analyst of turbulent Somali affairs. His pal, Abdi, with an aged M-16, covered my back, but my real security was Ali's gift as a divining rod for potential trouble. His unfailing answer to everything was "Why not?" When he said it quickly, with a smile, no danger lurked. If he looked worried as he said it, things were risky but possible. When he scratched his head and demurred, it was time to slam into reverse. A half-dozen times, he waded into gun barrels to dissuade assorted militiamen and freelance thugs from ruining my day.

By the time I returned in December, he had been promoted to field marshal, supervising the AP's fleet of eight rented vehicles. A string of successors had their own Ali stories; all of them owed their lives to him. He had long since sent his wife and kids to Kenya, and his new colleagues were his family. I left again and, back in Paris, found that Ali had made the AP wire. He had taken three technicians into Mogadishu's minefield of a market to buy fruit. One wore a gold chain, and someone snatched it. Ali jumped the thief, but the guy's friend had an AK-47.

The story on wire was by Reid Miller, the Nairobi bureau chief, who, like the rest of us, looked on Ali as a brother. It recalled a remark Ali had made that he would do anything for the AP. "He kept that vow," Reid wrote. "He died for AP."

Chapter 5

# Snappers

Greg Marinovich, an AP photographer of considerable talent, offered some sensible advice to a colleague who turned up in Somalia. "Watch out for the port," he said. "Everybody's got guns, and they'll shoot at you as soon as you start to raise your camera." Later, I asked someone if he knew where Greg had gone. "He's out taking pictures," the guy said. "At the port."

Correspondents like to nurture the image of being crazy, but few of them are. Photographers are crazy. Show me a perfectly normal, housebroken snapper who looks both ways before crossing the street, and I'll show you a lunatic. Trust me on this. At one time, taking pictures abroad took only technical skill, stamina, good sense and some courage. Now you've got to be nuts.

When hot bits of metal pepper the atmosphere, sane people keep their heads down. If TV camera crews or photographers did that, they'd have no pictures. Anytime an enraged crowd surges toward you behind a blur of waving spears, your instinct is to remove yourself rapidly from the scene. Unless you're holding a camera.

Marinovich, who is crazy but not stupid, is always thinking. "You don't take unnecessary chances," he explained, "but you do your job." His photos of rioting South African blacks setting a man alight won the 1991 Pulitzer Prize. Reporters, who might work for months on a project worthy of a Pulitzer, tend to suspect that the photo prize comes from a fleeting lucky break. Marinovich knows better. "Luck," he said, "is being in the place where luck happens."

David and Peter Turnley, twins who work separately, always manage to be where luck happens. They got to Bucharest in time to watch Nicolae Ceausescu fall. Romania, suddenly free after forty years, imploded with emotion. Young men scampered onto tanks and fought pitched battles with hidden snipers. Casualties backed up in the hospitals. Women stuck flowers into gun barrels. But the Turnleys each had the picture of the revolution, a single face, before they even got into town.

The airport had closed, so the brothers decided the fastest, smartest way into Romania in turmoil was on a relief convoy from Bulgaria. It was the first outside assistance, a sign that the world was with their uprising, and Romanians lined the streets to watch it roll in. From a truck, each Turnley spotted the same middle-aged man. His face, trained over a lifetime to hide feelings, collapsed into a shapeless, tear-streaked form. For a fleeting second, joy, relief and fear all jostled for room on that same face. David shot him vertically; Peter, horizontally. The pictures were otherwise identical.

It was all in a day's work. David had forgotten about the picture when his newspaper, the *Detroit Free Press,* found him months later in Johannesburg for a conference call. He figured he was being fired in the ferocious cutbacks sweeping the industry. Instead, his editors told him he had won a Pulitzer. Peter worked for *Newsweek,* and magazines did not qualify. He won the year's other awards.

David put himself in luck's way again during Desert Storm. He produced what turned out to be the only real combat picture of the war under circumstances photographers will debate for years. He got himself into a separate puddle of a pool when the ground war started. Up front, he met a colonel from Texas who had lived in Paris. The Turnleys' base is Paris; David made a friend. He was allowed to cruise the front lines in a helicopter.

In the heat of assault, David watched a U.S. M-1 tank blast a Bradley fighting vehicle, one of those cases of friendly fire. He was aboard the medevac helicopter that carried out the casualties. As the trip started, he watched a wounded soldier who was almost giddy with nervous relief. He was hurt but was headed to safety, out of the war. An unknown soldier lay beside him in a body bag. He was saddened at that, but in an abstract way. Once he gave his buddies a high five, with the cheerful bravado of someone who has beaten death in a close match.

Suddenly, he found out who was in the bag. It was his closest friend. For an instant, his face reflected all of the horror of what war is really about. Turnley's lens, snatched up and focused in that same instant, caught the picture. It showed none of the fancy weapons or the expressions of men who were killing at a distance. The frame showed a wrapped body and the face of a dead man's friend. It was Desert Storm, up very close.

Since David's access to the front had begun with the pool system, he felt obliged to show his negatives to the Joint Information Bureau. Officers asked to hold them until next of kin could be notified. Time passed until it was evident that the officers were stalling. They refused to give back the film. Until then, the Pentagon had managed to sell the war as some sort of giant video game, a war that was not hell. Here was dramatic evidence to the contrary.

Finally, David insisted on getting his film back. A colonel told him he could have it on the condition that he not use that picture. David only grunted. After debating the moral issues with himself for a few moments, he transmitted the photo to Detroit. Soon, the world saw it. Nothing more was said. A year later, when he asked for Pentagon permission to accompany U.S. flights to Sarajevo, Pete Williams himself, the assistant secretary for public affairs, came on the line. Since David had done such good work in the Gulf, Williams said, he would do his best. He did his best, or he didn't. David did not get his permission.

The Turnleys are storybook examples of American kids growing up to be what they always wanted to be. Yet another brother, in fact, is a Washington-based television cameraman. They come from Fort Wayne, Indiana, the sons of liberal-thinking antique dealers in the Amish country. Peter can launch a bolt of temper from time to time, but both rely more on charm than bluster.

During the last years of the Soviet Union, Peter got to be Mikhail Gorbachev's favorite snapper. He was invited on trips and had unmatched access to the Kremlin. When hard-liners tried their coup, Peter was back home in Indiana. But he was at work in Moscow by the next morning.

Their omnipresence has gotten to be a joke with the Turnleys and me. Anytime I think I am somewhere ahead of the game on a major story, I look up to find at least one set of reddish curls and freckles. Often, two sets. During the Gulf War, in the off-limits Saudi town of Hafr-al-Baten, I walked around a corner to find a jeepload of U.S. soldiers. Fearing a challenge, I tried to sneak by. Safely past,

I heard a voice call, "Hi, Mort." It was David in military drag; the soldiers were snappers.

In Baidoa, Somalia, I finally had them. The world's event of the day was a convoy of U.S. Marines and French paratroopers rolling in to save starving Somalis. The Turnleys were not around. Just after dawn, seventy vehicles rumbled past the swarm's photo position behind a huge American flag. The AP's Jerome Delay and I shot out ahead of them in a Range Rover. We waited among a crowd of Somalis as the convoy approached. Suddenly, it turned right to skirt the town. Mad Abdullah, our driver, set out cross country to catch them. We rocketed through grass that masked the windshield. Abdullah lurched over rocks and ruts, flat out. Finally, we caught the convoy's tail end. Weaving among armored vehicles that tried to ram us, we got near the front.

Only the lead vehicle, the one with the flag, was still ahead of us. Abdullah pointed the jeep into a gulley of boulders and stomped on it, sailing ahead onto the open road. Jerome leaned out the front window and shot backward. Nothing else was near us except for two matched Toyota pickups that had been ahead of the convoy the whole way. There was a Turnley in each Toyota.


As a group, photographers are even more diverse than correspondents. Even among U.S. news organizations, not many are Americans. Some are highly schooled, and others are barely literate. A few have personality traits that would get them committed to institutions, let alone fired, if they were only reporters. That is fair enough. Their job is harder.

Correspondents only have to know what took place. If they oversleep or take a wrong turn, they can get a fill. Photographers must not only witness the moment but also get it on film, whatever the light or the tumult at hand. This means finding the right time and place, and lugging the right gear, before the moment happens.

Their job, obviously enough, is vital. Old-time reporters remember the days when photographers were those nuisances with the bulky Speed Graphic flash cameras who tagged along to do as bidden, to snap a mug shot of the interview subject or one more photo of a car wreck. That changed a long time ago. No matter how much we wrote about the great African humanitarian tragedy in Biafra, in the late 1960s, we stirred little interest. A single photo on the cover of *Life,* the now-familiar baby with swollen belly and matchstick limbs, rocketed the story to world consciousness.

The danger increases by the year. In many societies, people don't like having their picture taken. Some cultures fear that the camera is stealing their soul. Others have a more practical worry: Authorities, or enemies, might identify them and seek to settle a score. More and more, reluctant subjects make their point in convincing ways.

At Medina Hospital in Mogadishu, Santiago Lyon of the AP made a single quick snap of clan warriors bringing in a wounded comrade. He had just arrived and had not had time to learn how touchy Somali gunmen were about pictures. But that probably would not have stopped him, anyway. Lyon slipped back into the hospital's emergency ward, and the men burst in to find him. They wanted the film. He rewound an unexposed roll on a different camera and gave it to them. They left, grumbling.

Moments later, they burst in again. The leader, no darkroom technician, had pried opened the film can and examined the long strip inside. When he found no pictures, he assumed Santiago had tricked him. Santiago had, of course; the guy was right for the wrong reason. It took the intervention of four doctors, several drivers and half a dozen others—and an hour of waiting inside the hospital—to dissuade the gunmen from opening fire.

In Lebanon's turbulent 1980s, in the Shouf Mountains, another photographer whipped out his high-tech light meter and took a reading on some Druse soldiers at a checkpoint. One of them grabbed it to take a look. It read f/16. The man jammed a gun into the snapper's guts and announced that the photographer was a U.S. Air Force ground spotter. He had proof: the guy had called in a strike by F-16 fighters.

Once they get the picture, photographers have to get it out of town. During that Romanian revolution, a handful of snappers from a French agency chartered a plane from Paris and arrived on the first night. Fighting was vicious. One of their friends, a French television cameraman, was so caught up in his work he did not notice the tank that backed up and crushed him to death. The photographers shot back at snipers with telephoto lenses. All the next day, they risked their lives to collect images. Finally, it was time to ship. The airport was closed, and one of their number was delegated to take everyone's film to Paris by train.

At the station, a group of insurgents thought the photographer was acting funny. He might be a Securitate agent trying to escape. As the Romanians approached, he panicked and ran. They caught him and took the film. He was roughed up, but that was nothing compared with what his colleagues did later.

Photo agencies are a clearinghouse for freelancers who are too busy working to sell their own pictures. Each has a stable of regulars who work on assignment for a specific magazine or who market their photos as they come in. The product is perishable, and negotiations go fast. Higher paying editors get first crack in competitive areas, but the best pictures are sold in different markets around the world and then resold from the archives.

A lot of photographers work out their own deal. David Turnley has a staff job at the *Free Press,* but he also sells pictures through Black Star. Peter Turnley is freelance, but he is on contract to *Newsweek.* He, too, works through Black Star. On important stories, big newspapers often send a photographer or two from home to work with a special writer. Mostly, however, newspapers depend on the news agencies.

As it is on the words side, news agency photographers are the profession's beasts of burden. They seldom can afford to get lost for a few hours, or a week, in search of the perfect shot. Thousands of newspapers depend on them to illustrate the day's breaking story and each of its subplots. If a reporter writes about the guy who invented collapsible chopsticks, editors want a picture. When big news breaks, they want lots to choose from.

Major papers subscribe not only to the AP's photo service but also to those of Reuters and possibly Agence France-Presse, AFP. The competition is brutal. Winners are determined by who is best, but more often by who is first.

That first night in Romania, Laurent Rebours, a Frenchman who shoots for the AP, was working alone. He had powerful pictures, but news agencies cannot wait for trains. Rebours returned to his hotel room to develop and file. Wire photographers travel with a computerized transmitter which sends pictures as electronic bits. They only have to develop the film in a small metal cylinder and zap it with a hair dryer. Negatives are sent directly, without prints; the quality and speed are astounding. By working a few keys, photographers can edit frames and balance color. But they need a working phone line. Often in dicey situations, it is hit or miss. In Bucharest that night, it was all miss.

Rebours was in a classic bind. If he stayed inside waiting for a line, he could not shoot. If he went out to take pictures, he could not file. As it turned out, the competition had more people in town. His pictures were better, but he lost the first day's play.

A year later, Rebours was part of the AP's photo team in the Gulf War. Like a lot of others, he decided he would be the first into liberated Kuwait. After repeated trips from Dhahran to the border, he found a tiny apartment to rent just south of Khafji. When troops finally moved, he moved faster. Rebours knew the desert tracks that skirted checkpoints. He pushed the limits, getting as close as he could to retreating Iraqis without being invited at gunpoint to go along with them. About the same time that Tony Horwitz of the *Wall Street Journal* got into Kuwait, so did Rebours. But, traveling light and pretending to be part of the military, Laurent had no photo transmitter, let alone a satellite phone.

With Rebours, hanging out around the border, was a resourceful cluster of British and French journalists. Excluded from U.S. military access, they had no choice but to find their own. When the ground war began and military officers tried to drown the Americans in pools, these guys were safe and dry. An AFP team had a jeep ready to go, with transmitter, satellite phone and generator, already past the checkpoints. Once across the border, they pulled over and set up an electronic darkroom. In the middle of the desert, with war hardly a mortar lob away, they sent pictures.

Mostly, Rebours creams his competition. For reasons that social scientists might explain, French news photographers tend toward one extreme or another. They can be arrogant, pushy, pretentious and selfish. Or they can be like Laurent, the opposite. When there is danger, he wades in without bravado or posturing. It is no test of courage; it is only getting a camera to where the picture is. When the story is complex, he figures it out and finds a symbol to represent it.

Sent to cover the Sarajevo siege, Rebours spent some time thinking. "I told myself, 'Laurent, you will not cover the war,' " he said. " 'You will cover people. Soldiers fighting, you can see all the time. This is about people.' "

Behind the burned out Marshal Tito barracks, he found rickety buses loading up with children and women, the first convoy to safety after months of shelling. Not much happened as people slowly said their goodbyes and climbed aboard. His inner voice clicked on again. "Something said to me, 'Laurent, you stay,' " he recounted.

" 'Just stay.' " He stayed, cameras ready. Just as the bus was about to go, a little boy put his hands to the window. His father reached up and laid his hands on his son's, separated by the glass. Rebours focused in tight, on the touching fingers, with the youngster's tormented face behind them. That picture was worth a lot of words.

"It was all over in three seconds, no more," he said. With a chuckle, he added, "The Reuters photographer was rewinding her film."

With today's gear, the skill is even less in technique than in timing. For years, no one used anything but Nikons, and Rebours still does. Now the trend is toward Canons and other automatic cameras which do the focusing and parcel out the light. Snappers concentrate on the shot and let microprocessors do the rest. "We're not photographers, any more," Laurent says. "We are framers."

For photographers, this means competition from reporters whose editors shove cameras in their hands before they go out the door. This is nothing new. In Vietnam, we all carried cameras, with a simple instruction from an AP stalwart, Horst Faas: "Shoot it at 500, f/11, and I save you in ze darkroom." Now all we do is point. Somehow, the photographers usually do it better.

Rebours started out studying economic science, but it bored him. Instead, he wanted to be a photographer. Working nights as a hotel clerk, he scraped up some savings. To succeed, he needed a scoop. Afghanistan was too cold. He went to El Salvador. With neither contacts nor experience, he floundered. In the end, his dream reportage was a feature on Nicaraguan coffee pickers.

"I learned," he said. "This business is a matter of making a mistake, learning, and then not making the mistake again." In Paris, he worked his way up among small photo agencies. Now, a star, he has more than he can handle. After five weeks in Sarajevo, he came home to an impatient wife. Then the phone rang. He was off to Somalia.

Asked about the deeper philosophy behind his work, Rebours gave a soft laugh, and he tried hard to satisfy a friend's question. "I guess I don't really think of it that way," he said. "I like people. I like news."

Crazy is sometimes the only word for it. Morten Hvaal, twenty-eight, freelances so much for the AP he is virtually on the staff. Not many guys will do what he does. A gentleman photographer, he wears a jacket in the evenings and dines as well as circumstances allow. But he wades into anything. In Bosnia, he slipped into Dobrinja one day and tried to get out the next day in a Muslim ambulance. Three left, and he took the third. He didn't know it, but the first two were raked by Serbian machine guns, and all six occupants died. Near a roadblock outside of town, the third ambulance was hit 172 times. The driver was hit in the thigh. A medic and his patient were wounded. Hvaal's flak jacket was hit six times by bullet fragments. He went home to see his new baby in Oslo and then returned to Sarajevo for a few more months.

Christopher Morris of *Time* spent five months in Yugoslavia during the worst of it. Accepting an Overseas Press Club award, he thanked the magazine for sending him in, again and again. "They kept asking, 'Why do you want to go back?' " Morris recalled in his brief speech, but he offered no answer. He probably has no answer.

In schools, the emphasis is on f-stops and framing. Normal-type professionals put most of their thought into finding some clever way to make a point or to outsmart light. Among news photographers, the main trick is to be there. Everything else is a luxury. And some will stop at nothing.

Wesley Bocxe, an American working for a French agency on assignment for *Time,* was among the first few journalists into Kuwait, ahead of liberating troops. Based in El Salvador, all he knew about the Gulf was in his encyclopedia. He saw Bahrain had pearl fishermen, so he flew there expecting to hire a boat to Kuwait. That, he discovered, was a dumb idea. In Bahrain, the swarm was getting no visas from the Saudi embassy. He booked himself a flight from Dhahran to Qatar and told the Saudis he was a terrified tourist trying to get home. He got a three-day transit visa to catch his flight and stayed three months.

At the International Hotel, he stole a major's uniform from the laundry room, thoughtfully removing the name and insignia. He smeared his rented Japanese wagon with cooking oil and sand. After hustling some accreditation papers and scrounging a blue police roof light, he headed north. It worked. When he needed to fool the Saudis, he was an official American. If he was dealing with Americans, he simply acted as if he belonged.

Once, his luck ran out. A passing Saudi soldier saw him photographing troops from the highway. Bocxe drove off, but a motorist chased him, pointing a pistol through the window at 50 miles an hour. He was handed over to the Alabama National Guard, who took him, blindfolded, for interrogation. He got baseball questions, right out of World War II movies. As it turned out, baseball was not his thing. Worse, someone found in his bag a novel in Spanish. "I thought you said you don't speak Arabic," the reservist said. He was held thirty hours.

Bocxe camped near the border and, at 6 o'clock one morning, BBC told him the ground war was on. He joined a Saudi convoy through the Saddam line and, by 3 in the afternoon, he was in Kuwait. That was two hours before television, he hastens to add.

For some, he went too far. If you can make someone think you are who you're not, what the hell. A little exaggeration, in seeking access, is a useful tool. But his tactics might be seen as giving news people a worse name than we have already, if that's possible. Then again, in other circles he's a hero. Bocxe is hardly defensive. "If editors had sent more people who work in the Third World, who know how to break rules and take risks," he said, "we'd have had better coverage."

Ethical questions are always there. Should a photographer save a life or just take pictures as the life slips away? Most will say they are there to reflect reality and not to change it. This was Horst Faas' answer when he leaned in close with a 21-mm wide-angle lens, for the AP, to photograph Bengalis torturing suspected traitors in 1972. The victims died. Faas and Michel Laurent, the AP colleague who was with him, won a Pulitzer Prize. They do not think they could have stopped the executions. If they could have, both said at the time, they were not sure what they would have done. Photographers and reporters are supposed to cover news, not shape it. But this can be a very tough call.

Nothing can define that set of responses that leads to a picture person's choices. One afternoon in Vietnam, Faas was in the darkroom when Nick Ut brought back film from up the road. South Vietnamese had accidently dropped napalm on civilians. The photos were compelling: a mother cradling a singed child, weeping victims, dramatic close-ups of a fireball. Horst went straight to a picture of a little girl running in panic ahead of the flames.

Correspondents tried to talk him out of it. The girl's pubic hairs were visible, and no one would print it; the photo was blurred. "This one," Faas said, ending the discussion. The picture, yet another Pulitzer winner, was the one everyone remembers from the Vietnam War.

The issues are never clear-cut. The presence of a lens, especially on a television camera, can create the news. When Iranian hotheads besieged the U.S. embassy in Tehran, they spent most of the time hanging around in good spirits. The moment anyone raised a camera, they were a chanting, angry mob.

With competition so fierce, there is pressure to deliver, to squeeze the most from a story and get it back before anyone else. In Haiti, journalists flew into mayhem in a back corner of the island. An Italian correspondent watched as a group of photographers clustered around one victim who was battered but still alive. She tried to convince them to take him to a doctor. It was too late, they argued; he was beyond hope. But she knew that he could have been saved. Their concern was catching the flight back to dispatch their film.

Television camera crews face the same problems as photographers, with the added complications of their medium. The gear is bulkier; the demand is greater to stand there and keep shooting; and if someone does better, everyone else knows it that night when the evening newscasts are put together. As a result, competition blots out other emotions.

At dinner in Mogadishu, before the swarm hit Somalia, I overheard two cameramen talking at dinner. One was telling the other about his good luck that day. "The girl's head was half blown away," he said. "Damn, I wish I'd gotten that," the other one replied, dejected but hoping for the best on a new day. "It was all quiet when I was there." Both certainly would have preferred that such tragedies not occur. If tragedies had to occur, however, better they should be there than someone else.


Like reporters, photographers are at the mercy of editors. On the biggest of stories, the AP may transmit a dozen pictures for each twelve-hour cycle. A half-dozen photographers may be shooting nonstop, each with three motorized cameras. Someone has to pick and choose. The selected pictures go by laser and electrons to each newspaper on the wire, and more editors compare them with whatever else is available. At times, one frame will be plastered across every newspaper in America. Much more often, negatives go in the garbage, unseen by anyone but a dyspeptic photo editor in London or New York.

Photo editors wield an enormous influence on news from abroad. If video captures immediate attention, the still frame is a lasting image. It defines a story and fixes it in the collective memory. Just as a lead paragraph describes what the news is about, a photo depicts it. What people often forget, however, is that a picture can mislead as easily as a set of words. When Asian refugees streamed out of Kuwait into Jordan, I went to the border each day to write what I saw. Photographers came along with instructions. Sometimes, a distant editor asked for tragic pictures. On other days, he wanted happy ones.

Most people forget to suspend their belief with photos on the theory that they are seeing the news with their own eyes. Not necessarily. Beyond the distortion of the editing process, the camera itself can lie as easily as a typewriter. New technology allows a composite of almost anything. Situations are easily faked—or at least pumped up a bit. One French agency man used to carry a teddy bear in his camera bag, just in case he had to photograph a child victim.

More often, mistakes are innocent, but they are still mistakes. Even in a hurry, snappers try hard to know what they are shooting and to get the facts straight for captions that connect their pictures to the story. But accidents happen.

The classic case was in 1959, when the Dalai Lama fled Tibet after an unsuccessful rebellion against the Chinese. Dennis Lee Royle of the AP and an old rival from UPI were assigned to photograph him as he crossed into India. Both chartered planes and set up motorcycle relays for a frantic race from the Chinese border to the nearest transmitter in India. They waited, propellers turning, for the historic moment. When the Dalai Lama emerged, each shot fast and sprinted for his plane. It was a mad scramble, in the air and through jammed city streets. The UPI photographer won.

For hours, Royle paced and fumed as his competitor sent picture after picture to New York for relay around the world. By the time he got to the transmitter, the first UPI photo was already in print. Royle went off to his hotel, crushed. Soon a cable arrived: "Opposition's Dalai Lama has long shaggy hair. Yours bald. How please?" In his haste, the UPI guy had photographed the interpreter. Royle, no longer so crushed, messaged back: "Because my Dalai right Dalai."

## Chapter 6

# Getting the Story and Getting It Out

Nicolae Ceausescu's hated regime was falling in a pool of blood, and a few of us got into Bucharest that night to watch it happen. Besieged on the sixth floor of the Romanian television building, I could see unarmed crowds surging in the streets below to face the gunfire of die-hard loyalists. I had a hell of a story to tell and no shortage of AP subscribers anxious to hear it. Except that the phones had gone dead.

I paced and fumed and fretted, rattling the cradle of every phone in sight, hoping for a miracle. "Jesus," I said out loud to the heavens in general. "Isn't there even a goddamned telex?" The heavens, well-known for tolerant forgiveness in the matter of profane correspondents, answered me: "Yes, in there." The speaker was an elderly man whose job was telex operator.

The heavens exacted their price. It seems the operator was taking brief leave. A rocket had blown open the telex room's outside wall, not only letting in a very cold night but also exposing occupants to snipers across the road. Still, manna is manna. Cowering under the table, I reached up and punched blind, guessing at things like whether A or S came first on the keyboard. Somehow, I remembered the routing codes to Vienna and Paris. New York wasn't thrilled at my typing, but it got the story.

In journalism schools, students learn how to cover a story, basic skills like interviewing and tracing documents. In real life, that is often the easiest part. Every reporter soon finds out the hard way that it doesn't matter what you know if you can't tell your desk about it. For the new breed from the laptop generation, this can take some getting used to.

Not long after the Romanian revolution, for example, the heavens came through yet again, but they neglected to allow for the new age. I had gone to an Armenian enclave near Nagorno-Karabakh, deep inside Azerbaijan, on the scariest flight I'd ever taken. Armenian irregulars, hung from shoulder to knee in heavy metal, crawled atop artillery pieces in a Soviet helicopter meant to carry a third of the weight it was hauling. As we bounced in the air, skimming mountaintops to elude Azeri gunners, the Armenians lit cigarettes and casually tossed their matches back toward the fuel drums.

By chance, the enclave declared independence while I was there, and a small war raged. It was a great story and, naturally, there was no way to file it. The next morning, I looked for the helicopter. Flights were infrequent, depending on the weather and enemy fire. You couldn't wait at the pad, because landing sites changed at last minute for security reasons. If all else fell in place, you were likely to get bumped for wounded soldiers or guys off on leave. After six hours, I got lucky.

The chopper reached Yerevan, the capital of Armenia, but, of course, the phones were down. I'd just begun my pace, fume and fret routine when inspiration struck: the airport control tower. Sure enough, a morose Russian was willing to deny me his hand-crank radiophone link to Moscow. That meant he at least would talk to me. After fifteen minutes of whining and begging, he relented. "You can try it," he said. "Once."

An operator put through the call smoothly and quickly. A colleague in our Moscow bureau picked it up on the second ring. I could hear her voice, clear and loud, as I waited for the operator's momentary clicking to stop so I could dictate the story. The voice, petulant, suddenly announced: "Bad line, call back." And the phone slammed down in my ear.

But there is the other side of the coin. Reporters who were weaned on the technology can usually make it work. Equipped with portable satellite links that Dick Tracy could not have imagined, they can punch a few commands on the keyboard and dump a two-thousand-word story to their desks in a few minutes. In the good old days, if you could find a phone, and it worked, and anyone would let you use it, two thousand words was at least an hour's dictation.

When Desert Storm moved into Kuwait, I was able to get into print the first dispatch from liberated soil. This suggests skill and cunning. Big deal. I used CNN's car phone. Agence France-Presse did better. Denied access to U.S. military pools, reporters from the French news agency hid out near the front lines. When the border opened, they charged across, fired up a generator for their satellite phone and sent back running reports.

The technology, in fact, has changed every rule. These lines are being written on a Toshiba 1000LE, which will be a Stone Age relic by the time this book ends up in print. An RJ-11 module connects it to the phone. Although the machine happens to be up a jeep-shaking French mountain road, where phones die at each heavy rain, it might as well be in Rockefeller Plaza. With a few key strokes, it can send a dispatch to newspapers and broadcasters with a combined audience approaching two billion people.

Before technology slanted the playing fields, the game went to the swift and sneaky. Reporters in remote backwaters were all in the same boat. If the phone worked, everyone had a shot at bribing the operator to get out the first call. When there was only telegraph, they shared even odds on getting stories home. Photographers looked for "pigeons," people to carry out film. At most, they chartered planes, often sharing to cut the costs. One reporter sometimes found a way to get through for a while until others caught on. But victories tended to be small and short-lived.

In a way, this forced a better sort of reporting than much of today's work. Stories had to be well-crafted; correspondents never knew when they would get through again. There was no, "Oops, sorry, Bobbi, they didn't really shoot the president." At the same time, reporters lost too much time sitting by inert telexes or finding an alternative. And editors were not thrilled at meandering color when telegraph rates were a dollar a word.

American correspondents date back only to the last century, when an undersea cable began relaying messages faster than the mail packets out of Southampton. Until well into the 1980s, when it became possible to direct-dial New York from the equator, a correspondent's only lifeline was often a capricious telex line.

The night Biafra collapsed, in 1969, pointed hints were broadcast on the rebels' shortwave radio station. Gen. Odumwegwu

Ojukwu, who had separated Biafra from Nigeria, would address his nation at midnight. I had a telex in my AP office in Lagos, but I didn't trust it. Instead, I waited at the cable office where I could spread good cheer should the need arise. It did. At 5 A.M., Ojukwu's recorded voice said he had left in search of peace. So long, suckers. In under a minute, I had a line to London.

I finished sending my story, and London confirmed receipt. As we chatted about coverage plans, the lights went out in Lagos. When they came on three hours later, my colleagues at UPI and Reuters each had a stack of backed-up messages, all screaming for news. No one, fortunately for me, had invented satellite phones.

Back then, a three-hour lead, if only blind luck, was momentous. But it was early on a Sunday morning. Anyone who offered a later but better story could wipe out my scoop. In 1992, elsewhere in Africa, the roles were reversed, and the peril was far higher. Reuters had a satellite phone in Somalia, before Operation Restore Hope, and I didn't. Until offices closed at night, I could wait in line to beg a few minutes on a United Nations fax. Or I could only hope that Reuters turned up nothing urgent.

When lines are scarce, competition is brutal. Much was made of Peter Arnett's refusal to let others use CNN communications from Baghdad. In a *GQ* article, he was quoted as telling some French correspondents, "Haven't you ever heard of fucking competition?" They had, of course. In those first days in Bucharest, two incorruptible operators booked calls from the Hotel Intercontinental. First-come, first-served, no exceptions. Each call took hours to come through. Callers wandered off, trusting colleagues to alert them. Toward deadline, several Frenchmen, far down the list, hovered around. An operator would say, "Daily Mail." A Frenchman would echo, "Daily Mail." A nanosecond later, he'd tell the operator: "Not here. Cut ze line."

The rules of the road are that you share your communications when you can. Someday, the situation will be reversed. Direct competitors might be touchy about this unless they are friends, which they often are. In Kuwait after the invasion, I was desperate for a phone line. A Reuters pal obliged. If his had been the only phone in town and the world had been hanging on what we had to say, it might have worked out differently. You never know.

Once a group of reporters flew to Niger to cover a minor African peace conference. The only resident correspondent, a Frenchman, shrugged off questions about how to file. He had a telex at home. If we were lucky, he gloated, we might find another, but he didn't think so. In fact, we found six machines at the post office control room. We also found the switchboard on which one of our number rerouted the Frenchman's line to the ozone layer. (French people also share phones; this is not a national trait.)

A resourceful reporter can usually find a line somewhere. The tricky part is convincing an operator to make it available ahead of the other resourceful reporters who had the same idea. Bribes usually work. Known as "gifts" in expense-account language, these incentives require a certain skill which upright journalism professors are ill-equipped to teach. In the old days, one correspondent in Laos got his copy through immediately, no matter how high the waiting pile. He wrapped each page in a banknote. It wasn't the amount which the operators appreciated but rather the aplomb with which it was given. In some places, perfume, cigarettes and a smile work better than ten-dollar bills. When television networks show up, however, the price skyrockets.

Gifts are especially useful for communications, but they can grease all sorts of wheels. Years ago, in the Congo, I sent in an expense-account item which read, "Buying life in street, $25." A soldier had jammed a gun barrel in my gut and demanded some cash. I fished out enough to satisfy him. The accountants did not quibble over whether they got value for money in the transaction, but then that was in a more profligate time.

The problem is greater when no public lines can be had at any price. Today, major news organizations at least share mobile communications on long-running big stories. A whole kit, dish and all, fits in a suitcase. This allows the best correspondents to flash home long, enlightening dispatches with little time lost to logistics. And it lets the worst ones deluge their desks in drivel. Even more, it has altered the way everyone works.

On the psychological level, more important to reporters than to reportees, the business isn't as much fun anymore. Computers dominate our lives. The little screens which glare in every newsroom find their way into the most charming of rat holes. When correspondents gather to unwind after a 36-hour day, talk is of modems not madams. If reporters can quickly reach their editors, the reverse is also true. The raven is always at your shoulder.

But there is a practical difference. When editors are not kibitzing needlessly, they bring important elements to the story. Reporters can react to events in Washington or other capitals. They learn fast when competitors have done a better job, if not always in the kindest terms, so they can match it. They also get their herograms quickly, adding a lift when conditions dishearten. By consulting first with editors, they can cast their nets in a wider arc, and their work is less likely to be scathed on the desk.

The impact is greatest on television. Crews carry not only their birds to transmit live but also editing consoles and the full range of transistorized toys. This means they can base in large hub bureaus—London is everyone's biggest—and blast off toward breaking news on a few minutes' notice. Time zones put them at least six hours ahead of New York. They can load up, travel, fly, set up, and feed before the evening news. There is time for everything but reporting.

Communications, however vital, are less important than getting to the story to report on it. The master at this, hands down, is the *Washington Post's* Ed Cody, the Bionic Correspondent.

After U.S. troops invaded Grenada in 1983, Cody flew from Paris to the Caribbean and puddle-jumped to the next island over. He convinced a boatman not to worry about the American threat to sink unauthorized small craft. A day after the assault, in spite of a ban on reporters, Cody was in Grenada with three colleagues who had joined him en route from Miami.

With notebooks bulging, Cody looked for some way to file. An obliging U.S. Navy officer invited the reporters to chopper out to the command ship to send their stories. Once there, the four were held incommunicado for two days. That's another chapter.

When Rajiv Gandhi was assassinated in 1991, I happened to be flying to Bangkok. It was easy enough to grab the next plane to New Delhi. As I interviewed mourning Indians, the only outsider among Delhi-based correspondents, I glanced up and saw Cody. He had flown from Mexico City, God knows via what route, at only slightly less than the speed of sound.

Bill Drozdiak, who replaced Cody in Paris, is no snail, either. He was touring Asian cities in 1989, as the *Post's* foreign editor, when he got a 1 A.M. phone call in Bangkok. The Berlin Wall had fallen, and the paper's correspondent was ill. At 4 A.M., he and several hundred wiped-out Germans were aboard a sex adventure tour charter heading back to Frankfurt. Before the evening deadline, he had two Berlin stories for the front page.

The old guys did it a little differently. Richard Harding Davis, not a light packer, once took this into battle: a large cart, two oxen, three Basuto ponies, one Australian horse, three servants and four hundred pounds of supplies and baggage, including a collapsible rubber bathtub. If you couldn't invite an officer to whiskey and sparklet soda and a spread of delicacies, he explained, your paper was suspected of being cheap and, since the war was popular, unpatriotic.

A century later, the necessities are simpler: a laptop and odd bits like alligator clips to attach onto disassembled phones, a shirt-pocket shortwave radio, some medicines and toiletries, a skinny flashlight, possibly a Walkman and decent road music and, for the priggish, socks and underwear. Luxuries include more clothes, files, and a collapsible rubber bathtub.

Every correspondent knows the basics: take everything on board; bribe, threaten, or whine; befriend airport managers and charter pilots; never give up. One overwrought television reporter had to get to Bangkok on an already full plane. He used every trick in his repertoire to get a seat. Finally, he invented some outrageous tale of woe, and the supervisor relented. But the plane was late. Pacing back and forth, he abandoned himself to a nervous habit of tearing up bits of paper and sticking them in his mouth. When the flight was called, he realized he had eaten his boarding pass.

The speedy arrival is paramount, even when a story is already swarming with reporters. Editors want good coverage. But more, they want their own coverage. Getting there before deadline is a point of honor. Decades back, a fabled Fleet Street stalwart managed to make it into Pakistan with only enough time to cable his byline, a one-line story and a three-word note to his editor: "I arrived in this war-torn capital tonight. Pick up agencies."

More often, correspondents are supposed to produce on the move. A reporter's most useful tool is the ability to dictate good copy into any telephone which suddenly materializes. Early one morning, I was alone in the Saigon bureau when word came that John Paul Vann had died. As a maverick American adviser, he was a key figure, later the subject of Neil Sheehan's *A Bright Shining Lie*. At 3 A.M., I woke Arnett at his hotel. Without a moment's pause to wake up, he reeled off a thousand words which captured Vann exactly, complete with dates, exact figures, quotes from memory and a moving account of Vann's impact on the war.

The hardest part is being in place before the story happens. This takes logic, instinct and, as always, luck. In July 1990, Carole Murphy of the *Washington Post* had an uneasy feeling about how Iraq was handling its tiny Gulf neighbor. The U.S. ambassador to Baghdad went on vacation, but Murphy went to Kuwait. When the Iraqis invaded, she was alone, and her dispatches won a Pulitzer.

Sometimes trips come up suddenly because some despot wants attention. Moammar Khadafy is famous for his short-notice news conferences. Invitations go mainly to women. One reporter left her job partly because an editor joked as she headed for Libya, "Show a little leg." Another received a midnight visit to her Tripoli hotel room from a goon in a doctor's coat, brandishing a syringe. Khadafy had decided she would be his next conquest, and he sent the guy to administer an AIDS test.

This sort of turbocharged life can wreck you as a human being. You can always spot correspondents, even they when manage a leisurely vacation. They are the ones who elbow aside old ladies, sprint to immigration, stagger past customs with a hundred pounds of carry-on and are showering in their hotel before most passengers get off the plane.

After the flight in, the next question is where to stay. Princess Grace died suddenly in Monaco during the off-season, and journalists did not manage to fill the luxury hotels. More often, the story breaks in a place where the best hotel has as many guests as fleas, both at overcapacity. (Full hotels are not always a drawback. Late in 1992, Vicky Graham of the AP found Baghdad's El Rasheed Hotel jammed, and she went somewhere else. The next day, an American missile shattered the lobby.)

Ever since mythical reporters crowded into a leaky-roofed dump in Evelyn Waugh's imagination, a noteworthy collection of hotels has shared the distinction of playing host to the hacks. A clause of the Geneva Convention stipulates that wars must be fought only in cities with an Intercontinental Hotel; that held for Managua, Dhaka, Amman, Bucharest, Zagreb, Belgrade, Tehran, Peshawar and Kinshasa, among others. There were Famine Hiltons in Khartoum and Addis Ababa. San Salvador's Camino Real, where you had to worry if the story would come to you, was a Westin. Several of the most notorious, however, are hearty independents.

Connoisseurs rate the Continental Palace in Saigon as the all-time favorite, with its seedily elegant colonial-style rooms and its grandfatherly roomboys. Throughout the Vietnam War, the terrace café, known as the Continental Shelf, was clearinghouse for every rumor and solid tip in town. Miraculously, it always managed to escape the bombings which terrorized Saigon. When the war ended, reporters confirmed their suspicions about why. The waiters reverted openly to their main jobs, as Viet Cong agents.

Throughout the tumult of Lebanon, the Commodore in Beirut was a time-out zone. It provided drivers, telex lines, visas, banking facilities and edible meals when the city around was ablaze in battle. Bar bills were laundered, as laundry charges. Various militias and the Palestine Liberation Organization were paid to lay off the place. Its well-stocked bar featured a parrot which whistled a flawless imitation of incoming artillery. Sometimes, the noise wasn't the parrot. A *Los Angeles Times* correspondent, breakfasting on the terrace, noticed a fragment of shrapnel neatly puncturing his fried egg.

One Easter, the manager left a chocolate egg on each of his guests' pillow. An agency correspondent, back from too long at the Commodore Bar, flung his out the window. Moments later, the desk rang up. "Sir," a polite voice said, "there is a militiaman down here covered in chocolate who is on his way up to kill you." The reporter hid under his neighbor's bed.

The Tehran Intercontinental slid downhill with the Islamic revolution. One night, correspondents stood downwind and sniffed ruefully as guards smashed the contents of the wine cellar, a thousand bottles including some better years of Mouton Rothschild.

At the Amman Intercon, during the 1970 Black September war, one old pro filled his bathtub for the coming water shortage. An hour later, he found his roommate happily soaping himself in the tub. The Dhaka Intercon was the tallest building in town when Indian jets strafed Pakistanis at the birth of Bangladesh. At each raid, all sixty reporters rushed to the roof, to the horror of the staff, who feared that long lenses looked too much like gun barrels. For six weeks, the hotel served only chicken curry.

The Federal Palace in Lagos, the press camp for the Biafra War, thoughtfully listed prostitutes as "misc." on the bill.

For nearly a decade, the Camino Real supplied the hot showers and cold beer for a resident press corps of about a hundred in El Salvador. Everyone had offices on the second floor: three agencies, three networks, the papers and magazines, the Europeans and Japanese. The hotel's bar was the rumor exchange and center stage for machos on parade. Its parking lot was marshaling yard for the

Russian jeeps and vans that took *los periodistas* to war. One morning, someone delivered the news, dumping a body out front.

More people, however, know the International Hotel in Dhahran, Saudi Arabia. For much of the Gulf War, television viewers thought those turquoise cloisters behind the anchormen were some kind of high-tech weaponry pods. They were plastic swimming pool changing rooms. The rest of the circus was not on television.

Journalists turned the two-hundred-room hotel into Space Central. Wires snaked across the carpets, held down by gaffer's tape, and wound in a snarl of copper spaghetti down the emergency stairs. By the time the ground war started, seventy-nine cables stretched from upper rooms to the flyaway ramps outside. The only press casualty was a guy who tripped and broke his arm.

Outside, twelve satellite dishes stood in a line, each perched on a plywood deck plastered in network logo decals and littered with editing consoles, half-eaten sandwiches, folding chairs and $700,000-a-year television correspondents waiting to relay the day's military handouts. The really heavy birds lurked out past the garden where a grateful host threw barbecues that everyone was too busy to attend.

Television people pitched tents everywhere, on the grass, on terraces, on the roof, to shield equipment. People were a more serious problem. Soon the hotel filled to impossible, and even the crummiest backups were jammed. Early on, a few voluntarily chose to join the French at the Méridien Hotel. It was luxurious, it was on the water and the food was in a different universe. But it could not match the International. Distance from the military was a minor drawback. Much more, it simply was not the place.

During the first few days of trouble, AP photographers colonized a sprawling suite just off the ballroom that housed the military information circus. It was the best room in the joint, right off the stairs and overlooking the largest airfield in the theater. It was soon the AP news and photo bureau, with a back room for the guy who ran things around the clock. Much later, CBS arrived, anchorman and entourage, and cased the hotel. Who's in there? a senior person asked the manager. Told who, the guy replied, We'll give you twice as much. The manager laughed.

U.S. military security agents scanned the place regularly for bombs. The only known explosion, however, was a homemade bottle of Chateau (Brian) Calvert, overfermented in an NBC room.

Room service was an early war casualty. Some of the waiters and the people who were supposed to make the food taste good had stopped coming to work. But in a country not known for nightlife, the International offered a regular show down in its concrete bowels. Funny masks were *de rigeur*. Later, the air raid shelter follies were immortalized on T-shirts: "Appearing Nightly, Saddam and the Scuds."

In an earlier time, correspondents carried credentials which gave them access to trouble. Press cards told the police who they were and why they were nosing around. This was always fairly iffy. The last illusions evaporated on June 20, 1979, when ABC correspondent Bill Stewart, thirty-seven, pulled up to a roadblock in eastern Nicaragua. Anastasio Somoza Debayle's National Guardsmen ordered him to kneel. He held out a white flag and a perilously thin little Nicaraguan press card. Neither did any good. A guardsman kicked Stewart and told him to lie on his stomach. Then he took a step back and executed him.

The scene was filmed and shown on ABC. It helped bring down Somoza. It also changed a lot of reporters' devil-may-care attitude toward going up the road. In 1990, three NBC people stopped on a Salvadoran highway to interview peasants. Their van was marked "TV" in huge letters. Guerrillas were nowhere around. A Salvadoran army helicopter swooped low and circled, and the left-door gunner sprayed them with machine-gun fire. All survived, and they filmed the chopper, with its tail number plainly visible. El Salvador had only sixteen helicopters, and their crews were U.S.-trained. Despite NBC protests, the American embassy made no investigation.

These days, papers are as likely to get you into trouble as keep you out of it. Reporters who cover both sides of the Middle East check carefully to ensure that no stray Israeli shekels get lost in a side pocket. Most correspondents carry an extra pariah passport for visas which may cause them trouble elsewhere.

Danger is seldom where you expect it. No braver journalist than Neil Davis emerged from Vietnam. First a cameraman, then a correspondent, he went on patrols no one else would consider. He always knew the risks and how to minimize them. The war ended before Davis had used up his nine lives. He settled in Bangkok for NBC. There, as he was covering a failed minor coup on a sunny day with sidewalk strollers around him, he took a fatal bullet in the head.

Armed crazies are part of a reporter's life. The onl
is wing it. In the Shouf Mountains of Lebanon, an Amer
was asked where he was from. "New Jersey," he repli
wrong answer. Angry men cocked their weapons and stopped j
short of firing. At that moment, the USS *New Jersey* was shelling the
area from off the coast. Another time, not far away, an American
answered a similar question "Dallas." It seemed like the wrong answer. A wild-eyed soldier thrust his face into the reporter's and
stared at him hard. For emphasis, he jabbed at the terrified journalist with the barrel of his Kalashnikov. He had one more question:
"Who shot J. R.?"

The object of all these logistics is the story itself. This gets
back to sourcing. However they decide to write what they learn,
reporters must first learn it. They draw on a dizzying range of informants, from the airport cabbie to the president. Among news
sources, there is no order or logic. Head-of-state interviews are
treasured by editors, most of whom refuse to let correspondents
quote taxi drivers because they sound too easy. In fact, cabbies
usually reveal more.

Correspondents have two concerns. They know that the
sources they cite are the consumer's clearest clues to depth and
credibility. Who is quoted, what is reported anonymously and how
sources are woven together with personal observation are basic to
good journalism. In the age of swarm and high-stakes competition,
this subject grows more critical by the year. But all of that aside,
reporters must sort out reality in any way they can.

The most reliable source of news is the correspondent's own
eyes. As their own witnesses, reporters can be sure that no one is
exaggerating, making a mistake or lying. They can sketch out color
in confidence and draw conclusions from observable facts. Even
then, they can screw up. There was Rat Man, for example. One
reporter covering an earthquake in Central America wrote that people were so hungry they were reduced to eating rats. In fact, they
were eating small guinea pigs, a local delicacy in the best of times.
Ungenerous colleagues gave him a lasting nickname.

Occasionally, someone might get overenthusiastic. When Indira Gandhi died, her son, Rajiv, flew over the Himalayas in a C-130
to scatter her ashes. No reporters were allowed on board, only a

single Indian photographer whose pictures were given to everyone. But an American newspaper correspondent "covered" the moment in gripping detail. He described how the tense lines deepened on Rajiv's face and his moist eyes reflected sadness as he cast the remains of his mother over the top of the world. His account appeared next to a photo of Gandhi wearing a full-face rubber oxygen mask.

When their own eyes are looking elsewhere or are shut tight after a long night, correspondents often use their colleagues'. This is the hallowed "fill." The practice is questionable but too common to dispute. We all do it, but most of us are careful about whom we trust. Sometimes it bring us grief. At an OPEC meeting in Vienna, Ted Stanger of *Newsweek* was up early. He briefed Pat Sloyan of *Newsday,* who, in turn, shared his notes with Ray Moseley of the *Chicago Tribune.* Then Don Schanche of the *Los Angeles Times* wandered in at noon and got a fill from Moseley. His story ended up in the *International Herald Tribune.* In Southern Turkey, Jon Randal of the *Washington Post* passed on his best stuff to the *Philadelphia Inquirer* guy, who filled in the *New York Times.* Randal got a message asking for a matching story on his own material.

A common source is the one-on-one interview with a newsmaker. This basic tool, the correspondent's hammer, evolved as a give-and-take session to seek out frankness. The source makes a statement; the reporter challenges it to fill in all the gaps. Exchanges may be friendly or hostile, but they depend on a reporter's skill in asking the right questions and convincing the source to open up. Television correspondents have the added burden of keeping the subject articulate and on track. Print reporters can wander all over the block in hopes of pouncing on inconsistency. But television reporters also have the camera, a mysterious verbal laxative. This amazes us all. People, down deep, like to talk. Time after time, sources plead for anonymity, afraid to see their names in print. Later, these people show up on television, saying more than they dared to reveal in secret. Go figure.

In earlier days, fewer reporters competed for interviews. Like it or not, newsmakers who wanted to influence people had to deal with journalists on their own terms. Few reporters accepted the question-and-answer format, for example, which limited their ability to insert a paragraph pointing out why their source was full of sheep droppings. No one agreed to submit questions in advance.

Now competition is intense to reach newsmakers with tight schedules. Television has the edge; it offers direct access to viewers without additions of context or balance from the other side. For networks in constant battle, the privilege of being the first to offer this access amounts to a major coup. This has led to a worrisome menace: the dreaded word "exclusive," which can be even more distracting to workaday reporting than the word "Pulitzer."

Journalists are supposed to focus on what they think is important rather than on what wins them attention. They work within fixed principles. If these factors coincide to produce a prize, or an interview with a headliner, all the better. But angling for a prize at least requires some solid, resourceful reporting along with tactical maneuvering. Exclusive interviews, in many cases, are had at the price of shaving on principles.

When hijackers were holding a TWA airliner full of people on the ground in Beirut, in 1985, the networks scrambled to get the terrorists on camera. "Plates of cocaine, plates of cocaine," one reporter chanted, parodying the bidding that went on to secure that privilege. As Lech Walesa emerged in Poland, an unknown union man who rattled the Communists, he found himself deluged with gifts—snow tires and such—from reporters seeking his attention. Goods or money may not necessarily change hands. The price is often letting the source, in one way or another, set the terms. This can have an impact on the news report.

In a book called *Live from Baghdad,* CNN producer Robert Wiener explains how, early on, his crew got a rare look at how Iraqi troops occupying Kuwait were unprepared for war. But this weakness went unmentioned, he said, for fear of jeopardizing a requested interview with Saddam Hussein. The other networks were trying just as hard. The eventual interview was predictable. If Saddam could have been pushed into anything more than staged posturing, it might have been worth it. But this rarely happens. With so many reporters trying for an exclusive, the subject chooses the tone. He is less of a source than a sales gimmick.

Like almost every other despot with a dream, Saddam wanted coverage. Reporting might have been better served with a team of correspondents hammering away from different directions, none with any other motive than learning something. That is, a news conference. But this is speculative hindsight. More, it is heresy. Who turns down an exclusive with Saddam, or a Pulitzer?

The problem is not only with television. At the height of South Africa's crackdown on blacks, years back, Al Neuharth took his Gannett cavalcade to Pretoria, where he saw President P. W. Botha.

This, Neuharth boasted in print, was Botha's first full interview in years. That, Johannesburg-based reporters added among themselves, was because Botha knew that others who requested an interview would ask tougher questions and insist on answers.

Most stories include a range of sources, some easier to handle than others. Newspaper and news agency editors prefer to have a name on every quote. When that is not possible, most will settle for a brief description of the source and a reason for anonymity. Others, however, insist on identification. If identification is a laudable aim, with a sensible purpose behind it, a ban on blind quotes can prevent correspondents from reporting reality.

The issue is complex. Standard phrases once peppered everyone's dispatches: "usually reliable sources," "highly reliable sources," "a well-placed source," "diplomats" or "observers." These unnamed informants could be anyone or no one. "Observers said" was as much a dead giveaway as the old Henry Kissinger label, "a high administration source on the plane." It meant the reporter had drawn a conclusion and had no one else to hang it on. Unnamed sources covered laziness and sloppiness, and they allowed politicians to float ideas or take pot shots from safe cover. In foreign dispatches, editors had few means to weigh their true value.

Yet anonymous sources, cited by skilled, trustworthy reporters, also revealed crucial information which might not have surfaced otherwise. Corruption, secret diplomacy and economic duplicity were exposed regularly because people could unburden their consciences without risking their lives. The finest moment was Watergate, when the *Washington Post* used the hallowed two-source rule to bring down a President. But discomfited victims fought back, questioning reporters' credibility, and some inept or dishonest journalists played into their hands.

Sometime during the post-Watergate rebalancing, editors decided that readers no longer trusted them. Was someone making up all those colorful, sensitive quotes? To counter this fear, a few of them banned blind quotes outright. At best, some specific information could be attributed to anonymous sources. But anything approaching an opinion or an analysis died on the desk.

The advantage is obvious. Readers who see a name, any name, will assume that the person exists and is speaking with authority. The reader is protected from people selling a viewpoint without the courage to stand behind it publicly. Dispatches have a heftier feel with real voices in them. In fact, this assumption can mask reality.

People who are named are as likely—or more likely—to mislead as those who are not. Anyone with a job, a place in the community or a particular self-image tends to say what is politic. This is especially true with the government officials and company spokespeople who appear so often in dispatches. Their formal stand is important to the story. But, when assured of anonymity, these sources frequently unfork their tongues.

Often, I've had friendly sources reply to a question with "You want my on-the-record statement or the truth?"

The problem here is that handling such sources is tricky work. A reporter must filter out bias and self-serving remarks. Each unnamed quote must be set in context and qualified. Hardly anyone still writes "reliable source," yet the writer must believe any anonymous informant to be reliable.

Not every reporter is able to walk this line, and not every editor corrects for it. A few news organizations forbid all reporters from venturing into anonymity, even those who can do it expertly. This means, inevitably, passing up some important news. Other organizations ruthlessly purge their ranks of suspected cheaters and answer challenges with the standard reply of the profession: "We stand by our story." There are neither rules nor guidelines.

In all cases, readers should look out for themselves. A trained nose can smell good sourcing. Has the correspondent tried to give clues? Is there supporting evidence? The AP, which shuns unidentified quotes and insists that reporters explain why a source is not named, once carried a paragraph that read: "A spokesman for the ministry said there would be no immediate comment. He spoke on the condition of anonymity."

Each sort of dispatch has its own demands. Disasters are only police stories writ large, with official death tolls that lean toward the conservative and eyewitness accounts that don't. Here names and titles are essential. If someone contradicts the official version— someone always does—the obvious question glares: Who he? If authorities suggest a bomb or a political motive, which authorities? "Expert" is not enough. Who?

Atrocities demand solid sourcing and also a description of the sources' qualifications. Not only do people involved often lie, but sometimes they also hire professionals to manipulate the gullible and disorganized "media." When Saddam took over Kuwait, so many reporters wrote that Iraqis had pulled babies out of incubators that we did not stop to wonder how we knew. It took us a long time to figure out that the source was the daughter of Kuwait's ambassador to Washington at a congressional hearing, a masterpiece of a $11.5-million campaign by the public relations firm Hill & Knowlton.

At the hearing, fifteen-year-old "Nayirah" said: "I saw the Iraqi soldiers come into the hospital with guns. They took the babies out of the incubators . . . and left the children to die on the cold floor." Bush quoted her often as he squeezed out Senate votes to approve war. Hill & Knowlton not only set up the testimony but also produced a video news release for Medialink, a public relations network that serves seven hundred television stations. NBC "Nightly News" used some of the release; all told, thirty-five million Americans saw it. A lot of fools like me mentioned the incubators when writing about Iraq. Later, H & K said there was no reason to doubt her word, whoever her father was. No one visited them to punch noses. Like the others, they're still at it.

Political upheaval is even harder to source. Coups d'état routinely start at the radio station, and many finish there. Deposed leaders insist they are in power until they cut and run with their money. In such cases, reporters can only to listen to all sides and watch developments. Turmoil at the top demands inside sources who cannot be named. But these need to be sprinkled with grains of salt. Correspondents on the ground long enough to develop trusted contacts can assess their informants. Others cannot.

Most reporting is more general, and sources are a mixed bag of officials, intellectuals, resident foreigners and ordinary folk, along with the local papers, television and radio. It depends on where you are. In Thailand, squash at the Royal Bangkok Sports Club can produce the prime minister, the CIA station chief, the top Thai drug cop and towel boys who know everything there is to know.

The mixed bag is always changing. In Czechoslovakia, under the Communists, Henry Kamm of the *New York Times* visited his favorite sources as they were finishing their shifts at factory boiler rooms. After the revolution, he saw them at Hradcany Castle. "Little did I know that I was going from the boiler room of the foreign minister to the boiler room of the president," he said. "It was a great satisfaction to see the triumph of friends who convinced you they represented the people."

When Michael Dobbs moved to Moscow for the *Washington Post* in 1988, officials were just beginning to agree to be quoted by name. Mostly, it was the old style. Government handlers took weeks, or months, to produce an interview subject who spewed doctrine. Reporters watched for clues like a hunter seeking spoor, scanning photos to assess party clout and deducing trends from asides in the nightly newscast. Dobbs' predecessor, Dusko Doder, realized Yuri Andropov had died because lights were burning late in the Kremlin.

Travel restrictions kept reporters from covering ethnic turmoil, which was just starting around the country. But Dobbs worked the telephone. A new direct-dial system meant he could call distant cities and ask questions. Then, with a new parliament, things began to change. The Soviet tanks that rolled toward Russia's White House passed by Dobbs' window. He worked the street, just as he would have anywhere else. When Boris Yeltsin leaped onto one of the tanks, Dobbs was a few feet away.

Early in 1993, I asked Dobbs how access had changed. He had just called the Russian foreign intelligence press office to request an interview with the chief, equivalent to the CIA director. Someone called back within ten minutes to ask if 4 P.M. the next day was soon enough. It was no surprise. In 1990, as the first foreign journalist allowed into the KGB, he was whisked inside and shown around the place. Months later, in Washington, he showed up for an interview at the CIA. He waited for hours while guards ran a security check; they were about to call off his appointment. It was far easier to penetrate Lubyanka than Langley.

Although access to sources can be limited, reporters are most restricted by their own inability to communicate. This can be a serious problem. Correspondents usually speak several languages, but these are not necessarily understood by anyone they need to interview. Translations are always difficult. In French, a word-for-word rendering into English usually comes out wrong. At best, nuances are missed.

In most countries, speaking the language is taken as a sign of courtesy and culture. It helps to earn trust and open doors to the inner circles where all the serious business and fun happens. Without it, reporters can't eavesdrop, scan the local headlines and or see what people are watching on television. Without the language, a reporter is left with Americans, if any are around, or a small group of people who learned English for a particular reason.

Interpreters, never quite good enough, can be awful. This badly hampered our reporting in Vietnam. Even reporters who had spent years there could hardly order a beer in Vietnamese. I once came across an old woman in a hamlet which had been raided by the Viet Cong. Squatting by the smoking ruins of her home, she told her story. She jumped to her feet to emphasize a point, gesticulating wildly and spitting out words. Her voice rose to a wail and dropped to a choking sob. She imitated gunfire and grenades. After five minutes, I stopped her and asked a Vietnamese friend to translate. He replied, "She say she is unhappy."

Investigations are more complicated. When a correspondent tries to reveal wrongdoing which has gone unnoticed, finding sources is only one problem. Sometimes a bigger hurdle is getting the story into print. Editors, who may be reluctant to draw the heat which these stories inevitably bring, want to be convinced that the story is clad in iron. Some of them are not unhappy to find an honorable excuse to kill the piece.

By the time a reporter is ready to write, he may be his own best authoritative source. He will have fragments of information, bits of documents which add up to a picture but mean little on their own and the confirming testimony of people who are risking a gunshot in the head if they are named. But to make the story stick, each part of it must be attributed to someone and, if possible, backed up by "the paper"—documents. Since crime is usually involved, the best sources are often criminals. This, of course, allows the culprit to point out that a felon cannot be trusted. "The paper" is always a problem. People who betray public trust or steal money tend to avoid writing things down.

In principle, when a smoking gun cannot be found, a roomful of powder-burned weapons ought to suffice. Reporters are not prosecutors. It is enough for them to point out glaring questions so that prosecutors, or some other legal entity, can ask them.

This was how Watergate unfolded. The *Washington Post* revealed the first intriguing pieces of the puzzle. Other papers picked up the scent. Television weighed in, and eventually enough facts emerged so that the original pair of *Post* investigators could administer the coup de grace. It helped that Watergate was a Washington story. And that was another age of reporting.

Iran-*contra,* more significant in its way, was never pinned down. Much of it took place abroad, and correspondents could not produce sources to satisfy editors who feared criticism that they were ganging up on a U.S. administration. Every so often, a piece of the story broke. But other news organizations, if they did not knock it down, simply ignored it. Investigation was left to a special prosecutor with no reporters on his staff. In the end, he threw up his hands.

At different times, reporters tried to hail down a story related to Iran-*contra*. Central American allies and thugs on the CIA payroll used the *contra* supply line to smuggle cocaine into the United States. On a CBS "West 57th Street" report, pilots described on camera how they had flown drugs into Homestead Air Force Base in Florida. But they were in jail. Hardly anyone followed up. Honduran military officers and U.S. officials admitted that Washington had condoned massive drug trafficking because Honduras supported the *contra* policy. But none would be named.

When the pieces fell into place, evidence suggested that CIA officials had known all about it. More importantly, so had operatives and aides who were in contact with Vice President George Bush. Either the White House knew and looked the other way, or it was being deceived by those who carried out Central American policy.

Senate investigations were hampered by partisan concern and lack of access to official records. No other agency took a hard look. Some reporters published their findings in magazines. Others helped authors document books, which caused little stir. Some made damning films. But the story never got into the mainstream. Later, Robert Gates, who was deputy to CIA director William Casey during Iran-*contra,* was made chief of Central Intelligence. Alliances continued unchanged. Honduran military officers made yet more money from the drug traffic. Attention was focused instead on Manuel Noriega. In his case, quotable sources were easier to find.

If Iran-*contra* and links to America's war on drugs went uncovered, blame falls heavily on often forgotten but primordial parts of the process: editors who keep the gates and proprietors who are reluctant to make trouble. The whole episode showed to what extent an American administration controls reporting, not directly but by skillful use of our own system.

The initial break on Iran-*contra* came not from an American reporter but rather from Lebanese journalists. No one got very far with it, even after the U.S. attorney general had confirmed it. The *San Francisco Examiner* took some of the first bites into the story. Seth Rosenfeld revealed the Frogman case, in which cocaine smugglers and drug money were turned loose with the help the CIA. Unlike Watergate, there was no resonance; few papers followed up. This got to be a pattern around the country. If one reporter ignited a few embers, competitors poured water on them or at least let them die out.

Frank McCulloch, nearing seventy, was the *Examiner*'s managing editor. Well-seasoned as a correspondent and editor, he knew what his reporters had. He sent them up the trail to Washington and beyond, but the story was more than one paper could handle.

"God, I wish we had the resources to follow that one to the end," he said later, with a slow shake of the head. But he was not surprised. The problem, he said, begins with American apathy: people do not rise in outrage against political wrongdoing. In such a climate, a new class of executives and managers no longer finds it prudent to publish and be damned. Challenging power invites controversy, and that endangers the bottom line. Nervous editors try to judge the mood, an insidious sort of self-censorship. Even the bold ones depend on their budgets.

"Look," McCulloch told me, "you cannot make the case to people who don't have the calling. It doesn't add up for them. If you have a story that will upset the government, that might bring reaction, maybe legal action, their reasoning is simple: You will not add readers if you run it. You will not lose readers if you don't. It is a costly, needless headache. How do you make them understand?"

This is not new. A. J. Liebling, in a classic set of essays, *The Press,* observed in the early 1960s: "Many proprietors have a prejudice against news—they never feel at home with it. In this they resemble racing owners who are nervous around horses."

But it is getting worse. A fresher reading comes from Kevin Buckley, respected by colleagues since he ran *Newsweek*'s Saigon bureau. His book on the Panama invasion explained much of what got left out of the newspapers about Noriega and his neighborhood. "Strategic coverage of these things was nonexistent," he said. "No editor I know of ever put the whole story together. They certainly didn't put Panama together. Seymour Hersh laid out the framework for strategic coverage, but his [*New York Times*] editors didn't do it. They dropped the ball. The American journalistic leadership is terrified of a scoop, of giving offense. They withheld Oliver North's name as long as they could."

The difference since Liebling is that government strategists have seized the meaning of this fear, and they play on it. They know how the pack works. Someone has to sink teeth into the quarry's neck. Until the first blood, the others hang back. Damage-control experts have to neutralize only those closest to attack.

Correspondents can usually come up with the sources. But they need not only time and expense money but also backing from the top levels of their own organizations. Someone not only has to call the President a liar but also stand there squarely in the slime that is sure to follow. If no one else goes after the story, it is all that much harder.

This is tricky ground, and no generality applies. A lot of publishers and broadcast executives can dispute this point with a clear conscience. But few disagree that pressure is applied. It might be as subtle as dropping names from the White House barbecue guest list. It is sometimes as complex as close personal or business ties. And it is almost always impossible to demonstrate.

The implications are serious. Correspondents are supposed to play an adversarial role. Not hostile, but critical. It is that simple division of labor, dating back to John Peter Zenger and other American editors who defied British colonial authority. Their job is to lie; ours is to catch them at it. The more that news executives fall down in this role, the less people expect correspondents to raise questions. In the end, the public sides with officials who want to stay in office and against "the media"—that is, against their own independent ears and eyes.

The correspondent's job is to get the story and get it out. Minor obstacles such as bad weather, bombs or a shut-down phone exchange are quickly overcome. When the obstacles are out of the correspondent's hands, the story dies. The information might filter out through back channels, but most people miss it.

All of these obstacles, human and logistical, are more than a personal challenge to reporters. Journalists are the only ones who can provide citizens with an independent account of what might affect their good name, their treasure and, in the extreme, their sons and daughters. Sometimes this essential reporting is lost to natural causes, but too often it is stolen—by authorities, news executives, editors or even correspondents themselves. Citizens who do not report the loss must share in the blame. It is a simple enough concept: If we're not there, you're not there.

Chapter 7

# Censorship and Other Assorted Pressures

When the Pentagon readied its invitation-only war in Saudi Arabia, the U.S. headquarters were in Riyadh, but most reporters were in Dhahran. Information officers set up a giant screen so we could watch the briefings on closed-circuit television. Tony Clifton of *Newsweek* watched the first one for a few minutes, then shrugged and tuned out. "In Vietnam," he muttered, "at least they lied to us in person."

In Vietnam, they also had the grace to lie to us with trepidation. When we caught them at it, they apologized. They knew that if they tried to tell reporters black was purple, someone would be out the next morning to check up on it. That is, if they stole our news, we'd go find it. The military hasn't changed much since then, but the news business has.

There is some serious irony here. For as long as the world has known government, leaders have sought to influence what is said about them. That is only human nature. Over the years, foreign correspondents battered away at the barriers. When some leader froze them out, they took the trouble to find out why. Thin-skinned despots were identified as such. Finally, reporters made their point. In much of the world, official access is getting easier. Governments know that censorship is mainly about image, not national security. Many find that they are more embarrassed by hassling the press than by anything that free-ranging correspondents might learn. But this only applies where the majority of reporters refuse to be hassled. Operation Desert Storm was not such a case.

From the beginning, all of us bought the myth that a nearly naked emperor was clad in triple-ply armor. Few reporters had taken a good look at Iraq before the crisis, which is our fault. But the Iraqis' record against unarmed Iranian teenagers should have been a clue. The more the Pentagon rolled out its high-tech toys and warned of overwhelming numbers, the more we got caught up in the game. With no intelligence to tell us otherwise, we worried about nerve gas. As a result, we missed the point. The threat was not military, it was political. Within two years, in a rebuilt capital, Saddam Hussein would be posturing for his Arab peers as George Bush slipped quietly out of power.

As Iraq's defenses collapsed, a friend from Reuters and I slipped away from the pack and sped up the two-lane blacktop from Khafji to Kuwait City. Almost without noticing it, we passed the dreaded Saddam Line, the belt of steel and inflammable oil we had described to our nervous readers, time and again. My friend looked at the puny coils of concertina wire and a narrow trench of black goo. "Exactly what I thought," he grumbled. "Just another fucking Arab army."

The AP's Washington bureau chief, Jonathan Wolman, sifted the evidence in hindsight and drew a similar conclusion. "There is no way that things could have been misread so badly by the administration," he said. "This was by thorough deliberation." For its own purposes, the government exaggerated the threat. And rather than providing question marks, we chose exclamation points.

Americans are hardly the worst offenders in a world of authoritarians who attempt to control what is said about them. At the extreme, there is what Peruvian journalist Sonia Goldenberg calls censorship by death. Governments simply kill noisome reporters, baldly or in secret. A ham-handed few still use classic means, subjecting outgoing dispatches to a censor's office. These days, however, defining censorship by counting up blue pencils or newspaper closings misses the point.

The most effective news management is by manipulation, artful shielding of real sources and lying in a convincing way. Many countries now hire outside advice. Big public relations agencies can shape almost anyone's reality for a price. Low-rent freelancers seek out gullible reporters who have not yet learned to be on guard. Some of the best of these manipulators are on the American public payroll, experts who can con newspeople to play along and like it. Their finest hour was Operation Desert Storm.

To follow the Gulf War, old hands demanded briefings like the Five O'Clock Follies in Vietnam, grill sessions where midlevel spokespersons ran scared. The idea then was to ask the same question until the major got tired of evasive action. War was serious business, and the people back home who provided the blood and money needed straight answers. But in Riyadh, television cameras turned a vital reporting tool into public theater where newspeople were pilloried for doing their work. For the first time, questions were scrutinized more than answers.

Instead of majors, we got generals. Rather than operational details, we got generalities, cooked statistics and tightly edited gun camera film of the day's successes. The more we pushed for the boring little facts which were clues to the bigger picture, the worse we looked. Those of us whose job is writing, not talking on camera, came out as stumblebums. Like a lot of processes, ours is messy. No hotdog maker would choose to operate in a shop window.

It did not help that some editors sent jerks. Many were as Henry Allen of the *Washington Post* described them: "dinner party commandos, slouching inquisitors, collegiate spitball artists ... a whining, self-righteous, upper-middle-class mob jostling for whatever tiny flakes of fame may settle on their shoulders like some sort of Pulitzer Prize dandruff."

But the First Amendment allows for jerks, just as it protects money-grubbing proprietors who squeeze juice from sensation. That is the point of a free press; no one needs a license. A journalist, whether a stringer in Singapore or the president of NBC News, is merely someone who produces a journal and convinces other people to pay for a look at it.

When executives back home insisted on the people's right to know, a lot of military minds dismissed it as a sanctimonious plea for the right to make money. That this criticism had a grain of truth in some cases did not alter the principle. But the "media" were on the defense. Just as White House manipulators were about to waver, a "Saturday Night Live" skit which mocked reporters convinced them to hold firm.

A Times-Mirror poll said 57 percent of Americans thought that reporters were too pushy and that press controls should be tougher. Sympathies lay with the lovable bear of a commanding general, who talked past journalists to a broader audience. Instead of dead bodies, he spoke of KIAs and collateral damage. Slick Air Force footage focused on the hits, not the misses. On the day U.S. aircraft pounded civilians in Baghdad, he showed an Iraqi driver barely escaping a bombed bridge, "the luckiest guy in Iraq."

Those of us who talked to pilots knew that more bombs were missing than hitting. As it turned out, 70 percent of the bombs were off target. The other myths, like the Patriot missiles' prowess, exploded when most people were no longer looking.

At the time when answers mattered, viewers complained to CNN that correspondents were messing up the briefings. The reporters ruined the public's communion with the military. Why were they doubting the word of our leaders? Gen. Norman Schwarzkopf had announced, "We are happy to report that we have destroyed all of their nuclear capability." Who could argue with that?

Reporters had to jeopardize their credentials, and their lives, to see the war for themselves. The Pentagon set up pools, and grown professionals fought among themselves to jump into them. News executives back home maneuvered for a better spot at the trough. Pros like Bob Simon of CBS tried it the old way. He and his crew drove toward the front to see what they could find. They found Iraqis who captured them. Instead of respecting their dedication to the job, many people insulted them.

Most correspondents padded around a hotel ballroom, watching snippets of the war on television while they awaited press releases and the odd field trip to some rear-echelon unit.

"What is going on here?" thundered Leon Daniel, a grand old wire animal leading United Press International on a last charge after a hard-fought career on the road. Freshly arrived in Dhahran, he had just seen the JIB, the U.S. Joint Information Bureau, and the jiblets who ran it. It took him three minutes to size things up: "This is the Stockholm syndrome."

The Gulf War showed with grim clarity the price we pay—correspondents and consumers alike—for leaving the world uncovered on the theory that reinforcements can be marshaled as needed. There is no such thing as an instant foreign correspondent. Reporters from home have their own flawed news-gathering system. One main failing is that when ordered to stay put, they tend to stay put.

Another is that for reasons difficult to understand, many of them believe what authorities tell them.

Like any specialty, covering foreign news requires its own brand of skepticism. When the news is war, experience helps. Every reporter must start somewhere, and it is up to editors, not other correspondents, to decide who gets sent where. However, this gets to be everyone's problem when everyone must depend on pool reports from untried newcomers.

By the military logic, a media person is a media person. Editors with responsibilities to fulfill and reputations to protect do not see it that way. Each evening, serious newspaper people tried to piece together news from the front with field contributions reading, "Color quote (from a general): 'I don't eat salads. I eat meat and wear wool.'"

One night, I looked at photos from a pool visit to a forward U.S. Marine base. Telltale silver cannisters were hanging from fighter wings. I hurried over to a Marine officer attached to the JIB, a veteran who shared our contempt for excessive restriction.

"I know you can't say anything," I said, "but smile if you're using napalm." He grinned. After a little fencing, in which he broke no rules but confirmed my remarks on the properties of napalm, I called our man in Riyadh. He told the chief Marine spokesman that we were going to report on the napalm and needed his comment. A denial, he added, could be embarrassing. The reply was: "Napalm is used in the theater but it is deployed against installations, not personnel."

I tracked down pool photographers who said pilots had told them that dead Iraqis were the inevitable collateral damage of napalm. Then I told my Marine source that we wanted to make no mistakes on the wire. "You're using this stuff on bunkers but not people?" I asked. He chuckled and answered: "Have you ever seen the inside of a bunker hit by napalm?" I had. Our story carried the Riyadh statement but also reflected reality.

Late that night, a young television anchorperson from the South banged on my hotel door. She was furious that I had said Marines were using napalm.

"They told us they're only dropping it on gun emplacements, not people," she said.

"What do they man those things with?" I asked, a little uncharitably. "Chimpanzees?"

About that time, many Americans who opposed the war were stunned by evidence of Saddam's depravity. A British video report showed pathetic sea birds trapped in an oily mess which Bush blamed on opened valves at the Sea Island terminal. Greg English, an AP photographer, and I raced to Khafji to check it out. We found the birds and tracked the spill. It could have come only from shore installations hit by allied bombing. The Sea Island mess was still far from the coast. At a briefing, the AP's John King and I tried to pin down the truth. Spokesmen evaded our questions. Other reporters, instead of pressing, changed the subject.

Pete Williams, the Pentagon spokesman, came to Dhahran to see how the pools were working. Reporters told him. Nick Horrock of the *Chicago Tribune,* speaking as coordinator, said, "It is a far worse disaster than anybody ever contemplated." Reporting on the only ground action to date "was probably the worst account of anything the American people have had in thirty-five years." Williams listened, took notes, and later wrote in the *Washington Post,* "The press gave the American people the best war coverage they ever had."

Some coverage was good, with little thanks to the Pentagon. In the beginning, news organizations had to beg the Saudis for visas. After all, said U.S. officials who were mounting the massive occupation, it was the Saudis' country. When access eased, reporters poured in. The AP covered the war both ways, joining as many pools as possible but also fielding "unilaterals." I put thirty-five hundred miles on a rented Japanese power wagon, sailing through Saudi roadblocks with a smart salute. U.S. MPs took the trouble to tell me I shouldn't be there, but most seemed happy that I was. I cruised for hours across open spaces, wondering how anyone could take seriously the ludicrous notion that a war zone is too small for a few hundred reporters. I was the intruder, despite having signed security guidelines, while mysterious Bedouins drove their pickups unchallenged through U.S. installations. Some war.

Once, JIB officers told us that reporters could stay with a unit, outside of the pools, if a field commander agreed. I set out with an AP photographer who knew public affairs officers (PAOs) in the 24th Infantry Division (Mechanized), out of Fort Stewart, near Hinesville, Georgia. They were in deep hiding, but we knew we'd find them. Along the highway, we saw a broken down tank, stranded for eight days, with the 24th's "V" on the side. The crew told us roughly where to find headquarters. In the town of Hafr-al-Baten, a French photographer gave us more precise directions.

We followed the highway looking for clues. A wooden sign with an arrow, marked "Hinesville," did not take Mensa-level deduction to figure out. On the dirt road, we stopped an officer and asked him to advise the PAO of our presence. He was the MP colonel. With extreme politeness, he put us under guard. With the same courtesy, a lieutenant told us we'd be fired on if we insisted on leaving. The short version is that we were freed three hours later, to the chagrin of a public affairs captain.

As luck would have it, the captain had accompanied me months earlier on an official field trip to the 24th. Although I chose not to report some alarming equipment failures, I mentioned low morale. He was upset that I had written a "negative" report when I was supposed to be cheerleading. By then, the 24th was notorious. Gen. Barry MacCaffrey shaped his image carefully. After James LeMoyne of the *New York Times* mentioned morale in November, he closed the division to journalists. As the war approached, MacCaffrey slipped his favorites into the pool, which screwed reporters who had waited their turn, according to JIB rules. This time a 24th flack had me.

"You're in deep shit," the captain advised.

"Unless there's been a coup in Washington," I replied, "you're in deep shit."

I shared the irony with him. In twenty-five years of covering wars around the world, the first time I was held prisoner was by Americans. His colonel turned us loose but reported us to Dhahran. JIB officers gave our names to the Saudis, along with some other "unilaterals," so that we might be expelled. The Saudis, fortunately, had read the First Amendment. Three times near the front I ran into Americans I had quoted earlier in stories, with their permission. They had talked about themselves, not military operations. All three had been hunted down and disciplined.

The AP's pool people spent weeks and months in the trenches, sometimes advancing into Iraqi fire, but it was the unilaterals who got their stories on the wire. Pool dispatches were invariably late. The only significant battle, at Khafji, was an AP scoop. We sent three reporter-photographer teams, in relays. The first pair inadvertently went past Iraqi lines before slamming their jeep in reverse. Marines took photographer Peter de Jong into the heart of battle.

When the pool was finally brought to the outskirts of Khafji, Brad Willis of NBC spotted unilaterals. To one of them, Robert Fisk of the London *Independent,* he uttered words which went into the annals, along with, "Dr. Livingstone, I presume": "You asshole, you'll prevent us from working. You're not allowed here. Get out. Go back to Dhahran." Then he squealed to the minders.

U.S. officers seized film from a French television crew, which had nothing to do with the Americans. France was there, too.

What reporters learned up close was the opposite of the account in Riyadh. It was not heroic Arab allies who had run off the Iraqis and certainly not the Saudis. It was Marine artillerymen and three iron-nerved forward spotters who had hid in a tower and called fire to within yards of their position. When my turn came, I found a Marine gunner who laughed when told the official version. "Are you shitting me?" he said. "We passed those guys going about a hundred miles an hour in the wrong direction."

The issue here is far larger than correspondents' travails. When it was all over, Gen. Colin Powell sought to calm the protests. "It will all come out in history," he told a television panel. But, of course, it won't. For the most part, history will be the official record. In any case, history is supposed to come later. The present demands reporting.

From the first, the Pentagon sold the image of eager young men and women anxious to help the cause of democracy. "Media personnel" were to be on the team. Early on, I visited a Marine outpost. Sitting with some troops around a wooden table, I asked what they thought. One of them glanced at the captain over my shoulder and told me everyone was happy, thrilled at helping allies in trouble. I drew his attention to the table top in front of us. Someone had carved, "Fuck the Saudis."

Image-tending was sometimes bald. Frank Bruni of the *Detroit Free Press* wrote that pilots returning to a carrier had been "giddy." A military censor made it "proud." Sometimes the whole business got ridiculous. One officer crossed out a reference to captured Iraqis eating potatoes, onions and dates.

As the war went on, a U.S. naval commander just shook his head at some blatant lie by a fellow officer. "It's like that movie about the bridge over the River Kwai," he said. "Some of these guys get so caught up with what they are doing that they lose sight of their purpose."

Toward the end, JIB bulletin boards were dotted one morning with a photocopied handbill, unsigned. Someone had sneaked them up during the night, in the same way those first daring slogans were painted at Democracy Wall in Prague. It was a quotation from Col. Hal Moore, one of the enduring heroes of Vietnam: "We are an army of free men, defending a nation of free men and women who have a right to know what we are doing in their names."

When it was over, Col. Larry Icenogle, the affable Army tanker who was charged with coordinating the pools, acknowledged that they hadn't worked. Too many field commanders cared more about their own image than the people's right to know. "In the end," he told me, wagging his head in disgust, "where the rubber meets the road, the system broke down."

There can never be a replacement for correspondents who get close, ask questions and weigh what they see. Anyone who thinks government handouts and briefings are enough might recall this short communiqué from Vietnam, our supposed Golden Age of war reporting:

> ELEMENTS AMERICAL DIV. 11 LT INF BDE., MADE CONTACT WITH EN-
> EMY FORCE UNKNOWN SIZE 9 KM NE QUANG NGAI. INF SUPPORTED BY
> USA HEL GUNSHIPS AND ARTY. SPORADIC CONTACT CONT UNTIL 1500H
> WHEN CONTACT LOST. 128 KIA/2 US KIA. 4 WIA (MEDEVACED) AND
> 6 WIA TREATED RETND TO DY.

It was years before Seymour Hersh translated that into English: U.S. troops had masssacred several hundred men, women and children at a village called My Lai.

In the Gulf War, it was only after the yellow ribbons had been put away that we learned how deadly our own "friendly" fire had been to American and British troops. Perhaps when investigative reporters get around to it, we will learn how many Iraqi draftees were buried alive as our flag advanced behind the doctrine of over-whelming force. The lesson, in the end, is that official tampering with the citizen's right to know is as great a threat to U.S. national interests as a Middle Eastern land grab.

Much has been made of Gulf War coverage, but the main point is often lost. War is news, whoever is fighting. If the United States is a combatant, the rules of journalism cannot change. We foreign correspondents treasure our passports. We vote, pay taxes and dream of sunsets in Colorado. On the job, however, we are reporters, not Americans. When the U.S. military services do not provide access to their wars, we have to push until they do. Failing all else, we find some way to make them wish they had. As the Vietnam hero Hal Moore put it, free men should have nothing to hide.

Schwarzkopf's own reputation was made in Vietnam because Joe Galloway of *U.S. News & World Report,* then with UPI, was around to see his exploits. Schwarzkopf gave Galloway privileged access to the 24th Infantry Division in the Gulf because he remembered Joe's stories. But from the first weeks of deployment in Saudi Arabia, his staff sought to muzzle most of the media. He canceled interviews with reporters whose dispatches had irritated him. His press aide, a bureaucracy-minded Navy captain, decided at the start that all correspondents would have to be escorted everywhere. Instead of standing firm, news organizations jockeyed for position. Their executives were negotiating along a line of compromise that began in 1983, after Grenada.

During the U.S. invasion of Grenada, generals who feared embarrassment simply banned reporters. This had worked for Britain and Argentina in the Falklands War the previous year. Why not try it? But they were no match for Ed Cody of the *Washington Post.* On the first day, he and three others island-hopped until they got close enough to hire a boatman to make the harrowing run to Grenada. By the time Navy helicopters began diving around the little craft, it was too late to turn back. On shore, the four reporters interviewed Grenadans and watched desultory resistance to the massive U.S. invasion force. Then they tried to file.

All communications were down on the small island. Ham radio operators were not about to invite a silencing artillery shell. A Navy officer suggested that the correspondents might want to send their stories from the admiral's flagship. They accepted happily. Mysteriously, their stories were not sent. The helicopter that was to take them back to the island somehow never lifted off. They were held as involuntary guests for two days. No one else made it during the first two days. The only record is the Pentagon's.

Afterward, news executives negotiated on their reporters' behalf. A Pentagon pool was set up, which gave the military power over an official delegation of reporters. After a worrisome bad start during the Gulf tanker war, the pool had its first real test in Panama in 1989.

The sixteen members of the pool arrived late and never caught up. They saw virtually nothing. Reporters were given history lectures while fighting raged. They were closed up in rooms, shunted to sideshows and taken to see the cold remains of action. In the military's protective cocoon, they saw no Panamanians. But since there was a pool, foreign correspondents were judged superfluous.

Arthur Lord, a senior NBC producer who covered himself in glory during the Vietnam War, shepherded an L-1011 full of reporters and photographers from Washington. Network people and others chartered the plane, which had permission to leave but not to arrive. The Pentagon neglected to warn Howard Air Force Base; or perhaps not. When the charter landed, a master sergeant gaped at it. "My God, what are you all doing here?" he asked. But it was no problem: All 167 journalists were locked up in the recreation hall, with two phones and floor space. They stayed inside three days and went home. A few managed to see Manuel Noriega's headquarters being blown up in the distance, too far for pictures.

Other reporters got in on a CNN charter from Costa Rica. A few braved the overland route. They joined the others in the recreation hall concentration camp, about three hundred in all.

A handful of reporters were already in Panama, mostly at the Marriott Hotel. Noriega's "Dignity Battalions" took some captive and then released them. The journalists knew there would be another round. Editors at home asked the military for help. This was seen as evidence that reporters were merely in the way. Then again, if an American force decides to invade someplace, part of its mission ought to be security for the U.S. nationals and other foreign civilians it puts in danger. If generals disagree, they will still find correspondents happy to take the risk.

After Panama, correspondents expected pools to be scrapped for good. Instead, the pools evolved into an Orwellian nightmare in Saudi Arabia. Handlers referred to us as "media personnel" and called our attempts at reporting "pool product." Quasi-official Desert Storm team members—the lucky ones who found a spot and passed the physical—were given hand-picked opportunities to collect words and pictures. When pools stumbled upon news which officers chose not to call sensitive, it was often delayed until it aged into history.

Martha Teichner of CBS spent thirty-two days in the trenches on the front line. The only four of her reports that made it to Dhahran were carried by CBS people; pool handlers lost the rest. Once, the official escort even lost the pool. Reporters and their minder spent a night wandering in the desert. Teichner returned to Dhahran before the ground war, certain the system would collapse. She was right.

Tony Clifton told me that he had never been so restricted. Even the Iraqis had let him see more during their war with Iran. But in the end, he wound up in a front seat, advancing up the coast under fire with the Marines. He sent back daily pool reports, all of them rich in color and context. The Marines loved them, eager for families back home to read of their exploits. When Clifton got back to base, he found all of them, still wrapped and unsent, waiting for him. A signalman had misunderstood orders.

John Kifner of the *New York Times* scored big in the pool system. He lucked onto an enthusiastic PAO who wanted deserved glory for his Army division. But it took a Kifner to make it work. For a while the pool was paralyzed. The general refused to provide transport. Gee, Kifner remarked, in lovable gnome mode, the Marines are getting all the press. Within minutes, a helicopter materialized.

In the months following the war, five Washington bureau chiefs met repeatedly with the Defense Department to find common ground. They agreed that independent reporting would be the principal means of covering U.S. military operations. Pools would be restricted to bringing a small group along on the first wave and to situations where physical space made them necessary. The military would help with transport and communications but would not hinder journalists who worked out their own logistics.

But the touchy subject was prior security review of news and pictures from the field. In short, censorship. The Pentagon retreated slightly, but questions remained about what would happen when the issue was next put to a test. With a new administration taking power, the debate stopped. Months after Bill Clinton took office, nothing had been settled. One of the negotiating bureau chiefs answered with a bitter laugh when I asked where things stood. "We agreed to disagree," he said, "which means they won. No one has any naive expectations. They'll do what they want."

Whatever happened in Washington, correspondents knew, the old struggle would start all over again. They would demand more access than the military wanted to give them. Clashes were inevitable. Among the press corps would be some of those whom Robert Brown of *Soldier of Fortune* called "the biggest bunch of boobs and dorks I've ever seen," which included, in the view of some, Robert

Brown. PAOs would remember their elaborate lessons in masking bad news.

Mal Browne of the *New York Times,* whose experience with battlefield news management goes back thirty years, summed it up in a letter: "As for future U.S. censorship and restraint of reporters in new wars, I think it's inevitable and deplorable, but if our country remains willing to sustain a free press—by no means a sure thing— we'll still have a fighting chance. For wars that last only a few weeks, the Pentagon will always beat us. But for bigger, longer wars, no uniformed fact-suppressor will ever equal the ingenuity and persistence of a determined reporter."

In military matters, access always ends up as a tug of war between journalists and generals. Authoritarians simply dictate guidelines after determining where their best interests lie. Democratic leaders do the same thing, but they look for a softer verb than "dictate."

Britain, despite its long tradition of a free press, has a custom of voluntary cooperation with the government. Under the D-notice system, if officials suspect that an editor is about to release sensitive information, they can invoke national security. A D-notice is not legally binding, but in Britain's peer-driven society, it is almost always enough.

When Margaret Thatcher sent a fleet to run Argentina off the Falkland Islands in 1982, journalists who went along were placed under tight censorship. Few objected. No one was allowed on the islands until British forces decided it was time. The government used the BBC to confuse the Argentines, and everyone else, with disinformation. The result was an uproar similar to the one the Pentagon faced after the Gulf War.

All of this gets complicated in states which fall between the extremes of democracy and authoritarianism. The Israelis walk a tightrope, censoring reporters while they curry their favor. Under threat from its first days, Israel was shaped by Jews from Eastern Europe and North Africa, where control of information was a matter of course. State journalists reflected an official line; Jewish journalists worked toward their cause. But Israel's constitution assured free expression. A new breed of reporters and editors, many from America, called things as they saw them.

When Israel fights, correspondents and local reporters go wherever they have the guts and ingenuity to go. As Israelis rolled into Lebanon in 1983, CBS crews lost three rented cars on the first day: one was crushed by a tank, another was hit by artillery and Palestinians stole the third. In general, reporters have free run of the place. Israeli officials and politicians discuss sensitive matters. An energetic press office helps with translations, interviews and trips. Big-deal visitors believed to be sympathetic get lavish personal attention. The catch is that every word and picture going out of Israel, in war or peace, is subject to censorship.

Back when correspondents filed by telex and leased lines, they encountered mysterious garbling if their copy neared a nerve. Now, with modems and satellites, the censors seldom watch. It is up to journalists to submit material beforehand or take their chances. Broken rules can mean expulsion. In theory, censorship is strictly military, to deprive enemies of information that might give them tactical advantage. But this criterion is subject to interpretation. Censors argue that a dispatch which somehow puts the Israeli Defense Forces in a bad light can diminish its fearful reputation, threatening Israel. By this definition, the sky is the limit.

During the 1983 invasion, I watched Israeli jets strafe and bomb a Palestinian refugee camp near Sidon. Their objective was a gun position near the camp. If Palestinian fighters were hiding behind civilians, the Israelis reasoned, the fighters were responsible for any innocent victims. That seemed to be like bombing a subway station to kill bandits in the crowd, but it was not up to me to judge. I only reported what had happened. Soon afterward, the Tel Aviv bureau told me censors had killed my dispatch. I was mistaken, my colleagues had been told. The jets had been hitting near Beirut. Please tell them, I said, that I can recognize an air strike, especially when I'm standing under it. An hour later, Tel Aviv said the story had died for security reasons. Tell them, I said, that Palestinians don't need to read the AP wire to know that bombs are landing on their heads. The story stayed killed.

Later on, a *Newsweek* correspondent heard Lebanese complain that Israeli troops had stomped through their mosques, wearing boots and bringing in dogs; Muslims are pretty touchy about this sort of thing. Israeli field officers confirmed it, and the reporter included the incident in his story. In New York, editors asked their bureau to recheck with the Israeli high command. Oh no, they were told, we don't that. The incident was edited out.

The issue arose in 1992 when live shells were used accidentally in a training exercise, and five young soldiers were killed. At the time, though no one was supposed to know, Israel's top military people were there to watch. Correspondents heard about the incident, dug out the details and wrote about it. Carol Rosenberg of the *Miami Herald* went the furthest, colleagues say, and her press card was suspended. Others were also punished. But Rosenberg and the others continued to work. Ted Stanger of *Newsweek,* whose credentials were pulled before the Gulf War, had no problem reporting from Jerusalem two more years without them.

Here was that tightrope. Clyde Haberman was among those who reported on the embarrassing accident, but he escaped reprimand. He works for the *New York Times.* Later, he told an Israeli paper that he never submitted copy to the censors. Neither do some others. The advantage of press control, the Israelis know, must be weighed against a $3-billion annual infusion from Americans, who, up to now at least, have preferred their news uncensored.

News management is most evident during hostilities, but it is hardly limited to war. In almost every country, some type of government pressure on journalists is a daily fact of life. Scores of reporters are killed each year. Hundreds more are assaulted or arrested. Not all are the victims of government thugs. But many die because people have learned that bullets and bombs work better than letters to the editor.

Foreign correspondents are hardly the worst off. They can generally hop a plane and go home. Local colleagues stay put and face the pressure day after day. In Colombia alone, dozens of journalists have died in the drug war. Courageous reporters and editors across Latin America have stood up to death squads, threats to their families and advertisers' boycotts to fulfill a mission that some news executives in the United States talk about only in abstract speeches at annual meetings. It is a risky business. In Asia, Africa and the Middle East, local reporters push the limits, for themselves and for foreign correspondents who may be less sure of their ground.

At the height of El Salvador's guerrilla war, a caravan of foreign journalists and local television reporters hurried into the hills to meet with senior rebel commanders. When they came back several days later, government troops detained them briefly and said they would be killed if they reported on the rendezvous. That was enough for most. But Salvadoran television stations broadcast hours of interviews with rebel leaders condemning the government, the army and the oligarchy behind them. Using fragile freedoms still available to them, local television directors stood up to the worst form of pressure, self-censorship, by not giving in to unspecified fear of reprisal from mysterious forces, usually linked to the government. At Channel 12, a privately owned station in San Salvador, general manager Narciso Castillo Hernández told the *New York Times* that the guerrilla interviews had brought nothing worse than a warning, but that defiance had its limits. "We have a brick wall in front of us," he said. "The critics want us to throw ourselves at the wall. But that just bloodies us. Like a prisoner in the cell, we have to use a spoon to scrape at the mortar and loosen one brick at a time. We have to work slowly to take down the wall."

Courageous local journalists are the correspondent's best sources in closed societies. Whether or not they can report sensitive information, they always have it at hand. They can feel it as the tacit boundaries harden and ease back again. Often, they can help correspondents get visas or permission to travel to restricted areas. If not, they can at least brief foreign colleagues on realities they might be missing.

To the surprise of veteran correspondents, access is now easier in much of the developing world than it was in the past. Partly, this is Cold War fallout. Despots have lost the useful option of declaring themselves socialist, with all the Soviet assistance that once implied. Most are deeply in debt to Western bankers they are seeking to impress and addicted to foreign aid from countries which insist that they feign democracy. Also, some leaders have found that the occasional bad press they received was better than no press at all. Bald pressure has given way to more subtle measures.

A favorite option is to spend money badly needed for basic services on expensive public relations firms. Not only countries but also international organizations use these spin artists. During 1992, I wrote about a confidential internal report which criticized the U.N. World Health Organization's Global Program on AIDS. It listed areas needing improvement. Later, someone leaked a fax from Marshall Hoffman, a Washington public relations man. He warned WHO officials that my dispatch was "dangerous" since it might provoke interest among other reporters. It seems Hoffman earned more than $100,000 a year in public money from WHO.

Later, the reelection of the WHO's director general, Hiroshi Nakajima, showed how poorly equipped our news-gathering system is when it comes to investigating allegations of official wrongdoing. International organizations are protected by a collegial understanding that dirty laundry should be kept out of the public eye. Member states have conflicting interests which usually outweigh the business of any one agency.

The WHO, which spends nearly a billion dollars a year, is responsible for fighting not only AIDS but also tropical diseases which kill vast numbers of victims. It looks after primary health care programs for billions of people. It was the agency which beat smallpox and developed life-saving vaccines. Nakajima's detractors say he has demoralized the professional staff, driven away experts and made new recruitment more difficult. A survey by the Staff Association overwhelmingly confirms low morale.

Nakajima has strong political support at home in Japan. And Japanese officials are eager to assert their national presence in the U.N. system. Toward the end of 1992, Japan began a major offensive to ensure Nakajima's reelection by the 31-member WHO Executive Board in January 1993; his confirmation in May by the 183 member states would probably be assured. The United States and European members, charging poor management and lack of leadership, wanted someone else. Reporters became interested when WHO officials and diplomats accused Japan of using threats and foreign aid incentives to influence the voting. Third World sources confirmed some of these charges.

WHO officials who opposed Nakajima revealed privately that some Executive Board members had been given lucrative contracts. They also gave details of what they called outright bribery, payments of up to fifty thousand dollars by unspecified parties. Documents seemed to support them. Western diplomats seconded the allegations but had no proof. It was a tough story to write. In the election, seven African members agreed to back a Nigerian candidate on the first round, as is normally done, and then vote individually if he did not win. But in secret balloting, no one voted for the Nigerian, not even the Sierra Leone delegate who had nominated him. The Sierra Leone delegate, suddenly without a job, was offered a WHO consultancy (which a WHO executive blocked as improper). Nakajima won, 18–13.

Afterward, reporters obtained an outraged memo from the internal auditor, a Norwegian, who said the Philippine delegate had gotten an irregular and "quite deplorable" $150,000 contract to write a history of health care under President Corazon Aquino. He had other examples. With fanfare, the WHO ordered an external audit. This confirmed "shortcomings." Auditors said they had to fight for access to records of Nakajima's expenditures; computer files were blocked for weeks. But nothing in the report linked improprieties directly to Nakajima. If there was bribery, auditors found no trace on the WHO books.

One set of U.S. officials wanted to press a campaign to block confirmation. Department of Health and Human Services officers charged bribery. But the State Department was undecided. It had other reasons to keep the Japanese happy. This same dichotomy troubled other Western governments. Privately, a range of sources insisted that Japan and Nakajima had bought the election. But few would be named, for fear of reprisals. Reporters might have drawn more attention to the controversy, but they had little on paper. The internal audit, saying rules were "seriously breached," came out only in May on the day Nakajima was confirmed, 93–57.

Insidious pressures reach deeply. In 1981, I gave up my job as editor of the *International Herald Tribune* because I could not convince the publisher to label as advertising special sections which the ad people sold to governments. In a letter I found, a salesman told the president of Sierra Leone he could "dictate" the contents, an apt verb for the leader in question. I knew I was in trouble when I saw a China section in preparation. The bylines were all Chinese from a country with no independent reporters. "The government helped me find freelancers," the editor of special sections told me. When I objected, he added: "Don't worry, I went through and took out all the propaganda."

But the biggest threat is still direct action. More than a third of the 180 countries a reporter might want to visit exercise careful control over visas. Some require a specific invitation and months of paperwork. If the reporter has been there before, chances are he or she won't get back; any such paranoid regime is likely to take offense at something. Even tourist visas can be difficult. In the Congo, you need a certificate from a mayor saying that you have lodging, and it must be countersigned by immigration authorities.

In parts of the Middle East, especially, getting in to have a look requires patient, often humiliating, supplication. Press authorities have long memories. A correspondent who writes something unflattering or, worse, reveals an incident that the government wanted to suppress might be barred for decades. Once inside, reporters may be assigned minders to dog their steps, steer them toward happier sights and intimidate their sources.

As tension mounted in the Gulf, Iraqi minders found a useful technique for rattling correspondents. If reporter asked a question judged to be penetrating, a minder might remark: "Oh, you are an investigative reporter? Bazoft was an investigative reporter." Farzad Bazoft, an Iranian-born British reporter, was hanged as a spy the previous year.

China swings widely in its policies toward correspondents. Until the early 1970s, it was covered by periscope from Hong Kong. A Reuters correspondent, allowed in, was held in humiliating house arrest. By the time of Tiananmen Square, reporters were relatively free. Then they weren't. Early in 1993, authorities banned any reports which could endanger "national security, unity or society's common interests"—that is, anything the government decides it does not like.

Sudan jailed and tortured Mike Kilongson, a Sudanese BBC reporter, because he had reported famine in the southern part of the country. He fled to Kenya, in fear of his life. That was in 1986, but Sudanese authorities still crack down hard when displeased at having been embarrassed. They are far from the only ones.

When societies close down, we could cover them through the looking glass, quoting diplomats, human rights agencies, exiled politicians and intellectuals, and refugees. This would pressure leaders to open up to get their side across. In fact, most states can slam the door and apply the thumbscrews in peace. We seldom push. A simple axiom applies, whether to Washington or Pyongyang: The less we fight for access to news, the more governments gain by censorship. Then again, nothing is that simple in this business. Look, for instance, at South Africa.

Over decades, South Africa tried to win friends and stifle people. Journalist visas took months to obtain. Past writings were scrutinized, and references were checked. Visas specified the subjects to be covered. Once correspondents got inside, reporting was easy. They visited townships and homelands. But outspoken South Africans were sometimes banned to the press. And if correspondents stepped over the line, they did not come back.

Some reporters based in Johannesburg censored themselves and missed what was obvious. Others pushed the edge, with their visas always in doubt. In 1986, when violence turned nasty, authorities clamped down hard. Under emergency powers, they prohibited cameras in townships. Reporters could be jailed for ten years under a sweeping set of rules. Pictures stopped, as authorities had expected. According to one thoughtful insider, the government lost as much as it gained. Rian Malan, an Afrikaner journalist with an open mind, established his credentials in a book called *My Traitor's Heart.* In 1989, asked by the Freedom Forum Media Studies Center to assess American coverage of his tormented homeland, he let fly. With objective passion, he dissected a situation in South Africa that can serve as an example of similar distortions of reality elsewhere.

Malan had just watched Oprah Winfrey finish a program by declaring: "We said we'd never let it happen again, but it is happening. It's happening in South Africa today. Another holocaust is under way . . ." Photos of bloodied, broken African bodies appeared as music welled and the credits rolled. Beyond her disturbing inability to distinguish degrees of evil, Malan wrote, Winfrey did not know what she was talking about. He explained:

> What really irked me was her assumption that South Africa is still convulsed by ghastly police violence, the way it was three to five years ago . . . when images of South African bloodshed and repression were a nightly staple on network news. That era ended abruptly on June 12, 1986, the day the Botha government kicked the cameramen out of the township, barred journalists from covering any "security force action," and started rounding up all the anti-apartheid organizers and activists it could lay its hands on. South Africa then vanished from the world's television screens, and since nobody informed them otherwise, many Americans assumed that carnage carried on unseen. This was not the case.

Massive detentions broke the back of rebellion, he wrote. By 1988, whites could drive from one end of Soweto to the other, scarcely seeing a policeman and finding no white soldiers at all. South Africa had returned to its own brand of normal, with torture and terror and mysterious murder, but Oprah's visible holocaust was not taking place. Except for the ban on cameras in townships, correspondents ignored the totalitarian restrictions and covered the news. The government made an occasional example when it wanted to make a point. The game was cat and mouse.

In September, a month after the Oprah show, township violence returned to the screen. In the heat of elections, police killed
at least twelve protesters in Cape Town. "The onward march of
history provided American television networks with a morality play
of the sort it handles best—an apartheid morality play in which white
villains suppress black victims and innocent people die gruesome
cinematic deaths," Malan wrote. "Give the networks a story like that
and they'll go into the townships, shoot 'illegal' footage of police
dispersing crowds with birdshot, and show it on the evening news.
And then Archbishop Tutu will appear on 'Nightline' to explain it
all."

In this case, Ted Koppel remarked, "We've seen more violence
today than we've seen in several years." The *Los Angeles Times* made
the same judgment. But at least two thousand people had died in
political violence over three years, Malan continued, mostly blacks
killed by other blacks who were less likely to arrest American media
attention.

"The flow of news from South Africa is governed by two forms
of censorship," Malan wrote, warming to his subject. "One is the
Banana Republic goonsquadism of apartheid's security apparatus.
The other is one you may not have heard about—an invisible force
that acts on the hearts and minds of well-intentioned Just White
Men. On the basis of the record, it's sometimes hard to tell which
is the more powerful of the two."

Winnie Mandela, he said, was a case in point. For years, she
captured headlines as her imprisoned husband's consort, the brave,
noble and selfless "Mother of the Black Nation." The *New York
Times* ran twenty-two stories on her in 1986, and she appeared seventy times on American television. She was showered with honorary
degrees and nominated for the Nobel Peace Prize. "The real Winnie
could be ravishingly charming to Western ambassadors but treated
ordinary people with imperious disdain," Malan said. "She issued
peremptory orders and screamed if they weren't obeyed. Her retainers were so cowed that they stood up when she entered the
room. . . . She used the proceeds of books and movie rights sales to
build a $250,000 palace for herself in Soweto and tried to sell mer-
chandising rights to the Mandela name to Bob Brown, a black Republican so conservative that the Reagan administration considered
him for an ambassadorship."

While she accused foreign investors of complicity in apartheid,
Winnie Mandela kept her own money in South Africa's largest white

bank, personally managed by a man the African National Congress had declared an enemy. Most of this was overlooked in American papers. Soon she was hard to ignore. Her private palace guard strutted around Soweto, demanding free drinks and the attention of young women in the name of the freedom struggle. In 1987, some of her retainers were arrested on charges ranging from murder to torture to armed robbery. The local press could not write it, Malan said, and the foreign press did not write it. Reporters, suspecting possible disinformation, gave Mandela the benefit of the doubt. She remained the heroic mother of her nation. In July 1988, she made thirteen U.S. television appearances, once as ABC's Person of the Week.

Then Mandela's young lions raped a high school girl, and students marched on her house and burned it down. "The neighbors looked on indifferently, none bothering to throw so much as a cup of water on the flames," Malan wrote. "The *New York Times* and *Washington Post* noted the incident, but their reports were so devoid of details as to be virtually meaningless. CBS attributed the attack to 'black gang members,' and NBC led with the arson story, presenting it as yet another apartheid atrocity. Trevor Tutu, the archbishop's son, merely insinuated 'the system' had done it, but Reverend Allan Boesak said it outright: The white racist regime was to blame. And finally, Winnie herself appeared on the screen, talking about her lifelong 'struggle for justice.' "

In the following months, South African papers were full of trial testimony. Witnesses described murder and mutilation. "Winnie 'Served Tea' to Youths Tortured in Her Backyard," one headline read in the *Weekly Mail*. "These stories stunned South Africa and mortified the internal opposition, but they were completely ignored by the foreign press," Malan wrote. Later, four more teenagers were abducted and taken to Winnie Mandela's backyard. After days of brutal interrogation, one got away. Church leaders saved two others, but a fourth, Stompie Mokhetsie, 14, was missing and presumed dead. This, too, went uncovered.

Finally, the *Weekly Mail* published an explosive account in which prominent black leaders condemned Mandela and excluded her from the movement. Suddenly, Stompie's torture-murder was a story.

"So the truth about Winnie Mandela went untold for two years, and as soon as it was published American liberals rushed into print with damage-containing rationalizations . . . ," Malan wrote. "When she started veering off the rails, nobody dared to criticize her, no matter how badly she behaved. She lived in a total vacuum of censure."

Malan's message is not that there was a conspiracy of silence or mass dereliction of duty; it is more realistic: "It's hard to be a foreign correspondent in South Africa." The blacks' cause was so palpably right it was difficult to fault them for being wrong. Besides, no one is sure the outside world wants to hear. South Africa was the one place where good and evil were supposed to be clearly demarcated. The world was in chorus on apartheid, and one was fearful of hitting a flat note.

An independent television producer, Danny Schechter, went further in a similar remark: "Restrictions are placed on correspondents not only by the government but also the limitations of culture, class, color and consciousness, which are harder to detect."

Such sweeping judgments always overlook individual cases of fine reporting, in newspapers, magazines and on the air. Some dispatches made it plain that Winnie Mandela was no saint. In 1986, she supported necklacing, the punishing of suspected black collaborators by flinging tires full of burning gasoline around their necks.

In South Africa, so little understood by outsiders who nonetheless hold definite convictions, correspondents faced enormous challenges. For one thing, they could not trust what they heard. The government was diabolically clever at news management, and all sides had something to sell. "There was so much disinformation put out from Pretoria that it was only until legitimate anti-apartheid leaders condemned Winnie Mandela that we felt comfortable believing these stories," said David Crary, the AP news editor at the time.

Malan faulted reporters for not explaining the nature of political violence. When white police shot blacks, he said, headlines were assured. But a vicious Zulu civil war was followed only sporadically, with little analysis or detail. Yet outsiders cannot fathom South Africa without understanding its internecine violence. White South Africans, one writer put it, are paranoiacs stranded on a desert island in what they believe to be shark-infested waters. They won't venture off until they think it is safe. Blacks fighting one another scare them to paralysis.

But this is one of those pressures of our news-gathering system. The Zulu war did not go anywhere. Editors were bored by it. They wanted an update from time to time. If there was a major turn, reporters covered it. In the meantime, few desks wanted to make space for running accounts of the story, however anxious reporters were to write about it.

Similarly, Malan accused reporters of ignoring the cultural and ideological landscape. In most readers' stereotypes, South Africa is separate from the continent it anchors. Yet 45 percent of black city dwellers, and 80 percent in the countryside, practice ancestral African religions. In April 1986, African National Congress youths in rural Sekhukuniland came to believe that local women were using witchcraft to hold back freedom. They rounded up thirty-two and hurled them into firepits. The *Los Angeles Times* covered this, the worst mass murder in South African history. The *New York Times* gave it four brief sentences along with fourteen paragraphs on a Desmond Tutu civil rights speech, Malan said, and most American news organizations missed it entirely. Unless reporters explain the cultural underpinnings, carefully and repeatedly, a complex set of African nations is seen in terms of Alabama the 1960s.

Ideology is badly understood, largely because of shorthand codes which travel so poorly. When Nadine Gordimer came to America to promote her novel *Burger's Daughter,* talk-show hosts kept describing the hero as a "noble white liberal." He was an Afrikaner who devoted his life to fight for black liberation. But he was a Communist, Gordimer tried to explain. No one seemed to hear. In American civil rights terms, the good guys are liberals; Communists are bad guys. "This was not a matter of misreading or misunderstanding," Gordimer said. "It is the substitution of one set of values for another." Real liberals fell out with the anti-apartheid resistance, which was "socialist" and "revolutionary." But these last are heavily loaded words.

Here again, reporters faced the same obstacles. The *Washington Post*'s man was Bill Claiborne, a veteran of India and the Middle East, who knows about cultural bridges. Reporters, he said, faced yet another pressure: the need to explain in the tight space available. "Very patiently in every story, you had to explain the misconceptions about South Africa and apartheid, power sharing and the blacks," Claiborne said. "It was almost a function key on the computer. It is a very complex place. You need a hell of a lot of patience to conduct little history courses, political science lessons. You have to show how it is not a good-guy, bad-guy place. TV can't do it."

Malan's conclusion was that whatever is said, how South Africa is portrayed in America has an enormous impact on events. Hardliners hold back in fear of bad publicity. Black resistance figures are equally sensitive. The future of South Africa, and much of Africa beyond, hangs heavily on how much reporters can hold all culprits' feet to the fire.

Soon after Malan wrote, Nelson Mandela was free. South Africa opened to the world. The Zulu war flared, one of a series of brutal conflicts among blacks in the waters around the whites' desert island. The country got to be freer but more tense and restrictive all at once. Hatreds and frustrations grew more virulent. Authorities allowed camera crews to go into the townships, but few of them dared. For the reasons Malan and American correspondents have outlined, many readers and viewers were caught unprepared. This was a time not only for sensitive, comprehensive reporting but also for room to display it.

The luck of the draw equipped South Africa with a highly competent press corps. But the world was aflame elsewhere. Reporters were called to the Gulf and beyond, then Somalia. South African events were crowded out to make room for other news. As a result, only some feet were held to the fire. The system might have worked there. But every sort of pressure pushed it out of shape. Anyone who followed events and developments during that turbulent period had to work hard at it. It was not easy.

Of all the pressures, nothing is more direct than artillery shells dropping on your head. In Sarajevo, through month after month of siege, the newspaper *Oslobodjenje* continued to publish every day from an atom-bomb shelter. The twin nine-story glass and steel towers that had housed it before the war collapsed in a heap and melted in the fires that followed. Dug in a hundred yards away, Serbian gunners continued to pound the rubble and rake the streets at the glimpse of any vehicle. Using everything from tank guns to night-vision rifles, militiamen aimed at anyone who entered or left.

First the paper circulated all over the city. Then the distributors stopped coming to work, and the seven hundred kiosks that sold it were blown up or smashed by bullets. With no one else to do it, the journalists themselves took over. After writing and editing, they tossed bundles into their cars and sold them on the streets. It was the only consumer item still available.

It was an impressive case of adapting rapidly to circumstance. A month before the war, I visited Kemil Kurspahic, the editor, in his comfortable upper-floor office. Pouring out a tumbler of good whiskey, he explained why the stock label of "Muslim" was so misleading. Bosnians, from the same ethnic stock, had always lived together, he said. Radovan Karadzic, the Serbian zealot who vowed to confound that principle, was a force to be resisted at all costs. Kurspahic sent me to his bureau chief in the lovely old city of Mostar, a courtly Muslim poet who could not believe that the republic's intricate society would collapse.

At the time, with peace in the streets, it seemed academic. Eight months later, I read Blaine Harden's dispatch on *Oslobodjenje* in the *Washington Post*. The editor said to Harden: "Why do they hate us? Because we symbolize a Bosnia that they say is impossible. We still have 30 percent Serbs (roughly the prewar percentage of Serbs in Bosnia) with bylines in the paper every day. They hate us for that."

Kurspahic's right leg was smashed in a car wreck on his way to the office. Doing ninety miles an hour, the usual speed to elude snipers, he hit a police car. He went on leave and turned daily control over to Gordana Knezevic. A Serb.

# Chapter 8

# Gatekeepers

A correspondent for a fair-sized American paper, covering the famine in Somalia before most people paid attention to it, got a call from his top editor. The guy had a great idea. The reporter was to find a village where everyone was starving and about to wander off in a desperate search for food. Then he would stay with them until, lost in the desert, they all died.

Professional that he was, the reporter said he would look into it. It is bad form to laugh at your boss, however tempting that sometimes may be. Besides, the man also had better ideas. Good or bad, editors shape the process. Though often forgotten by outsiders, they are the ones to decide who goes where and, less directly, who says what. Agency editors filter what goes on the wires to the newspapers. At each paper, others determine what gets into print. A ham-handed desk person can wreak more havoc than a team of censors. A good one needs less than a sow's ear to make silk. Together, they pass judgment on words, on dispatches, on subjects. A correspondent might file clean copy well ahead of the deadline. But without their collective nod, it won't get through the gate.

At the top are the glass-office editors who have gravely voices in every film that touches on journalism. For readers, these are the ones to reach, the executive editors and managing editors. They determine the mix, divide up the editorial budget and hire the rest.

They get involved with foreign stories only if the news is very big or sensitive. Correspondents see these chiefs mainly at lunch on home leave. More pertinent to them are the foreign editor, or national-foreign editor on smaller papers, and the lower ranking people who actually handle the copy.

A correspondent's dispatch may pass through half a dozen sets of hands before getting into type. If it is from a news agency, another six sets may have already had a crack at it. Everyone down the line has a different function, but most share a common belief: With a few deft key strokes, they can make an illiterate boob sound like a pro. Sometimes, this is true. Few reporters admit how many times a sharp editor has spared them embarrassment, or worse.

Together, these editors dissolve into a single collective, "the desk." It amounts to a prism through which every dispatch must pass. If it is well-cut and polished, and held squarely to the light, it channels with clear intensity. If chipped or clouded or off on a cock-eyed angle, it throws out a blur.

Beyond the words, the desk handles people. The best editors keep a correspondent focused and in touch with the system. The good ones know that reporters at the end of a long line operate on alternating current. They need to feel the electricity humming both ways. On direct current, like their radios and computers, they run down. These are the editors who spring you from prison, cheer up your disappointed kid or remind you that Bart Simpson was not Madonna's first husband.

But desks vary widely, and not every editor is a wise, calm voice. The lore is rich in stories of the other kind. Once, for example, a news agency reporter got a call in London. It was a foreign desk editor, fresh from a domestic bureau and in training to be a correspondent herself. She was supervisor that morning.

"Um, Ed," she said (the quotations are approximate), "I see you filed a story about someplace called Gibraltar. Our atlas only shows a Gibraltar Flats, Minnesota, and . . ."

"It's a rock," the reporter replied. "In Spain. Belongs to Britain."

"Oh," she said, and hung up. Moments later, the phone rang again. "Um, Ed. If it's in Spain, why does it belong to Britain?"

"That's what the story is about," he said, beginning to warm up around the neck muscles. After another question, he snapped: "Look, you're the only person in the world who has never heard of the Rock of Gibraltar. Just put it on the wire."

At a newspaper, a young editor was puzzled by a reference to the Druses in a dispatch about warring religious factions in Lebanon. He thought for a while until he realized what the correspondent must have meant. He fixed it to read "Druids." All by himself, at a desk in New York, he turned a sect of fiercely independent Muslim hill people into ancient Celtic priests.

The initial editing process is as important as covering a story in the first place. If raw copy is not spiked stillborn, it is worked over before going on to the next tier of editors who make decisions about its fate. The desk must weave in essential background and context. And correspondents in a hurry cannot avoid mistakes. One particularly good writer rushing out a dispatch about a terrorist assault in Israel sent this to the desk: "The howl of ambulance sirens mingled with the groans of the dead."

Often, editors feel that things are not explained simply enough. Or they just may want to contribute to the literary process. In any case, once they change a dispatch, their supervisors seldom get to compare the original with the edited version. If a mistake is written into the copy or an important element is lost, the damage may not be undone. At the same time, if an editor improves a dispatch, the writer usually gets the admiration. It is tough job, professionally and psychologically, and it requires experience.

However skilled they may be, editors are not eyewitnesses. They seldom know the cultural nuances or the political context, let alone the geography. There may be time for them to clarify points with the writer. But when they make changes, they are bound to surmise. Some blunders are classics. In 1960, as Algeria fought for independence, Charles de Gaulle granted self-determination. French hard-liners rebelled. De Gaulle appealed for resistance to cease. Reporting this, an agency correspondent also wrote that de Gaulle had urged his army to wipe out Algerian rebels who continued to fight. A faraway editor rewrote the dispatch and gave it an "urgent" priority. The result was headlines announcing that Charles de Gaulle had told his troops to kill Frenchmen.

It often works the other way, as it is designed. Editors save their organizations from serious grief by suspecting a mistake and demanding that correspondents go back to recheck. A desk editor, sitting at the keyboard in a warm office, can buff up a dispatch written in haste under fire. But the interplay is always delicate. The editors' purpose is to tighten, to solidify, to dramatize. Besides accuracy, they demand clarity. This is not as simple as it might seem from a distance.

Sometimes, for instance, reporters choose words carefully to describe unidentified sources. The idea is to offer readers enough information without giving the source's foes too many clues. If a reporter uses mushy wording to protect a source's life, however, it is still mushy wording. It needs fixing. Someone who does not realize the consequences, by dint of having been in similar circumstances, is tempted to take an easier way out. A dispatch might refer to "diplomatic sources who passed through Peshawar." This is awkward, and the desk might make it, "a Western diplomat in Peshawar." But if there is only a U.S. consul based in Peshawar, the mask is pretty thin.

Editors must be confident and experienced enough to know when to break the rules, to see things from points of view they may not have considered. Their boot camp stresses the need to attribute as much as possible to named official sources, recognized authorities or the police. In much of the world, however, these are the last people to be believed. Although they belong in the story for balance, reality is more important than form. Inexpert editors tend to add weight to comforting official voices. This damages a correspondent's credibility. Worse, it misleads the reader.

But here is a serious weakness in the system. Although people who want to be correspondents seldom want to be editors first, it is good training if they are. So news agencies and some newspapers require overseas-bound reporters to pay their dues on the desk. If they prove themselves, they move on. Stuck at headquarters, they must make their mark on someone else's copy. Often, twenty-five-year veterans cover complex events only to be second-guessed back home by a twenty-five-year-old editor. The point is neither age nor inherent talent, but exposure to the world. Most know about the Rock of Gibraltar, but a home-based bias often shows.

When Mikhail Gorbachev made his inaugural address in the Kremlin as general secretary of the party, one editor asked Moscow what language he had spoken. Another editor at the same news agency expressed surprise to the Budapest bureau that Hungarians had their own native tongue.

I started this way, eager to earn my spurs. During my first week, a dispatch from Geneva mentioned the U.N. headquarters, the Palais des Nations. Flexing my embryonic French, I messaged that perhaps it should be Palais *de* Nations. No, Geneva patiently replied, *des* takes an "s." It might have occurred to me that even if a reporter whose first language was French could not spell a simple preposition, his office was in the building in question.

Mistakes are fewer when editors ask first. But often an editor cannot reach the correspondent, or simply doesn't try. Editors have three choices. If they leave unchanged something which is not clear to them, they risk rebuke higher up the line; once the copy is in their hands, it is their responsibility. If they cut out the offending passage, they may leave a hole in the story; again, someone may call them on it. The third road is to guess at what the writer meant. The de Gaulle incident, like countless others since, shows that this is tricky business even for the practiced.

The other problem is literary, often more an irritant to correspondents than a loss to the reader. Editors can't show skill by changing facts, but they can sharpen up the writing. This can be an unhappy experience. From Prague, one reporter filed a mood piece about how Czechoslovaks savored the word "freedom" on their palates. An editor, jumbling the lead paragraph, made it "lips." The result sounded as if the reporter had missed a scientific scoop: Here were people with taste buds in their lips.

Rules of political propriety can get carried to extremes. During the Gulf War, a reporter who spent the night on an aircraft carrier flight deck wrote about the lurking shapes which sprang suddenly to life with a jet blast that could "blow a man overboard." It came back "blow a person overboard." He messaged the desk that not only were all persons aboard the carrier men but also that the naval term evoked was not "person overboard." Nor did anyone ever say, "Person the lifeboats."

For balance, many desks are anchored by old-timers who have been there and come back. Some of these seasoned hands have a tendency to prejudge based on outmoded assumptions. More often, they guide the neophytes and add a broader view to dispatches which can use their help. They know why seemingly trivial distinctions are crucial to a story. And few of them suffer from a chronic desk disorder, the two-inches-on-a-map syndrome. (Oh, you're in Bangui? Hop over to Entebbe this afternoon. What, that means flying to Paris and then London and then back to Africa to go two hundred miles? But it's only two inches on the map.)

The big papers try to keep a heavy load of veterans on the desk. The *Washington Post,* especially, makes a point of bringing correspondents back, sometimes earlier than they want. The advantage is that old hands like Jackson Diehl and Ed Cody handle copy. That sort of editor anticipates a correspondent's problems and clears the way for more reporting time. Reporters in a hurry feel comfortable trusting the desk to work in background.

Also, there are editors whose career is editing, people who have never been tempted to report, at home or abroad. Their professional challenge is readable copy, free of libel or slurs on any collectivity, before deadline. Many organizations work hard to develop a stable of well-paid, highly educated desk people. Simon Li at the *Los Angeles Times,* who mixed his journalism training with broader studies in England, knows what people eat for lunch in the Rann of Kutch. Some others seem to hire anyone who knows a tense from a tuna sandwich.

Good copy editors are horrified not by the smouldering wreckage of an Airbus but by dangling participles and misspelled names. They work over copy like undertakers touching up the loved ones of strangers. Famous correspondents may impress readers but not editors. That big byline may be just another manic-depressive who can't keep his hands off the semicolon key. At the big papers, a desk editor might spend an hour on the smoothest of dispatches from the most trusted and experienced correspondent. It's all copy to be put into English.

Though they are as important to the process as the writers they oversee, most editors are beyond the public's view. Reporters have bylines, and their personalities emerge in their daily dispatches. They are boasted about in house ads. Top editors get their names on a masthead and eat chicken à la king with the Kiwanis. But desk people are elusive. Once newsroom visitors could at least see them, clustered around a traditional horseshoe desk, the rim, where they flexed their wit in a common energy pool. Now they work alone, electronically, muttering back at their computer terminals. Hemorrhoid cushions are gone; the new badge of honor is a wrist brace to relieve carpal tunnel pain from too much time at the keys. For a brief time, you could pick out the important ones, at least the males, by their bright red Ben Bradlee suspenders. Now there is only the old way, to look for harried expressions; the more harried, the further they are down the ladder.

One legend of his craft was Harris Jackson, who retired after three decades as the AP's "early" foreign editor. Jackson came in before midnight, in opera dress or a ragged flight jacket, and began sifting through what had landed from bureaus around the world.

The procedure remains. A supervisor and assistants decide what will die and what might live. A few survivors are selected for the PMs Digest, the menu of important stories in the works sent to afternoon newspapers. (It is the same for AMs.) Others go to the foreign editor for possible future use. But after Harris Jackson, the style changed.

Jackson was precise and brutal. He knew the larger picture and followed each twist and turn at the edges. He could not only spell the Court of St. James's, he had been there for tea. Woe befell any kid, on the desk or abroad, who could not keep track of "s" 's and apostrophes. Jackson filled in holes from his own prodigious knowledge or a reference shelf at his elbow. During Vietnam, he charted every skirmish on the map. Again and again, he went back to the clips of earlier stories. If all else failed, he launched a harrowing "Jackson message."

One night the London bureau wrote coyly that the new Oxford dictionary included some fresh dirty words, but it did not name them. "What words?" Jackson messaged. London replied that they were too vulgar for the wire. Asked again, London demurred, saying there were ladies in the office. Exasperated, Jackson fired back: "Are they among the following . . . ?" and he listed every obscene word he could recall, which was a lot.

Little impressed him. When Richard Nixon opened up China in 1972, the AP sent Hugh Mulligan, its star. Dazzled by historical significance, he wrote a dispatch about the great city of Shanghai, from which most foreigners had been banned for twenty-three years. He waited as a Chinese operator connected him to Rockefeller Plaza, half a world away; this would have been unthinkable only a few months before. The phone rang, and Jackson answered. Hugh heard the familiar nasal roar: "It's Mulligan with more of that Peking shit. Who wants to take it?"

Foreign editors, where they exist, ride herd on the copy. Some papers use what they call a universal copy desk, which runs all stories through the same chutes without any special expertise. More often, small to medium-sized papers lump national and world news under a single senior editor. At newspapers with their own foreign staffs, the editor has an extra role as correspondents' alter ego and, if any good, father/mother confessor.

Jim Yuenger of the *Chicago Tribune* once interrupted his birthday party to take dictation from Sarajevo. I saw him in Paris en route to buy furniture for a Berlin correspondent who was bouncing around too fast to do it himself. Yuenger was also working. A former UPI correspondent, he travels and writes often to keep in touch with the world. He sees the foreign desk not only as an editing center but also a support system. "We are the lifeline for a lot of courageous and hard-working reporters who are out at the ends of the earth," he said.

Yuenger's people produce because they respect him but also because they have no choice. If an agency reporter does a good story in a place his own people are also covering, he'll put it in the paper. As he sees it, his responsibility is to the reader. With a dozen or so people, he is able to throw troops at every major story. They write the main leads and also background sidebars, giving the *Tribune* something besides agency copy. But with his own staff he can also leave the hard news to the wires and let a correspondent dig up something no one else has. This is how the system ought to work.

Alvin Shuster at the *Los Angeles Times* has more staff reporters than anyone else, and he is prepared to let a story go if circumstances demand it. His paper has already buried two correspondents in a decade. Unwilling to risk anyone's life in Sarajevo, Shuster settled for dispatches he could get elsewhere. His East Africa correspondent had Somalia on his beat but was not eager to go. Shuster did not push. This subject arose when Mark Fineman and Scott Kraft arrived to cover Operation Restore Hope. Colleagues wondered aloud about earlier coverage. "At the *L.A. Times,*" Fineman said, "we think people are more important than stories or prizes."

At the *New York Times* and the *Washington Post,* the other papers with big staffs, correspondents speak warmly of their foreign editors. Cody remembers calling Mike Getler at home for permission to spend that six thousand dollars on a charter to Lockerbie when the Pan Am flight went down. It would skew his budget, late in the year. "I could just imagine him watching his bonus fly out the window," Cody said. "But he said, 'Aw fuck it, go ahead.'"

Not every foreign editor has been so popular. Some time back, a Paris correspondent for a large daily got a call from his editor about a story he had seen. The editor talked about the subject and concluded: "I can't remember where I saw it, but it's something I want right away." The implication was, Why did you miss it? My friend reminded him where he had seen it; it was a story the correspondent had sent two days earlier which the editor had filed away on hold.

To handle correspondents, editors must be part trail boss and part Nurse Ratchet. Along with serious concerns, there are always turf wars and bruised egos. At one large paper, a major story in Africa went uncovered. The correspondent in whose territory it was wanted to keep it on ice until he got back from an extended vacation. Others were eager to volunteer while it was a story, but they were waved off. Noblesse oblige.

Occasionally, editors have to explain the facts of life to people higher up the ladder who attempt to bend their arm. Some are more successful than others. After Mexican publisher Mario Vázquez Raña bought UPI, he called in Sylvana Foa, the foreign editor. UPI's Mexico correspondent was "not very polite" to the government, he said, and he wanted her replaced. When Foa argued and stalled, he told her to learn Spanish. You only need two words, he said: *Si, señor.* She refused to use them and was fired. He later sold UPI.

At every paper, foreign editors fight constantly for space. Some have an easier time of it than others. At the *Los Angeles Times,* a world focus is a given. "Readers equate quality newspapers with their coverage of the world," Shuster said. Each day, the *Times'* front section has at least thirty-six columns of empty space which is up for grabs between foreign and national. That is about thirty thousand words, a third of a reasonably sized book. If China erupts, there is room to say why. If the National Guard storms Chicago, world news gives way.

On a normal day, the foreign desk selects fifteen to twenty pieces; two or three of those are offered for the front page. Most are from *Times* correspondents, about thirty of them, but there is also agency copy and dispatches from other papers' news services. At one time, up to forty dispatches backed up from the bureaus, awaiting space. Now most *Times* copy eventually gets into the paper, Shuster said, but correspondents sometimes must write less. About a third of the time, the foreign desk hits Column One, a front page feature spot with steady readers.

Big news from abroad has no trouble getting page one display in the *Times.* Lesser news has a chance. An analysis or a story about a potential problem might also make it. It depends on a process similar to what happens each day in every newsroom in the country.

Section editors gather to consider a list of stories for page one. In turn, they pitch their favorites. The managing editor or the executive editor makes the choice. National and metro usually do the best. Business and sometimes sports get in a whack. Foreign is the floater. It carries weight, all right, but newspapers have to look after their own hometowns.

The day I attended the *Times* meeting, in July 1992, foreign pushed a single story, slugged "Yugo": the Bosnian president had pleaded with President Bush to break through the Serbs' siege and use aircraft to silence the guns that were shelling Sarajevo. It was a tossup against a metro story about a black hole, "Hole." The prize was a little chunk of space at the bottom of the page, with a jump inside. I'm not sure what Hole was about, and neither was anyone else. That, most likely, is why Yugo won by a nod.

Wherever a story goes, at least one of the foreign desk's sixteen copy editors works it over hard. "We emphasize the basics, interesting stories, with a lot of focus on making the stories human," Simon Li, the deputy foreign editor, explained. "We have a lot less of the 'spokesmen say' kind of story." For years, a sign hung over the desk: "Consider Gus." Gus was the faceless reader who picked up the paper, a sort of cousin to the Kansas City milkman, immortalized in a classic news agency novel of that title. The sign is gone, but editors still consider Gus. "Sometimes we ask ourselves, 'Is Gus going to understand that?' " Li said. Often the response is no.

"People don't understand bylines and datelines," he explained. "They call up and want to speak to the correspondent, expecting to find him here. They don't understand the difference between editorials and news stories." A sharp line divides the news columns, which seek to be objective, and the editorial pages, which don't. But readers who object to an opinion expressed often call the foreign desk to complain. A lot of things that journalists take for granted are missed by their readers.

"The wrong response is to dumb it up and give them what you think is wanted," Li concluded. Instead, good editors make the stories clear, even if they are complex. A low common denominator loses the informed readers and does little to educate those who would like to be informed.

This is Holger Jensen's philosophy at the *Rocky Mountain News* in Denver, but he has a much harder time of it. Jensen, an AP Vietnam correspondent who went on to spend years abroad for

*Newsweek,* is international editor of the *News.* He is a strapping Dane who fit right into the turmoil of Beirut and South Africa. Now, preferring his log cabin at ninety-one hundred feet and a yard slick with elk droppings, he is an editor. He writes a twice-weekly column and tries to stuff a heap of sausage makings into a tiny skin.

The *News'* circulation is 355,000, and it runs to 140 pages, but sometimes Jensen has room for no more than three inside story slots. "It is absolutely impossible to explain what is happening in Somalia in six inches," he said. "You can't do it." The *News* gets the AP, Reuters and the German agency, DPA, along with Scripps-Howard. The rival *Denver Post* has locked up most of the other supplementary services. Even so, he uses 2 percent of what crosses his desk. On average, 4 to 5 percent of the news hole goes to foreign articles.

Down in Fort Worth, Jensen's old AP colleague, Jim Peipert, has a similar job at the *Star-Telegram.* With a smaller circulation than the *News,* it devotes 12 to 15 percent of its news hole to the world. And Peipert complains.

There is no guide. The *St. Petersburg Times,* with roughly the same number of readers as the *News,* pours resources into foreign news. It has a Paris bureau run by Wilbur Landrey, UPI foreign editor in the good old days, a roving Latin American reporter and a senior editor who travels. Some bigger papers have almost nothing. And no one beats the space crunch. Take the *Philadelphia Inquirer,* which tries hard to cover the world. During a typical twelve-hour cycle in 1992, AP foreign bureaus sent 182 stories to New York. Of those, 60 moved on the wire. The *Inquirer* used edited-down versions of 9 of them, along with 5 from Reuters, one from the *Los Angeles Times* and 2 from its own correspondents, in Moscow and South Africa. The other available material, hundreds of thousands of words, was deleted electronically. It did not even make the garbage can.

At the *Atlanta Constitution* I met Randall Ashley, who speaks with a slow, southern charm and works at the speed of a crazed hornet. He smiled apologetically when I introduced myself and he recognized a name from the wire. "I've read a lot more of your stories than I've printed," he said. As foreign editor, he supervises five full-time correspondents and a team of stringers. He also sifts through the AP and Reuters, as well as services from the *New York Times,* the *Washington Post–Los Angeles Times,* Knight-Ridder–

*Chicago Tribune,* Scripps-Howard, and the *Financial Times* of London. Then there is his own chain's service, the Cox wire.

He tries hard to make good use of tight space, encouraged by an editor who is committed to world news. Once the *Constitution* put four reporters on trying to show how Yugoslavia was not such a remote place. But there are always those limits. I saw him in the summer of 1992, when editors knew that Somalis were in desperate trouble but the place was not yet a story. "I'm holding a Somalia piece now," Ashley said, with his slow rueful grin. "It's primary season. What shall I say?"

Workaday editors do much to define the shape of the world. Even when a story thrusts itself upon them, they determine the orders of magnitude. When the killing began in Bosnia, AP editors chose to base the running death toll on tabulations by health authorities. No one could argue with body counts. At the end of 1992, the total was eighteen thousand. But the same officials listed more than one hundred thousand missing, many of whom were dead. They did not count deaths in areas beyond their control or reach. The AP's toll, if defensible, might have been a fourth of the actual number. In 1993, the AP changed to the higher figures for dead and missing.

As the air war approached in Baghdad, editors pulled home correspondents who were anxious to stay. Some were driven by concern for their people. Others thought of the responsibility of getting back a "guest" from Saddam Hussein. A few must have reflected on what one London editor admitted on BBC: Keeping people "behind enemy lines" meant political heat. Newspapers may have feared damage suits from reporters' families. For whatever reason, war in Baghdad started with only pictures, no written words.

(There were words, but few editors choose to use them. When people talk of Peter Arnett as the only Western journalist in Baghdad, a few remember to add Alberto Rojo, of *El Mundo* in Madrid. That recalls Fawlty Towers, the BBC sitcom in which John Cleese runs a hotel, helped by a comical handyman whom he dismisses repeatedly: "Oh, that's Manuel. He's Spanish." In fact, Rojo wrote excellent copy, translated and distributed by the *Guardian.* He would have sent more had he been able to use Arnett's satphone.)

When editors decide to splash a story, everything at the edges is washed off the page. Willie Huber can tell you. In April 1991, he was running a school, children's hospital and orphanage in Mogadishu for the Austrian charity SOS Kinderdorf. When almost no one was helping Somalis, he found a Belgian military C-130 to fly five times a week from Nairobi to feed sick, starving kids. Then the Kurds streamed out of Iraq. Who could say if their need was greater, but they were the story. The Belgians diverted the plane to Turkey.

Bangladeshi cyclone victims in 1991 had better luck. Tom Kent, the AP's international editor, kept a reporter in Chittagong long after such stories are usually dropped. Perhaps not coincidentally, foreign relief supplies kept coming.

But these editors don't set policy alone. For anyone on the track of who stole the news, as far as papers are concerned, the trail warms above the level of foreign editor. Correspondents, almost unanimously, would like to write longer and see more of their work in print, better handled by the desk. It is not up to them. Copy editors are outriders who herd through only as much as the gates allow. Middle-level editors defend their own province. Managing editors and executive editors are the ones who count.

Any outsider interested in better world coverage should start with the chief gatekeepers on the top floor. Some of them need all the convincing anyone can muster. Others are already battling with their publishers and chain managers for more wherewithal to do better, and readers' letters give them more ammunition. There is a great deal of common wisdom to overcome.

James F. Hoge, Jr., who edited the *Chicago Sun-Times,* published the New York *Daily News* and now directs *Foreign Affairs,* describes what he calls a shocking long-term shift among newspapers. Most now see their prosperity hinging on subscribers rather than advertisers, and they are desperate to please. Over recent years, many papers have reduced national and international coverage in favor of more local and regional news. Editors who buck that trend need the backing of the boss.

Burl Osborne shapes coverage at the *Dallas Morning News* and is essentially his own boss. Osborne joined the paper as editor, leaving his job as AP managing editor, and picked up the additional title of publisher of the independent daily, owned by a Texas conglomerate. His peers elected him president of the American Society of Newspaper Editors. During six months in 1992, his paper's circulation shot up by 31 percent, by far the largest gain in the United States. This was in part because the *News* ran the *Dallas Times-*

*Herald* out of business. But that, too, suggests Osborne had sensed what readers want.

His attitude is that a good story is a good story, from wherever it comes. If people can see clearly why it is important to them, and not necessarily that same morning, they will be interested. "We've almost quit calling it foreign news," he said. "It's not foreign anymore. Mexico is local. Eastern Europe is almost local. With communications, the world has shrunk. The people who are our best readers have traveled, been to places, and television has made those places local. Tiananmen Square is a local place to people who have watched CNN."

Rather than overreaching with too many overseas bureaus, the *News* has looked for areas to focus on. Only a handful of its correspondents are based in Latin America and Europe, but others travel regularly. Seven went to the Gulf War, and four followed the collapse of the Soviet Union. This sort of coverage, Osborne and his editors believe, is critical to large regional papers.

The problem is deciding where to draw the lines. Far less than a measurable judgment based on reliable readership surveys, it is a question of conscience, a sense of responsibility and a belief in the readership. All of these have to fit into the financial balance, and profitability is impossible to measure.

"Take a number, say, $250,000," Osborne said. "It's very easy to get a handle on that number but not on what you get for it. And it's very easy for business people to say, 'I know where I can cut $250,000, and no one will even know.' But they will know. . . . We've been on this track for twelve years now, and our penetration is growing. We don't have any formulas, or perceptions. We only know what works for us. If we invest in good quality, a high productivity news effort, we will benefit on the other side." That is, make money.

The *News* is hardly alone among the bigger papers. Some small ones scattered around the country, like the *Star* in Anniston, Alabama, do noble service within their space and budget. Many others do not. Readers, in every city, must make their own assessment and protect themselves as best they can.

Overall, the trend is fearsome. Holger Jensen, watching a world he knows well from a mountaintop in Colorado, worries about the future. He has looked carefully at papers around the country. His judgment is harsh, but it is right on the money. I heard similiar remarks from disgusted professionals everywhere.

Except at the top six or seven papers, Jensen said, senior management people come mostly from a background in local news. "They sort of view foreign news and foreign editors as a necessary evil," Jensen said. "They need a bit of it for a modicum of respectability. But with the news hole tight all around, this leads to some really warped allocation. We have catchwords, like 'News You Can Use,' or 'Community Bulletins,' so you'll see a whole page on how to make a soufflé out of stale potato chips. And there'll be almost nothing for foreign news."

Papers have proven that when they spend the money on foreign news, they make it back, he said. People get to expect it, and they like it. If a paper is well edited, foreign coverage need not be at the expense of anything else. The challenge is not only finding more space but also making good use of what you have. The problem, Jensen said, is not a lack of interested readers but rather a misunderstanding by editors of what their readers want.

"Most newspaper managements are headed by people who are incredibly parochial but who profess to understand the reading public," Jensen said. "They simply can't grasp that other people can go beyond their own narrow interest. They're convinced that readers want less words, not more. We've lost the high-end reader who wants more and doesn't get it. These people see TV and they look for more in the paper. But they don't get it. They get the same soundbites, only written, without the impact of pictures. And now we're discouraging potential new readers by telling them they don't have to read."

The overwhelming presence of television has shaken up newspapers, forcing editors to look at how they do things. Many of them panicked and tried to design printed television. They shortened stories but used the extra space for splashy graphics and headlines. Instead of attracting readers into stories with a lively headline, they offer a simplistic alternative: little "at-a-glance" boxes—or "nerd boxes," to some editors—which sum up the contents. The success of *USA Today* won converts, but those who share Jensen's view call that a special case in a unique position for readers on the move.

"Instead of competing from their strong point, the ability to give depth and background, editors tried to outdo television," Jensen said. "That is doomed to fail because we can't match television's strong points. By reaching for the low common denominator, we only push it lower. Newspapers have a certain responsibility to inform as well as entertain. Nine out of ten people may prefer reading about Zsa Zsa Gabor slapping a cop than the Somali clan structure. But we have to give both. If we offer a steady diet, people will expect it and then like it."

For editors who believe in world news, television presents a deeper challenge. It has thrown time elements into turmoil. What people do not want, everyone agrees, is to read at breakfast headlines of news they saw live at dinner the night before.

When television news first started, producers assumed that people had already read about the main stories. Film could take days to come in from remote places. Television provided a visual backdrop to the news, taking viewers to places they had heard about but could not imagine. Now, with satellites and round-the-clock coverage, it is the other way around. When people read their paper, they are seldom surprised.

But not everyone is already forewarned. Broadcast news catches different people at different times. People listen with half an ear. Newspaper editors have to report the news cushioned in what the business calls a second-day angle. This is delicate work, especially with incidents and accidents that happen and then pass into history. Ask any wire animal about old standbys like, "Weary firemen poked through the smouldering remains of . . ."

Some serious newspapers have figured out how to play up their own strengths to fit in with the weaknesses of television. Their editors find that if television viewers are interested enough to look for more information in the newspapers, they want lengthy, thoughtful background. Reporters look for angles that television missed. During the Gulf War, when CNN blanketed the story, the *Los Angeles Times'* circulation tripled.

However editors deal with television, they cannot ignore it. "TV should be keeping us more honest," Osborne said, at the *Dallas Morning News*. "We might have gotten the sense right before, but we were not always exact. We didn't get the tone. Television raises as many questions as it answers, and we have to put in the context." Reporters must be more careful to reflect atmosphere, visual images and emotion in their stories, he said.

Television has also made the process part of the story. Speaking for journalism in general, Osborne added, "What killed us in the Gulf War was the juvenile behavior of some people. It absolutely ruined us." It certainly hurt us. People who should not have been sent on any assignment, let alone such a sensitive one, were seen as representatives of a profession to which they did not necessarily belong. One took it upon himself to apologize for his colleagues' rude behavior, as though he were the elected ethics commissioner of a bonded guild.

This points to a bigger problem. When the *New York Times* defied the Nixon administration to publish the Pentagon Papers in 1971, people understood what "the press" was supposed to do. Reporters had caught the government in a serious lie about Vietnam War policy; editors decided that such news ought to get through the gate. Readers, by and large, applauded. This was their watchdog barking. Later, during the heady days after Watergate, journalism school enrollments ranneth over. Every other kid wanted a piece of the glory. We had attention during the yellow journalism days, and we had occasional moments of glory over the years. For most of this century, reporters commanded a certain respect. But this was our Golden Age. It was brief.

With Deep Throats in short supply, many settled for shallower ones. Newspapers took some serious hits, including a Pulitzer awarded for a profile of a young drug addict who did not exist. The press grew into "the media," and everyone from Richard Reeves to Geraldo Rivera was dumped into the same bucket. Lobbyists weighed in from every side. Legitimate questions about the Reagan administration were attacked by guardians of the far right. Critics hammered away at the use of unnamed sources, the basic tool that had brought journalism to high esteem. Everywhere, editors felt their credibility at risk.

By the time Iran-*contra* surfaced, the Watergate backlash had done its damage. Few editors wanted to be seen to be picking on a President, particularly a lovable Republican whose friends included major political organizers, lobbyists and advertisers. Correspondents, the watchdogs, did little more than growl.

In this climate, editors went on the defensive, endangering their traditional posture of journalism without fear or favor. Then, with the Gulf War Follies, television offered up an antithesis to "All the President's Men," a sort of "All the Editor's Schmucks." In fact, nothing real had changed. The business was as it always had been, a cottage industry of individuals working with mixed success within a flawed system. But even more than ever, editors were apologetic, fearing more criticism.

Among some editors, the mood descends below excessive prudence. If an accurate and important story might draw fire—from government officials, from advertisers, from shareholders, from executives on a higher floor—is it really worth it? These days, answers can vary widely.

Yet another layer was added to this caution. Fear of political incorrectness terrified the managers. Newspapers stepped carefully to avoid any possibility of criticism from defenders of a gender, an ethnic background, spiritual beliefs, a sexual preference or physical characteristics. Some desk editors, zealots themselves, helped police the news columns.

The ramifications are great. One correspondent went to Dubrovnik in 1992, just as the siege ended. It was after Serbs and Croats had fought viciously in Croatia, after the ruthless Serb shelling of Vukovar. And the first signs of ethnic cleansing were beginning to appear in Bosnia. A million refugees were already on the roads.

In Dubrovnik, a young Croatian architect who would have to rebuild the city explained to the reporter how in Yugoslavia hatred was nothing personal. He went into history, going back to how, Croats believe, Serbia chickened out, and then sold out, to Turkey. He mentioned the lovable old lady they had just visited, a loyal Serb, as he put it, whom he had known for years. Then he spread his hands in a gesture of resignation. "But Serbs . . ." he said. "My father used to say that Serbs are the clods of dirt in the hooves of Turkish horses. They are animals."

It was a quote to kill for, rich Balkan imagery which touched on the roots of the conflict. The reporter put it toward the top of a sweeping dispatch which explained why feelings ran so deep in the remains of Yugoslavia and why things would surely get worse. His desk editor cut it out. When he protested, he was told, in the patient tones of the right-minded, that this could be construed as an ethnic slur on Serbs.

Well, yes. The reporter pointed out that it was in quotes, in the setting of a history of murderous ethnic hatreds, and balanced by others' remarks on Croats. The editor took the appeal to higher levels. When the story came out, the quote read only, "They are animals." That might apply in a lot of situations.

Thoughtful editors worry about how people will conceptualize news in the future. The nature of news is changing after the Cold

War, but the system is lagging behind. Readers are confused as their comfortable old benchmarks disappear. Whom do you hate, anymore? Fewer conflicts can be personified as good versus evil, and readers need more clues to replace old-style conditioned responses. Phil Bronstein, executive editor of the *San Francisco Examiner,* argues that newspapers have to seize the initiative, not hang back with their heads down.

"Newspaper identity has never been very forward-thinking," he said. "We are in a state of panic, and there is pressure to give the readers what we think they want. But we have some obligation to set the agenda. We have to include the DBI, the dull-but-important stories. We have to do stories that draw people in. If we abandon that, we abandon one of our charges."

Yet most newspapers still think in terms of headlines and world news briefs, while the developments that matter move at a slow pace, at subsurface levels. This is what Jim Hoagland of the *Washington Post* calls the creeping flash. The biggest new stories mostly move at an imperceptible pace: the environment, economic shifts, ethnic hostility, hunger. Each desk must decide what to do about them; most wait until they cannot be ignored.

This old pattern will be slow to change. Hardly any of the major crises of recent times surprised editors who had read what crossed their desks. But a lot of their readers were caught unwarned. "One of my greatest failures as a foreign correspondent was trying to get even the editors interested in Yugoslavia after Tito," said Dan Fisher at the *L.A. Times.* "I was a total failure at persuading this paper. No one else did much better."

There is only so much time and space. Birds suddenly dying in Tasmania ought to tell us something about the atmosphere, for instance, but they don't. It is as though we are watching the miner's canary keel over from poison gas but do not respond to the clear meaning. It is one thing for correspondents to see that as a story. It is another for people all along the line to let it through the gates.

This, again, is where the readers come in. What nearly all ranking editors agree on is that their feedback is sparse. A few people call in to complain. Fewer write. Even the *Los Angeles Times'* editors get only a handful of letters a week, crank mail excepted, on how foreign news is treated. And most suspect this is because people who might otherwise write fear it is a waste of time.

"Any serious letter certainly gets my attention, and it could be enough to trigger a policy change," Jim Yuenger, at the *Chicago Tribune,* observed. In fact, he was so impressed with one woman's letter that he called her up and stayed on the phone long enough to get some ideas he put into practice. Like Yuenger, most editors are old-time reporters, trained to trust the mysterious elements of feel over a bunch of expensive numbers from readership surveys. One voice does not make a majority, but it can lead to new line of questioning. A lot of voices can be stuffed together in a file folder to be brandished at the next budget meeting.

When I wrote *Coups and Earthquakes,* I interviewed editors around the country and determined that only six letters a week from concerned readers, addressed personally to an executive or managing editor, were enough to influence the mix in news columns. It was an arbitrary number. Shortly afterward, I was running my own paper, the *Tribune* in Paris, which reached 160 countries and drew a whole lot of mail. I realized I had made a mistake. A better number would have been four letters a week. If pushed, the gate can move with surprising ease.

# Chapter 9

# Television:
# Real Time

An old *New Yorker* cartoon tacked to my wall is not so funny anymore. In it, an anchorman is saying, "Owing to cutbacks in our news department, here is Rod Ingram to guess at what happened today in a number of places around the globe." These days, networks are reluctant to spare air time even for guessing.

No one can cover breaking news like good television people. Visual impact and immediacy are only part of it. It takes a certain mastery to race to a plane with half a ton of luggage, drop unbriefed into pandemonium and, after a few hours at most, bounce a polished piece of videotape off a satellite.

When an oil tanker ran aground off the Shetland Islands early in 1993, the networks excelled. Correspondents took viewers out over the wreckage, quizzed the ecologists, worked in the background. The dirty birds of the piece were real ones, from clips of past disasters nearby. It was a TV story, done well.

But significant world news seldom breaks. It sneaks out of dark alleys or percolates under the surface. The skilled television reporters still out there can keep track of this sort of news. Few, however, get the chance. The networks, no longer trying to match CNN, offer the barest minimum. And even CNN shunts aside what it must explain in favor of what it can show.

Hughes Rudd, an old-time newspaperman who was a pioneer at CBS before moving to ABC, used to call television news a comic-strip medium. "Any complicated or serious subject can't be explained on TV," he told Texas broadcasters in 1980, before new corporate owners began dismantling foreign bureaus to save money.

Yet two-thirds of Americans get their news primarily from their television sets. This means that the only superpower left, the nation which regards itself as No. 1, is desperately out of touch with the world it is supposed to be leading. Among the greatest threats to the United States, and the world beyond, is the squandered potential of American television.

The problem is not television as a medium. In fact, a study for a book called *Common Knowledge,* published by the University of Chicago, found that "television news succeeds better than newspapers in communicating substantive information." And "TV and magazine coverage resulted in significantly higher levels of learning than newspaper coverage." The sort of investigative work that Brian Ross did for NBC on drug trafficking and illegal money movement suggests that there may be something to this.

However effective it can be, television does not inform on what it does not show. For television, much of the world is a black hole. Undercurrents and creeping flashes are left until they turn into a story. What it does show is often too brief to make any sense. Television works best within a familiar context. On big stories at home, viewers are like fans watching football. They know when someone makes a first down or gets run off the field. In foreign settings, they have to fill in the blanks for themselves.

Television does not usually report the news it covers. Instead, it creates little sociodramas, known as packages, to represent the situation at hand. This can be effective if the creators are skilled, the pictures are riveting and the clock does not stop too soon. To depict the Sarajevo siege, Christiane Amanpour of CNN went to the zoo to show a tranquil eye in the storm. As it turned out, the idea worked out better than she intended. Heavy shelling started. With deft scriptwork to add context, terrorized tigers made the point.

Dick Blystone, one of the AP's best storytellers, shifted to CNN in its pioneer days. Bly caught on fast. He reports the old-fashioned way and then huddles with colleagues to make television. "It's simple," he explains. "You're in kindergarten. The teacher gives you a lump of clay, some pipe cleaners, a few gold stars, and puts you in the corner to make something for mommy." Television, he said, breaks open a window for people who want to find other ways to peer in closely. "Mostly it irritates the senses in order to get across the simplest of emotions. For sustained, serious information, don't even consider it."

But television's presence is overpowering. It has taken on such prominence that it casts a shadows over the news it reports, if it is not the news itself. I happened to be in Lubbock, Texas, when students arose in Tiananmen Square. The fact that Dan Rather was there, while Peter Jennings and Tom Brokaw were not, was talked about as much as the revolution in China.

Tiananmen Square was a story made for television. Students picked their moment, a well-covered visit by Mikhail Gorbachev. They unfurled a banner reading "Give me liberty, or give me death." In English. When China's aging leaders chose to give them the latter, cameras were there. Live coverage ended dramatically. Chinese officials barged in on Rather and on CNN. With the world watching, they pulled the plug. And then blood was washed off the vast square, which for days on end was the world's central stage, and China slipped back into the shadows.

Followed only by newspaper readers, the revolution oozed into whatever openings it found. The Soviet collapse quickened the pace. The Chinese freed their economy, if not their people, eager to trade in world markets. They smoothed ties with Japan, probed in Europe and looked elsewhere for friends. These currents affected a billion people, a once and future world power.

During the U.S. presidential candidates' first televised debate, the token foreign question was on China. Bill Clinton had some vague thoughts. George Bush, claiming to know the territory, warned improbably about isolating China. Then they returned to something more comfortable to their television-attuned audience: America's superiority in the world.


If correspondents had any lingering doubts, the Gulf War hammered home television's new place in the scheme of things. Dave Henderson of the *Milwaukee Journal,* waiting in Dhahran for a pool spot, grumbled, "I need a picture of myself, sitting in my hotel room drinking Perrier and watching CNN. War correspondent." Then he had a speck of action. The air raid sirens sounded, and he scrambled into his hotel basement shelter with two hundred others. Huddled in gas masks, scared as hell, they had no idea what was happening. The shelter had no television set, so Henderson found a phone. He reached his editor in Milwaukee, who, of course, was tuned to CNN. From the edge of Lake Michigan, the editor gave a running account of what was going on in the Gulf, directly above his reporter's head. Eventually, he relayed the all-clear signal.

This was "real-time" television in action, a reality session of news as it unfolded. During months of crisis, the ability to do this brought the medium to its highest glory and to new depths. The appeal is obvious; it is exciting to watch from up front. But the camera only shows what it's pointed at, and it explains nothing. Viewers still must take reporters at their word, although, in real time, they don't realize it.

At 3:45 one morning, a friend rang my Dhahran hotel room from San Francisco, frantic. "Are you all right?" she wanted to know. I asked why I wasn't supposed to be. "CNN," she said. Of course. Like any modern war correspondent, I slept with a remote TV switch in my hand. When I squeezed it, a familiar face filled the screen.

Clothed in bulky British chemical gear, the reporter warned of an imminent gas attack. This was a surprise since we had already been through the gas antics. Poison gas is nasty and, at first, we took it seriously. The same guy had fumbled to get into his mask on camera. NBC's Arthur Kent got famous by standing on the roof and shrugging off his anchor's pleas to take shelter; during the first raid, he had had the sense to join us in the basement.

We reasoned that Saddam Hussein had not figured out how to strap gas canisters to Scud missiles or, if he had, he would not waste them on us. But here was this reporter in full chem gear saying that he had been advised of an impending attack and that he and CNN were there for us. For a brief flash, I wondered if I was about to watch my own last gasps on real-time TV. "Hold on," I told my friend. I walked to the window and pulled back the drapes. There was CNN's flyaway, twenty feet away. The guy was in his gas suit. His crew were wearing T-shirts. (One read, "JTFC," for Just the Fucking Crew.)

From the first, the battle for ratings nearly overshadowed the war at hand. Each network tried a different angle. As the crisis dragged on, Bush gave Saddam until January 15 to leave Kuwait.

Fifteen days before, Rather airlifted his operation to the region for a daily "Countdown to Confrontation" which helped work up a fever pitch.

After it was over, I found an NBC friend who has logged decades of triumphs, a newsman who takes time to understand a story's implications and takes trouble to get them across. He had done his usual good work, but I asked how he thought NBC had done overall. "Well," he said, "we fucked up the beginning, we fucked up the middle, and we fucked up the end. Other than that, we did fine."

NBC suffered from trying to play by the rules, hanging back from "unilateral" coverage to avoid upsetting pool coordinators. One correspondent brought fury on his head by fingering reporters who had sought to slip the traces. The network could not set up communications from Baghdad and, at one point, had to show CNN tape, complete with Bernard Shaw. But old pros at CBS and ABC were hardly more generous about their own team's performance. Military restrictions and logistical nightmares did not help. Mostly, however, they blamed a system driven by ratings.

After allied troops crossed the Saddam line, ABC's Forrest Sawyer found a way around the pool, and he broadcast live from inside Kuwait. It was colorful stuff. But Sawyer, toward the rear and on the wrong flank, was hardly delivering a play-by-play of the siege of Kuwait. I asked an ABC producer why the network made so much of it. "This is a big deal to us," she said. "We're bleeding green. Something like this knocks us up a few points, and it means fifty people won't get laid off next year."

In the end, CBS scored the big one. Bob McKeown and his crew got to Kuwait first in a daring dash that, at one point, overtook the invasion force. Rather was down the road in Dhahran, but he got there fast, neck and neck with Tom Brokaw and Sam Donaldson, to take charge of his winning team. A month later, CBS closed down two overseas bureaus.

Depending on how you look at it, television correspondents were fast-thinking experts at rapid analysis or flimflam men, and women, with silvery forked tongues. At lunch one day, in Dhahran, someone yelled that Saddam had just announced a withdrawal from Kuwait. I raced to the office, fifty paces away, and scanned the AP wire. All anyone knew was from a vague radio speech delivered minutes earlier. Before making calls, I checked the television monitor behind me. My lunch partner was giving a well-reasoned, detailed account of Saddam's deeper meaning.

One star of the TV war soared and burned, an allegory of intensity in a rarified atmosphere. The friend who called me about the gas had a later request. Could I get Arthur Kent's autograph? I could, I said, but I wouldn't. Art, in the first stages of shock over sacks of mail piling up in his Rome office, did not want groupies. I had met Kent fifteen months earlier in Bucharest on the night Nicolae Ceausescu fell. We came in together from the airport. Working swiftly, I talked to some people and then headed for the besieged television studio to find a phone. Within minutes, I got inside. There was a phone, but Kent was on it. He had already fed dramatic narrated footage to New York. The guy was good, and he had balls.

Kent's Dhahran performance seemed OK, considering none of us had much to say. The leather jacket was no prop; it was what he wore. Suddenly, he was Scud Stud, with a *People* magazine reporter dogging his steps. When the war ended, viewers clamored for more Art. NBC people had a golden goose, and they managed to kill it. After a brief stint as a "Today" show host, Kent returned to Rome, with all sorts of promises from the top. He wanted to be chief European correspondent in London. Others felt seniority should count over sudden stardom. The desk wanted Kent to go where he was sent. An aggressive agent was involved.

As timing would have it, the venue for the showdown was the former Yugoslavia. Kent said he would not go on another story until his assignment was clarified. The network suspended him for not going where ordered, which was Yugoslavia. This, Kent said, implied that he was a coward and shirker. Things got silly, then nasty. Kent handed out leaflets outside of NBC in New York. The network censored his appearance that night on the Jay Leno show. Fired, Kent flew to London and got a BBC assignment to Sarajevo. His upfront reports aired on ABC and CBS. Thus having shown he was no chicken, he sued NBC for twenty-five million dollars for defamation. The story promised to be a long-running series.

Rather, no stranger to the big eye, had a simple fix on the whole episode: "The magnifying glass gets to be so big that if it turns the slightest bit, it will fry you to a crisp." Like the Scud Stud saga, the whole Gulf War episode was a magnified version of television reporting in general, showing its strongest and weakest elements. What made it so different from every other big story since the Crimean War was live coverage, war in real time.

"The trouble with live coverage is that it usually doesn't work," Blystone explains. "We do some things because we have the ability to do them, but that does not mean better coverage. Human events don't lend themselves to television schedules. It's great if you have a Berlin Wall falling, but that doesn't happen very often. Most of the time, you've got a parked car."

It is also unfiltered, misleading and often wrong. Atlanta wonders if Bly might one day make good on a standing threat. When someone cuts to him and asks, "What does it look like on the street, Richard?" he says he'll reply: "I have no idea what's happening because I've been standing on this hotel balcony for two hours waiting for you to ask me that question."

For many stories, broadcasting live is needless theatrics which wastes money needed elsewhere. In 1991, CNN sent Blystone and Amanpour to join Gary Strieker for a long, hard look at African hunger. They visited famine camps, talked to relief workers and explained the deeper causes of it all. But it was live. Truckloads of gear followed them in the desert, slowing them down and blowing holes in the news budget. Producers argued they could do a better job if the correspondents reported and the editors edited, allowing the team to craft a series of polished pieces which could be fed quickly by satellite. But then the marketing people could not boast that it was live.

Despite their advantages, live broadcasts limit coverage. Since everyone tries to do it on big stories, no one can risk not trying to do it. This ties up crews and expensive equipment and eats up the travel budget. By tacit consensus, networks decide what stories are big, and everyone piles on. If no one covers secondary stories, no one gets beat. Only the public suffers.

This carries over to print correspondents. Editors leave CNN glowing by their elbow, and they respond to news breaks like lab rats to an electrode. Few are prepared to waste many reporters on stories which common consent does not sanctify as news. In December 1990, two Arab tyrants vilified by Washington seemed ready to invade their southern neighbors, both of them thinly populated expanses of sand, clients of the United States. We heard a lot about the one who failed, Saddam Hussein. But Moammar Khadafy's proxy army of rebels swept across Chad and sent President Hissène Habré into exile. Anyone remember that one?

At the over-the-air networks, old pros kick wastebaskets in frustration. Their audiences still dwarf CNN's. CNN reporters, with notable exceptions, were watching "Sesame Street" when they set the standards for good coverage from abroad. They know that reporting means going to where news is hiding and kicking down doors until they find it. And, with reduced air time, hammered travel budgets and staff cuts, that is seldom possible.

ABC had only fourteen correspondents abroad in 1993, with no one in Latin America, and the others had fewer. "That's not many folks to get around on a big map," said Dennis Murphy, NBC's "Today" show foreign editor, based in London.

"In this league, you've got to bat .895," Murphy said. "There is no going out unless you've got a sure thing." Even then, that is not always enough. When a cyclone and tidal wave obliterated parts of the Bangladesh coast in 1991, killing what would surely be tens of thousands of people, Murphy loaded up for the airport. But somebody worked out the costs. Airfares and overweight alone would run over thirty-six thousand dollars. Independent contractors would be there, someone decided. It would be cheaper to buy it.

Television executives who might have thought no one would notice read about it in *Rolling Stone*. A new sort of profit-minded manager wishes that the news would go away, Jon Katz wrote. "Now every big news story is bad news. ABC was the only network to send a news crew to Bangladesh immediately after the cyclone. CBS eventually sent one after 'much hand wringing' about costs, said one producer. NBC simply bought coverage from BBC and Visnews. So went one of broadcast journalism's most sacrosanct commandments: 'Take your own pictures.'" Katz forgot to mention a commandment that is higher up the stone: Do your own reporting.

From the beginning, one fiercely held tenet of network television was that you shot your own film and asked your own questions. Anything else was unprofessional, if not dishonest. Television correspondents covered stories the way their newspaper colleagues did. They asked questions and wrote a script based on what they knew. Camera crews concentrated only on pictures. If there were any challenges, their editors' consciences were clear.

Much of that has changed. Each network has agreements with videotape suppliers, as well as ties with television people around the world. ABC owns 80 percent of Worldwide Television News, based in London, first set up by UPI and Independent Television News. NBC works with Visnews, owned mainly by Reuters and BBC. For years, NBC regularly used BBC footage, expanding its reach with dozens of British professionals whose breadth of coverage often dwarfed the Americans'. In 1993, however, BBC shifted its exchange agreement to ABC. Working together, the two networks consult daily on coverage plans to share the load.

CBS uses some videotape from both WTN and Visnews as part of a complex system of exchanges under which all networks can tap foreign broadcasters and freelance operators. It can be confusing for the viewer. In one report from Bosnia, marked "CBS News Exclusive," the correspondent kept using terms like "a nasty scrum," meaning skirmish, which sounded suspiciously as if he was addressing a British audience.

Contract suppliers often use crews whom editors have learned to trust over the years. But WTN calls on people based in eighty-six cities around the world, and Visnews' stringer network is even bigger. Desks are not always sure of what they will get. During one coup attempt in Haiti, a WTN editor sent an urgent request for coverage. A message came back saying the cameraman would be available in three days when he finished his voodoo ceremony.

Much of the commercial videotape is shot by people who are not reporters and don't have time to do much reporting. Mostly, they scribble notes for a "dope sheet" which they send with their film for editors elsewhere to turn into a narrative script. Facts may be wrong. Interpretations may be missed. Situations may be hyped, inadvertently or not. What often emerges is generic bang-bang, action pictures of something or other. The main purpose of journalism, learning root causes and understanding the impact, is lost to the procedure of collecting pictures.

It gets worse when news breaks in backwaters. "In the old days, when there was a foreign assignment editor in New York, if something happened in some remote place, we'd go get it," Art Lord of NBC explained. "Now, each one of these countries has a TV satellite, and they can make money putting it on Eurovision (a cooperative of European television stations). Instead of sending a crew to Jubangiland, you call Jubangiland TV, and they put it on the bird.

It's almost always government television, and everyone has some fix. It's not competitive."

The pressure is enormous for camera operators to produce dramatic video footage. Late in 1992, when Germans marched in Rostock to protest attacks against Romanian asylum seekers, police charged two television crews—one American and one French—with inciting Nazi sentiment. According to a spokesman, they paid some kids about $150 to give the Heil Hitler salute. Most crews recoil in horror at the thought of such practices. But unless editors know who is out there, they cannot be sure.

In the Gulf, I reminded a television pal of a favorite story from Vietnam. A network reporter had his Vietnamese cameraman shoot three different takes of him diving into a trench at the sound of gunfire. The cameraman, no fan of the correspondent's, sent all three to New York. The desk snidely thanked the reporter for his spontaneous leap, "all three of them." My friend laughed and said: "The worst part of that story is they used one of them."

The suppliers try to get it right. WTN found Bob Sullivan shoveling manure on his farm in Ireland, in early retirement from noteworthy work as a UPI man. He was made New York bureau chief to instill old-style news standards. But some days, one suspects, he feels he is back at the shovel. The problem, he says, is how the business works.

"TV stations want pictures," he said. "If they can choose between a serious discussion of some crisis or people being saved from a burning building in East Cupcake, what are they going to use?" Now, he worries, television has the potential to make its own pictures. A virtuoso at digital editing can put Goofy in a general's uniform and stick a smoking gun in his hand. "The possibility of faking is infinite," he said. "Some people have always lied, but before there were known limits."

The up side is that pictures roll in with amazing speed, under the hairiest of conditions. WTN's desk logs reflect a world on fast forward. "Just a quick handover," one begins, from an editor forced to neglect personal business. "My home's been burgled, and I have to get french windows mended, kill someone, or whatever." Like others, it notes crew arrests, beatings, visas delayed, commercial sabotage and double dealing. It lists the whereabouts of Yugoslav stringers, adding: "Ethnicity all okay." Croats had not been sent to Kosovo. A final item reads: "India. International Goat Conference. Sadly we forced to turn down."

When other people's footage comes into network hub bureaus, a correspondent is assigned to put together a package. "You use the technology, get all the elements from everywhere and you put together a literate script," Lord said. "You make a universal truth out of it. That's bullshit. It's not reporting. And the funny thing is they love it." He meant the money people.

The source may be a trusted colleague like BBC, but it is still someone else on the line. NBC routinely used BBC's Martin Bell in Sarajevo, once signing him off as "Martin Bell, NBC News." ABC had trouble rounding up volunteers for Bosnia. Instead, it found an untried but courageous young stringer to hire, and it was the only network to staff the siege of Sarajevo.

CBS covered Sarajevo sporadically, relying mainly on unidentified film narrated in London. Time after time, from the Middle East and Africa, familiar voices offered complicated analysis of pictures on the screen. Sometimes, the camera showed an Alan Pizzey or a Bob Simon in a stand-up, and the viewer knew that the network was there. More often, the piece ended with the dead giveaway, "Somebody Somebody, London."

It is the same at NBC. "The public is not well-served," one old hand put it. "We had an absolutely fantastic foreign operation and should be building it still. The feeling is that people don't care all that much." Steve Friedman, former executive producer of NBC "Nightly News," put it simply: "We're not in the overall killer coverage business anymore."

ABC tries hard to use its own people, but it also cuts corners to stretch a tight budget.

The other problem, equally serious, is the lack of air time. In Walter Cronkite's day, a half-hour evening newscast meant twenty-eight minutes of talking time. Now this is down to twenty-one and a half minutes. Commercials get the rest. Within that reduced time, large segments go to magazine-type features on America. The basic philosophy has drastically changed.

In his memoirs, *Out of Thin Air,* the former president of NBC News, Reuven Frank, writes: "When we started network news, we assumed those who watched already knew the news. So . . . we showed it to them. We transmuted into experience what had been information. . . . Never had Americans known so much about the world as in those years." Now TV takes the lead, and its agenda is thin, in experience and information.

Katz, in his *Rolling Stone* piece, explained why: "It wasn't just that the new owners of broadcasting cared about money. So did [network pioneers] Paley, Sarnoff and Goldenson. It was that they no longer could or would care about anything else. News had ceased to function as an ethical rationale for broadcasting. The government was no longer willing to regulate it; advertisers were less and less interested in supporting it; and an increasingly profit-minded corporate culture wouldn't tolerate its high cost and low return. Most devastating of all, viewers by the millions decided they had better things to watch."

At each of the networks, committed professionals struggle uphill. Cheryl Gould, who has seen most of the world and speaks several of its languages, is senior producer at "Nightly News." She knows NBC should do better. "You just grit your teeth and think about what you have to do," she said, "because if you don't you fall behind. And that's suicide."

Common wisdom holds that once television cameras got to the Ethiopian famine of 1984, the calamitous news was hurried to American homes. Had it not been for Gould, in fact, the story would have been crowded off the air. Michael Buerk of BBC did the report and, like most BBC footage, it was offered to NBC. Gould, shaken by what Buerk called a famine of biblical proportions, wanted to schedule the story. Her executive producer resisted. People are always starving in Africa, he said. They fought all afternoon. Finally, the executive producer grumbled that Gould could have her damned famine, and it was aired halfway through the newscast. The switchboards were lit for hours afterward.

For a non-scientific sampling, I watched an evening newscast as many viewers do, regularly over time but with inevitable gaps. I chose CBS for several reasons. One was history. CBS was Edward R. Murrow's network, a pioneer of serious broadcast news. It had the edge in Vietnam. For much of a generation, Americans watched Cronkite for reassurance before tucking in their children. Another was its audience. The French and Italians, among many others, watch the CBS Evening News with their breakfast, on local stations, six hours after it has aired in New York. It shows what Americans care about. The last reason was practical: I was in Paris; it was all I could get.

Some days, not a single foreign country was mentioned. One evening, five minutes were spent on a storm in Hawaii that had forced eight thousand people to evacuate their homes. At the time, nearly a million Pakistanis had to flee the country's worst flooding in a century. At least fifteen hundred had already drowned or died in the storm. Dikes gave way, damaging huge areas of cropland. Canals washed out. Two merged rivers threatened the most populous part of Pakistan, and the army mobilized to war footing. This I learned from BBC. CBS did not mention it. There was no foreign news, in fact, although the Sarajevo siege had taken a serious turn, and the Peruvian police had captured the guerrilla chief who terrorized the country for a decade. I learned, instead, that a Maryland man had been shot trying to steal an FBI agent's car.

The next day offered seven minutes on the Hawaii storm, which left three people dead and ten thousand uprooted, and some time on Hurricane Andrew, which battered Florida weeks earlier. In Pakistan, two thousand had died, and the entire nation was in an uproar. Food production and an entire development infrastructure were at risk, shaking the universe of millions. Not a word.

That same day, the first U.N. troops arrived in Somalia, a month late, and it was clear they could do little to help two million starving children. That was ignored. The show found time for a piece on American kids threatened by lead paint chips falling from the Williamsburg Bridge; that was worth covering, too, but at what price? The United Nations approved five thousand more troops to protect food conveys to Sarajevo. Nothing. "Eye on America" focused on hotel room intruders. A historic shakedown of European currencies put in doubt the new single market which might create a trade bloc of 320 million Europeans. That got a brief mention, from an American point of view: The dollar strengthened because the Deutsche mark was dropping after pressure from "Washington and other quarters."

My routine was the same. I'd watch CBS to the end, then I'd listen to "News Desk" on BBC radio. It was as if the two were reporting from different planets. If Americans had watched only the CBS "Evening News," and watched carefully, they might have seen themselves in a high-stakes global game but would not know whom they were playing, what the rules were or when either side scored. In a game like that, you don't even know when you lose.

Some days were better than others. At the worst, nothing foreign was mentioned, not even French fries. World news was always angled to Americans looking out at their own reflections abroad. This first struck me during the Panama invasion, in 1989. There was long, emotional coverage of U.S. casualties coming home. Panamanian casualties, far more numerous and important to the story, were barely mentioned. During 1992, among the few stand-ups from Sarajevo was a report on the U.S. airlift from Frankfurt. It was nicely done, a study of brave young Americans doing good. Then, after fifteen minutes, the crew left with the same plane. There was nothing about why the food was so desperately needed—and no mention of others who had brought much more than the Americans.

When Serbian leaders made a show of strength in answer to Bush's threat of military action, the newscast flashed a few frames of missiles, with a sentence of narration. There was a long report about a leather product, recalled with apologies, which had made some people sick. Like lead paint, this is important. The question is magnitude and priority. Looking at one woman complaining of a headache, in the face of a dying Old World city about to confront a winter with no fuel, power, water or peace, you had to wonder where we were headed.

I went to talk over my impressions with Dan Rather. It was to be a brief chat on a busy day. Ninety minutes later, it ended only when aides reminded him that he was due on the air. Rather, in his polished manner, wanted to get his disapproval on record.

"You never met anybody who believes in foreign coverage more than I do," he said. "We fight this every day, every week, every month . . ." When I mentioned that I could tell immediately from the tone of voice whether a correspondent was on the spot or in a studio narrating someone else's film, Rather winced. "All of us can," he said. "You lose plenty with this, but the more important question is, What does the viewer lose? The answer is double plenty."

Because of money pressure, he said, networks must decide how to get the biggest impact out of each dollar. Packaging news is cheaper than collecting it. Independent contractors cost less, with fewer people. "Increasingly," Rather said, "there is a belief that one is better advised to be in the news packaging business. I believe this is dangerous and erroneous. If you don't have your own person there, how do you know it is true?"

In South Africa, he said, he once got a report that police officers hidden in the back of a truck had driven into a black area and suddenly emerged to open fire. "It was critical enough for me to call South Africa and ask a CBS correspondent, 'Is this true?' He said,

'Yes, and we have the pictures.' When the predictable claim comes that it didn't happen—how do you know it happened?—I can say I talked on the telephone to a very experienced CBS person, and when he tells me it happened, it happened." But the cost per story is phenomenal from South Africa, up to three times the cost of a correspondent in a large bureau, he said. CBS now has no one anywhere in Africa.

Focus was the other problem. "The pressure is on to produce ratings," Rather told me. "We are constantly deluged with research [he added quote marks with his fingers] that says if you want to be compete well in the ratings race, you have to do domestic news. Foreign news is a long way from Broadway. Competition is so much fiercer, so much more unrelenting than it has ever been, that one has to think not only how to thrive, but to survive."

This is short-term thinking, Rather added. "The race will go to the experienced pro in the field," he said. "I'm hopeful that viewers and listeners will begin to reward the best experienced coverage. . . . The appetite is there, the market is there. The public knows the difference between quality and mediocrity. More than a public service, this is good business. Quality worldwide news gathering is good business."

Better television news is essential to America, he said. "In a constitutional republic based on democracy and committed to the idea that individual citizens make up their minds on domestic and foreign issues and then relay their feelings to their elected representatives, there is nothing more vital than to give the maximum amount of information," Rather concluded. "We all learned that in seventh grade civics."

Someone had cut class. I watched Rather on screen, minutes later. The only foreign item was twenty-five seconds on a Somali refugee ship reaching Yemen, chosen because of the powerful images. (It was French footage, and CBS had North American rights.) The viewer learned little about why people had fled in such precarious circumstances.

In our conversation, Rather had skipped over the underlying contradiction. He is anchorman but also managing editor, the eight-hundred-pound gorilla who earns a lot of bananas. When he said "they," you had to hear "we." If he can't reverse the tide, who can?

As 1993 began, the CBS "Evening News" was still a daily magazine of American topics which occasionally probed the wider world. One evening, after the turning globe that evoked the world in brief, five datelines followed. Four were in the United States; the fifth was about Americans in a Mexican bus crash. On another newscast, a one-sentence brief said that U.N. Secretary General Boutros Boutros-Ghali had been booed in Sarajevo on a trip that he called the last chance for peace before intervention. The next item, of the same length, said that two mobile homes were threatened by a sink-hole in Hernando, Florida.

As Serbian and Bosnian leaders gathered for a last-ditch try at peace, war threatened. A thousand shells landed on Sarajevo. France said it might go in alone. Radovan Karadzic refused to budge. Then Slobodan Milosevic, the Serbian leader in Belgrade, pressured him; already, Paris billboards were likening Milosevic to Hitler. Karadzic accepted but said he needed his parliament's approval. He would return in a week. If the answer was no, it could mean war. Fourteen minutes into that day's newscast, the briefs globe appeared. The Bosnian developments were all condensed to a single cryptic sentence. The next item was that National Guard snowplows were out in Utah after the second storm in five days.

A week later, when the Bosnian Serbs' parliament accepted the peace plan, but with conditions, the story was introduced: "President Clinton got a break in Bosnia when . . ." It was like the old *National Lampoon* parody of an American newspaper headline: Cleveland Couple Missing as Japan Sinks under the Sea.

My sampling ended on March 1, 1993. The United States had finally made a move in Bosnia, dropping some token food relief from two miles up. On BBC, I learned that it had missed the target. Rather gave the airdrop less than a minute, halfway into the newscast. Mostly, he covered the aftermath of a bomb at New York's World Trade Center. Americans suddenly felt vulnerable to terrorists but were still not looking to see which ones, or why. An image stuck in my mind: I saw an ostrich, head buried, waiting for someone to walk up in plain sight and kick its butt.

During the spring of 1992, Rather came back after the last commercial break with an item about "the remote and forgotten country of Somalia." Someone's footage showed desperate scenes. The narrator gave eighty seconds' explanation of clan warfare and famine. "Officials say as many as half of Somalia's eight million people may die of starvation in the next three months," the voice said, later ending, "Barry Peterson, London."

Talk about throwaway lines. If four million people were about to die, even in remote and forgotten Somalia, that sounded as if it was worth a crew's time to have a look. But CBS could not be blamed for not rushing down; hardly anyone else did, either.

Late in the summer, when people began to take note of the famine, CBS showed up for a week with a mountain of gear. The crew arrived with a hit list of story ideas: a hospital with American doctors, a refugee camp with a heroic white nurse, a market where stolen supplies were sold, a place where American aircraft would drop food. Each required a predawn hustle to load, haul, set up, write, transmit, drink and unwind with Wayne's World imitations. Spare time was short for going around asking questions and getting below the surface for details, which might only confuse the script.

"This is a news investment," explained Dr. Bob Arnot, the large, blond CBS medical correspondent. The idea was to hit the story hard, on the "Morning News" and the "Evening News," for a week. With only so much time and money, editors had made a classic triage decision on which group of desperate people would live and which would die. Somalia needed coverage, as Arnot explained it, and this was the likeliest calamity to drive up ratings. Then the eye would move on, leaving Somalia to starve unwatched.

But at least CBS was there, and Americans who watched that week got a close look at Somalia's desperation. Rather looked at it as a story that had to be done. "The way it goes now," he said, "you have to take judicious risks. The toughest calls are over what can we afford not to cover ... and when to shove in the stack. We're still in the news-gathering business. From time to time, we take a shot. We're going to do this particular story. Spend the resources to at least draw your attention. Perhaps it's not the staying power you'd like, but it's so important you'd better know about it."

At CBS, he said, there is still some commitment. "They don't say we have carte blanche, but if we want to do something extra, they say make your case, and we'll decide." It is not perfect, Rather said, but it beats what he called the "Potemkin village, ragtag pickup army" of a competitor he did not name. That would be NBC. Rumors circulate that NBC's owners want to dump network news. But NBC News does not act as if it were going out of business; it often does better than CBS. From an anchor who depends heavily on reporters forced to pretend they are covering the news, Rather's assessment seems a bit harsh.

At ABC, where there is clearly more commitment, similar factors apply. "We have not been frightened off from doing foreign news," Peter Jennings told me, "but it is a little hard when people are so preoccupied with personal affairs."

Evening newscasts are only part of it. ABC's "Nightline" routinely hones in fast when major news breaks abroad. At CBS, "60 Minutes" digs deep when something catches its producers' attention. ABC and NBC each has its own magazine-type program, and all do special reports when the world boils over. What suffers is the daily running account of events and trends.

This is no passing problem. In 1958, after William Paley canceled the pioneer magazine show, "See It Now," Murrow told assembled news directors in Chicago that a basic trouble with radio and television was that they had grown up as "an incompatible combination of entertainment, advertising and news." Top network managers had been trained in advertising, research or show business. "They also make the final and crucial decisions having to do with news and public affairs," Murrow said. "Frequently they have neither the time nor the competence for this." Soon after, he joined the U.S. Information Agency.

Arthur Kent, not necessarily another Murrow, made remarks in a similar vein after trying to do hard news on NBC's "Dateline." Nearly two generations later, the problem had worsened and the language had evolved. Kent's preferred term was "network skunks."

The conclusion is simple enough. Networks offer some powerful reporting. They weigh in on the biggest stories. Each has its strengths, but in any given situation, the crew on the ground is the definitive element. Altogether, the networks offer a fair sample of world news. But sampling is not coverage.

Robin MacNeil and Jim Lehrer cover as much as they sample, focusing closely on subjects which would send a lot of Rather's audience scrambling for the remote channel changer. Their "MacNeil-Lehrer Newshour" on the Public Broadcasting System is a solid alternative for people prepared to sit and listen. They buy videotape to make up for their lack of correspondents, taking care to identify their sources. Guests on the program pick apart crucial subjects. But, for many, the "Newshour" is too far at the other extreme from live television.

More and more, among outsiders, "television news" is fast being abbreviated to three letters: CNN. The upstart cable network has confounded all the experts who tried to laugh it off in the early 1980s. Its executives pumped money into the product, and whatever the national mood, they are opening bureaus in backwater capitals around the world. Editors cruise likely trouble spots to sprinkle goodwill for when the volcano lets loose. To a large extent, however, CNN is trapped within the expectations that it has whipped up about itself.

CNN's advantage should be the ability to dig into any story, anywhere, and surround it with resources. Its crews have a potential luxury which network people can only dream about. Without fear of competition, they can ask questions and shoot pictures until they have a piece which means something. All day long, there is space for it, and each repetition helps to amortize the expense. Instead, CNN feels that inexorable pull toward showbiz. Forced to choose, it leans toward showing what is happening rather than waiting a bit to say why.

From the television set side, it seems dramatic and close to the moment when an anchor cuts to a correspondent holding a microphone in the thick of things. At the other end, however, the reporter has been hanging around for the signal, wisecracking or scowling, while all of his newspapers pals go out to play reporter. He gets to the audience much more quickly than anyone else, but he doesn't always know what to say.

Ingrid Formanek, a Czechoslovak-born producer with a voice that endangers sound equipment, has brought glory to CNN from a lot a places. In Baghdad, she walked around with $250,000 in her kangaroo pouch, ready to put chunks of it to good use. She knows the value of live shots, but she knows their limitations. "I tell them to let us go out and report and feed every twelve hours unless there's some reason to go live," she said. Also, she wants CNN to dig deeper. "We should be doing more analytical pieces, but they're afraid people will go 'ho-hum.' We should ram it down their throats. It's important."

Live broadcasting presents some serious problems. A reporter's job is to toss facts, opinions and impressions into a miner's pan and shake it until only the big pieces are left. The process is common to the Brooklyn dogfight or a Chinese revolution. Reporters add context, check people's claims against reality and find the missing balance. Newspaper reporters have hours to do this. Television people, working at a turbocharged pace, can do it in minutes. No one can do it in seconds, which is what real-time reporting demands. It is not enough for people to see something as it happens, especially if they are not familiar with the context or setting.

A live microphone and an expectant audience amount to a powerful temptation. But it is unprofessional, often dangerous, for correspondents to reel off first impressions and unconfirmed reports—rumors—on the assumption that they can always be corrected later.

When Bush barfed mysteriously on the Japanese prime minister's shoes, CNN very nearly pronounced him dead. A stranger identifying himself as Bush's doctor called in to say the president had died. "This just in to CNN Headline News," the anchorman began, "and we say right off the bat, we have not confirmed this through any other sources . . ." A voice off camera said, "No. Stop."

It seems that an editor had realized "through the editorial process" that the tip might be a hoax. The anchorman finished: "We are now getting a correction. We will not give you that story. It was regarding some rather tragic news involving President Bush. But updating that story, President Bush is reported resting comfortably." Updating? Story? People around the world were left wondering what "tragic news" CNN had decided not to pass along.

Another problem recurs. When news breaks in some distant place, all reporters work the phones. We try to interview journalists or officials or diplomats. Whatever we get is tossed into that miner's pan. But every source has to be evaluated: Who is this guy? Why is he there? Does he know what he is talking about? Has he something to sell? Too often, I've watched anchors question these mysterious telephone voices as though they were trusted staff correspondents, and no one adds a note of caution. Some viewers add their own grains of salt. Most of them don't.

CNN editors know what they're up against. Paul Varian, a UPI editor who moved to television and took his skepticism along with him, warned, "Just because it's on video does not mean that it is true." Occasionally in television, the shot is phony, as when NBC rigged a pickup truck to feign an exploding gas tank. More often, a picture might be simply misleading. Tom Johnson, the president of CNN, insisted, "It is still vastly more important to get it right than to get it first."

Other international broadcasters keep CNN constantly tinkering with the mix. BBC World Service television, in a new spirit of competition, runs its own house ads with background music from a

James Bond film, "Nobody does it better . . ." A lot of people agree. In India, Sushmita Vijayan of New Delhi TV was categorical: "CNN gets into places faster, but BBC gives us a better report." I watched both, desperate for news of neighoring Afghanistan as rival rebels hurried into Kabul. BBC led with the story all day, with fresh footage and reporting. CNN repeated a two-day-old feature on nutrition and then did an Afghanistan brief with some WTN tape.

Pretenders in Europe and the Middle East sign up subscribers who resent CNN's American focus. One important newscast was interrupted around the world for a live broadcast of Bush switching on the White House Christmas lights. But not many competitors can match CNN's reach and resources.

No one surrounds a story like CNN when someone orders out all the stops. As Operation Restore Hope was gearing up, I bought a seat from Nairobi to Mogadishu on a CNN charter. Porters loaded two enormous crates of throat lozenges, enough to stock a clinic into the next century. I asked someone what they were for. "Oh, one of the correspondents has a sore throat," he said.

This presents a problem for people who have grown to rely on CNN as their yardstick for determining what's news. CNN was slow to explain the importance of Sarajevo. Like the over-the-air networks, it covered Bosnia only sporadically. Sometimes, reports were excellent. Often, major parts of the story passed unnoticed. According to senior correspondents, CNN had the same problem as everyone else. Few people wanted to go; it was a difficult, dangerous assignment. And, they said, headquarters was reluctant to spend the money. As a result, the war was not in real time.

All in all, CNN is a success story. In its early days, its newsroom was a converted barn-like puppet circus, and the anchor's backdrop was sometimes whoever happened to walk by scratching himself in an awkward place. Its correspondents were rumpled old pros, like Blystone and Arnett, who owned no hair dryers. Now other organizations have learned to respect the upstart network. Once hardly taken seriously, it is now a cornerstone of the business. Agencies quote it regularly as a source for news they have not yet verified on their own.

At times, CNN has to struggle to keep from filling too big a role. During the Gulf War, to the editors' consternation, the Pentagon acted as if it was a government agency. When Mikhail Gorbachev handed over the keys to the Soviet Union, CNN was called in to broadcast it live. Tom Johnson, also an AP board member, made a point of including an AP reporter and photographer to ensure that the event had news agency coverage. Gorbachev, however, signed the dissolution of the Soviet empire with Johnson's pen.

But, like every other news organization, CNN is only part of the package. Suspended belief and triangulation are advised. Stripped of its mystique, live television reporting is no more than the latest advance in journalism history. Foreign correspondents evolved from the 1870s after the telegraph gave them means to file copy. Until then, editors waited for mail boats. Any account was good enough; mistakes didn't matter much since no one could react any faster than the winds and tides. When Napoleon I fell in 1815, the guy who got the scoop was on a coastal schooner hired to intercept incoming ships; eventually, full accounts dribbled in. When Napoleon III fell in 1870, word came by transatlantic cable. This time, editors were no longer at the mercy of whatever fell on their desk. They could flash back the basic questions: What does this mean? Who says? Are you sure? With the ability to double-check, they tried to be as accurate as they were fast.

CNN is now at the top of this evolutionary chain. To its run of house ads, the network added an exciting video of its people at work in Atlanta. The newsroom is still a converted puppet circus, but now it is high-tech heaven. In the clip, earnest professionals jab at consoles and talk briskly in jargon, like television people at work. One at a time, they comment on their noble mission, often successfully accomplished. And the last one concludes: "We don't find out things any faster than you do."

Exciting. But frankly, it might be better to wait a minute until someone asked the old questions. Credibility, context and confirmation emerged as the bedrock attributes of journalism early in the twentieth century. Real-time television, and not just CNN's, can take us into the twenty-first century but also kick us back to the nineteenth.

Chapter 10

# Radio:
# Drive Time

When the Iraqis moved into Kuwait, Asian refugees streamed out, clerks and cleaners used to air-conditioned city life. They trekked for days to find the Jordan border closed. Desperate, penniless, out of food and water, they slept with scorpions in a desert no-man's-land. At one of their camps, I listened as a burly Indian pleaded for help from an American aid worker.

The Indian, a retired master sergeant, began with bluster. He demanded food, threatening violence if rejected. Then he switched to reason. People were starving. Patiently, the relief worker explained the foul-ups in Amman and promised to do whatever he could. Suddenly, the Indian broke into sobs. His family had no news of him. He would die in the desert, and no one would know. A crowd had gathered, and others shouted their own stories.

The aid worker was a veteran of the Afghan border, where refugees had routinely stuck guns in his face. He had watched babies die in famines. But this scene got to him. He could hardly talk, fighting back his own tears. I tried to help him calm the man, but my voice quavered, too. Finally, the wailing trailed off. I turned away and saw a radio reporter who had picked it all up in her mike. She was beaming. "Boy," she said, giving her Sony a loving pat, "it doesn't get any better than this."

She was no monster, this woman, but rather a radio pro whose obsession with her job pushed everything else into neutral. Thus equipped with such "raw sound," she put together a four-minute package, using her own narration to explain what was happening and why. Nothing I might write could convey what she had on tape. People driving to work, from Homestead to Hog Hollow, would be there in that desert. Still, I wanted to slug her.

For news from far away, radio can be the best medium of all. Deborah Amos of National Public Radio, asked what radio can do that television can't, was categorical: "Everything." She was probably right. And when it comes to those ten- to fifteen-minute pieces that NPR or BBC does regularly, radio can outdo columns of print. Its immediacy and flexibility are one thing. More important is the range of what it can convey.

Freed from the tyranny of pictures, radio people can concentrate on the story. A snatch of voice or the odd noise can draw in listeners, forcing them to stretch their imaginations. Interviews, when allowed to run, get across the original flavor and nuance. Little can match the calm explanation of a good radio reporter who knows and cares about the subject at hand.

"It's sheer emotion," Amos said. "You've got the emotion and the background at the same time. We can explain things, make them real. In radio, you speak to one person at a time. This is the thing that TV never gets. Television is like the movie in a small village, where everybody sits on chairs and just watches. They don't have to fill in any blanks. In radio, you're always suggesting. You have to induce them to listen, and they have to come along with you. I figure I've done my job well when people stay in the car to finish listening."

Time is jealously rationed on television, measured in fractions of a second. If a network newspiece runs twenty-one and a half seconds, every word has to justify its place in the script. On NPR, a single world news item can go on for twenty-two minutes.

But radio shares a major drawback with television. It is fleeting, and then it is gone. If a listener's attention wanders, there is no second chance. Often, it does not sink in.

"People always tell me, 'I heard you on the radio,' and I say, 'Yes . . . ? More . . . ?'" Amos said, imitating a situation we correspondents all know well, fishing for a compliment that just won't come. "And they say, 'Well, I heard you.' That's why I have to punch the emotion."

NPR, like BBC in Britain, does not have to earn a living in the marketplace. "Morning Edition" might reach fourteen million people during drive time, intelligent people caught in their cars with nothing to do but listen, and yet they fit no demographic pattern. Listeners are young and old, all colors and shapes. Advertisers cannot measure who is tuned in when, or why. As a medium, NPR is useless to the razor blade people.

On "All Things Considered," which runs for an hour and a half in the evening, Robert Siegel skirts what he believes to be a major failing of television. "TV overdoes it," he said. "There is a chronic underestimation of the American audience. Even when handed the most dramatic and important story, they need to hype. No synthetic excitement that you can create will match the story itself." He remembered the case of Felix Bloch, a U.S. diplomatic suspected of passing secrets to a Soviet agent in Vienna. ABC showed him handing over a briefcase and then had to explain later, with apologies, that it had been a reenactment. "They had essentially a John le Carré novel," he said, "and they still need to hype."

During the Gulf War, Siegel said, CBS Radio did a better job than CBS Television. "It was news shorn of some its more obnoxious effects." A story like that is a natural for radio, with fast-moving dramatic developments, loud noises and every sort of human emotion. ABC did an investigation of arms sales to Iraq that left Siegel, he said, "downright envious." But he described the disappearing standard hourly newscast as probably the least lamented form of American journalism.

NPR people think a lot about radio and its possibilities. "The stock belief is that Americans don't have the attention span to handle more than forty-five seconds before you have to shift the thing they're hearing," Siegel said. "In a five-minute story, you change voices, ambience. You're playing to the ear." The typical format of someone reading a long piece of world news, particularly with an odd accent, suggests that foreign news is something for foreigners. Voice-quality circuits are important. "A scratchy telephone line suggests something remote," he said. "There's a place in our brain that says if it sounds scratchy, it is far away. A good line suggests 'near me.'" Siegel looks for new ways to connect people to distant realities. "If other people are doing it, we shouldn't be doing it."

Commercial radio news, like television news, often falls far below its potential. It is a different sort of commodity. Stations subscribe to one or several networks, taking in hourly news summaries and short feature packages. At best, special reports from abroad run four minutes, about five hundred words, with tightly edited sound; more often, they are half that length. Routine summary spots are between twenty-five and forty seconds.

Complex events are boiled down to a few seconds of hopelessly simplified generality to fit into the package. World leaders are stripped of their names: "The French president visited Mars . . ." Political movements are assigned the nearest catchall adjective; Peru's Shining Path, like Britain's Labor Party, is leftist. The interviews which can be so powerful on radio are often sliced into a few free-floating words.

"In radio, you're either all-news, or you're no news at all," an old hand explained to me. Since he sells packaged news, he prefers anonymity. "Top-of-the-hour summaries are pretty much worthless for anything more than finding out what just happened." Even all-news stations amount to a string of quick hits, leaving the listener with stereotyped misconceptions of vital background.

"Mostly, it is too short, it doesn't tell you anything but headlines," Deborah Amos said. "Once the FCC said radio stations didn't have to have newscasts, they didn't. Now there is not much to radio." Good commercial broadcasts have all the advantages of NPR-type radio, she said, but few stations devote the time for crafted pieces, so the networks seldom provide them.

A lot of old radio pros dispute this point. Some consider NPR to be elitist, self-important and badly edited. Radio's real strength, they say, is the ability to keep people atop of events so they know when to look further.

Among ABC, CBS and NBC, television has long since shoved radio to the background but not out of the picture. "Radio is that lovely, unspectacular little medium that is always there," said Rob Sundae, who for years edited news at ABC's three networks, which supply twenty-three hundred affiliates around the country. With a satellite music network, the total goes to thirty-two hundred. When ABC people get squeezed off Peter Jennings on a busy night, they can always talk to radio. Correspondents work for news, not television or radio. Since television editors are focused on a single deadline at the end of the day, reporters stay in close touch with radio.

Fancy technology means a Sam Donaldson can tape a story and then update it on the network while he is still speaking on the air. Sundae can explain how it works. The result is that big radio works at blinding speed, even if it does not dig deep.

CBS News still has its own radio network. Like the larger operation, it relies on staff correspondents but also on regular stringers scattered around the world. NBC News sold its radio operation, name included, to Westwood One, a California company that packages entertainment by satellite. Westwood also bought the Mutual Broadcasting Network. NBC correspondents were supposed to feed the radio network, but few of them do.

CNN has entered the field, selling its audio portion to radio stations seeking to add a new dimension, or save money. It has mixed reviews. Competitors say it sounds like half a television broadcast. But it is making inroads.

The AP and UPI each runs a radio network. The AP's is larger, with about eight hundred subscribers around the United States. AP Radio has its own small team of reporters, but it draws heavily from the agency's correspondents all over the world. Anyone heading out for AP takes along a portable recorder. Some agency people discover a hidden talent, sending powerful spots whenever they get a spare moment. If not, there is always Q & A. AP Radio finds the poor sucker in deepest Tjunkistan and fires questions.

At the end of each spot, correspondents sign off with a name, a place and the tagline "AP Network News." After a pause, they do it again, with just a name and place. This gives radio stations the option of pretending they have their own staffs out covering the world.

Reporters recruited suddenly to radio duty find themselves plummeting down Alice's rabbit hole. Their reality changes. Comfortable old word patterns they use in writing sound awkward when spoken out loud. The names they struggle to learn, and spell correctly, are too big an earful for twenty-five-second spots. For example, Gen. Mohamed Farrah Aidid, commander of the principal Somali militia and clan faction, crucial to any negotiations, is "a main warlord." From this vantage point, it is easy to see how radio suggests simple situations, which require simple fixes.

But amateur radio reporters also realize what skill is required to say something significant in half a minute. Good or bad, those are the parameters. A radio spot, if restrictive, is immediate. People don't have to wait for the evening news or the morning paper to learn that their world has taken an extra spin. With only seventy words in which to tell a story, a pro can make them count. Above all, there is no room for a mind to wander.

Argentine generals bundled President Isabel Perón onto a helicopter and out of office in 1976. This was soon after the AP let me know that I, after a life of fingers on the keyboard, would also speak the news. For a day and half, I worked without sleep to follow events and write for the wire. Radio editors waited patiently for me to get around to them. At 4 A.M., I finally collapsed in sleep. And an hour later, with yet another news summary coming up devoid of a voicer, their patience ran out.

"Just do a simple Q & A," the editor pleaded, and I did my best. The first answer came out something like: "Uh, Mrs. Perón, the president, was, um, overthrown by the military who thought she, um, the president, Mrs. Perón, I mean, President Isabel Perón . . ." I've been called only infrequently since then.

In between NPR and commercial radio, there is Monitor Radio, maintained in Boston by the Christian Scientists' mother church in the spirit of its *Christian Science Monitor*. It has a substantial network of stringers around the world; their best work is squeezed into the hour-long, predawn "Morning Show." Correspondents report news developments in forty-second spots. When allowed to run long, they are limited to four minutes.

The idea is to provide the lively but serious coverage of world events which commercial radio does not offer. As far as it goes, it is a good idea. But providing news as a public service eats through the biggest of budgets.

In radio, the high mark is BBC. For correspondents of every nationality, it is a religion. Muslims pray only five times a day. Reporters kneel before their shortwaves, on the hour, from first light to last snort. The ritual is ancient, whether it is group worship around a jeep hood or a lonely listen in a monastic hotel chamber. First, the catchy hymn and the incantation: "The news, read by Pamela Crichton [or whomever]." Then three or four headlines followed by eight minutes of detail.

Often, a voice in the congregation yells, "Shit!" This would be someone who missed some important news angle that the BBC reporter did not. Sometimes, the newscast instigates frantic packing. Bigger news has erupted three countries down the road. Mostly, there is peaceful, satisfied silence. The world is safe for another hour. Or, if it is going to hell, at least it is happening across an ocean in someone else's territory.

Those clipped English tones can be tuned in by anyone with a shortwave. In many places at certain times, an FM radio is enough. For BBC junkies, as with all fans of serious radio, newscasts are only a part of it. Special reports, fifteen minutes or a half-hour long, probe the depths of stories that shape the world. Twice daily, "News Hour" covers high points and sidelights in telling detail. The range is wide. On Sundays, "From Our Own Correspondent" lets three or four reporters spill out their notebooks in wry pieces which tell about a place while explaining what it is like to cover it.

BBC's strengths are credibility and a straightforward presentation. It does not sell itself. No one shouts for attention or hokes up a story with vocal gymnastics. The people who write the copy concentrate on getting it right. Readers just read. It can put you to sleep. But, if you stay awake long enough, you are forewarned about what is headed your way.

BBC uses public funds but is administered by a separate trust. It has 120 million listeners in thirty-eight languages, many of whom with fiercely opposing beliefs. In India, longtime correspondent Mark Tully is better known than is Alistair Cooke in the United States. In one village, people swarmed out of huts to help a reporter change his tire; they saw a BBC sticker and thought he was Tully. But at a riot elsewhere, Indians in a mood to mutilate demanded of each reporter: "Are you Mark Tully?"

The Beeb is not always right; no one is in this business. When Terry Anderson finally turned up free in Damascus, he joked that he had followed his progress across Syria while listening to BBC from his cell in Beirut. Somehow, BBC jumped the gun. But it is close enough for most of us.

Americans have another choice, better in some ways, in NPR. The style is more familiar, the tone can be friendlier and the approach is usually as professional. Between "Morning Edition" and "All Things Considered," a lot of foreign news is covered in rich texture.

Amos is among the best. She began in television, working at a small public-access station in Florida and then moving to bigger jobs. Then, as now, radio had a taint of second string, regarded as outmoded in a television age. If you couldn't get decent work in television, the feeling went, there was always radio. Amos knew better.

"I'd had it with TV and moved to Washington, with no idea what to do," she said. "Somebody told me about a place called NPR. That was in 1977. We had no model for radio; it was all self-taught." NPR pioneers went to Berlin to learn from SFB, a public radio station that made its own rules. For a story on German Hell's Angels, SFB brought fifteen motorcycles into a symphony hall. Under the baton of a philharmonic conductor, they revved in full volume, one at a time.

NPR, if a little more conservative in approach, broke its own ground in reporting news from abroad. By 1993, it had a half-dozen staff correspondents abroad along with dozens of regular stringers. Amos is based in London, married to Rick Davis of NBC, but she is often on the road.

As young Nazis and murderous skinheads began to terrorize foreigners in Germany, late in 1992, every sort of correspondent took a crack at the story. Television showed what right-wing violence looked like, as well as the fear felt by Gypsies, Turks and other minorities. Newspapers had the space and format to explore historical meanings and psychological trauma in a Germany trying to emerge as respectable economic power. Magazines went deeper, focusing on individuals who reflected the larger picture. But radio took its listeners into the heart of it.

Amos and producer Michael Sullivan spent two weeks in Germany interviewing and harvesting sound. They did a five-part series, totaling forty-seven minutes. The shortest segment was five minutes; the longest, fourteen. Victims spoke more than a quick phrase into a passing lens. Angst and anger welled up around the words. Full sentences explained personal reactions and gave examples. Weaving together the eyewitnesses and analysts, Amos painted a vivid picture in words. Then she took listeners into the street. Skinheads, marching in their heavy shoes, taunted the police. Diners peered out of restaurant windows, curious at the noise. The mind's eye could fill in the rest.

For whomever they work, radio people run themselves ragged, scrambling around all day with a foam-covered mike and then huddling alone in lonely cloisters trying to edit hours' worth of tape. For print correspondents, a computer burst or dictation on a crackling phone line is enough to file their stories. Television crews travel with their own ground links and technicians to make them work. Radio reporters, who usually travel alone, have to hustle up a good-quality audio circuit for their feeds.

Ross Simpson, a full-time staff correspondent for Mutual, is a one-man crew. In Somalia, by the time he packed in a tape recorder, batteries, cables, a sleeping bag and extra underwear, he had little room for food and water. He existed for weeks on artful mooching, sometimes eating a can of tuna a day. To get around, he cadged rides. To file, he depended on someone letting him buy time on a satellite phone. It was a killer assignment.

AP Radio's foreign staff is Karen Sloan. From her base in London, if she spins a globe and jabs her finger at it, anywhere, that's her beat, unless she happens to be pointing at the United States. Sloan manages to cover it all. The way news works, many stations seem happy enough with solid coverage of the day's major story and snippets of the rest. When needed, reporters race out from Washington to help.

Sloan started like a lot of radio pros. She worked in a cheapo operation above a store where she had to race to the bathroom across the street and back before the record ended. Quickly, she hustled her way upward. Now, Sloan is everywhere, all the time.

Mostly, radio networks depend on stringers who live on a shoestring and travel on less. Michael Georgy of Monitor Radio, for instance, ekes out a living in Cairo. In his twenties, he was working for a newsletter in the United States, and he got restless. With limited capital, mainly a resonant voice and a will to suffer, he took himself abroad. "Why wait in the United States for ten years for some guy to decide to send you overseas?" he wondered. Why, indeed?

For listeners, radio's heavy reliance on stringers is a reason for extra caution. Major networks usually know whom they are dealing with, but it is difficult for them to maintain uniform reliability. The danger is greater with government-funded broadcasters, including Voice of America, which cannot always escape an overzealous official's penchant to push a particular line. Occasionally, outright propaganda slips by. In 1990, the *New York Times* exposed a covert Israeli program which hired radio stringers to send government-directed reports to stations around the world. "The [foreign] ministry pays me because the sort of stations I work for don't pay very well," one reporter told the *Times*. The program ran four years.

Editors at home seldom understand the pressures on their people. Many, not having worked abroad, miss the nuances of an intricate world. In Afghanistan at the height of fundamentalist fervor, Michael Sullivan of NPR filed a report on how fanatic elders unslung their Kalashnikovs to impose a dusk-to-dawn curfew. Their women, locked in behind walled compounds, wore veils with black mesh screens over their eyes if they had to appear in public. One editor, reasonably enough, wanted a woman's point of view. He asked Sullivan to find an English-speaking Afghan woman to take to his hotel-room studio for an interview.

Even the most sensitive editors have their own requirements in a hotly competitive market. Occasional clashes are inevitable. One correspondent in Asia went sleepless for days, collecting some gripping sound in his tape recorder and putting together a powerful script to give it wider meaning. But when he tried to feed back to New York, he could not satisfy the technican.

Over and over he fed the tape down what seemed like a relatively good line. The technician kept harping for something better. Couldn't the guy do something? Finally, the reporter had had enough. He asked the technician to turn his amplifier up to maximum. In a quiet voice, he asked, "Can you hear me now?" The technician said he could, but the level was low. The reporter told him to listen more closely. "OK," he said, "are you listening? Full gain? Ear in close? Ready? FUCK YOU!"

# Chapter 11

# Digging Deeper

In Somalia, I ran into my old pal, the Institution. When I first met him in Africa, twenty-five years before, he was already a legend at his weekly newsmagazine. This time, he had been a correspondent longer than his colleague, who would write the main story, had been a person. He was in semiretirement, which meant nothing in operational terms. It was the same old awful hours, the same heat and bugs, the same threat from overarmed lunatics.

"I've got pleurisy," he said, by way of greeting. This was not a complaint, merely the Institution's shotgun conversation style. Driving himself too hard, he had ignored a lung infection. Doctors said if he did not rest, he would probably die. "Sure, sure," he said, when I chased him toward bed and offered to cover for him. His magazine expected a story on the French Foreign Legion, which he had followed since before France lost Vietnam. It would mean a grueling night patrol. But he always delivered.

I next saw him days later. He looked like hell. Again, the Institution had a shotgun greeting: "They killed the story."

But the story did not kill him. Newsmagazine people are used to writing for the garbage can. All it takes is some late development elsewhere or a simple change of heart by an editor of rank. For the reader, this need not be a drawback. In theory, the most pertinent and best polished material rises to the top, to be wrapped around compelling photos in an attractive weekly package. In practice, however, editors often toss out bathwater and baby alike. Important stories, wrapped up and ready to go, never make it to the press.

With newsmagazines, you take what you get, and that can vary widely. *Time* is the biggest seller, but it not necessarily the one correspondents reach for when given the choice. *Newsweek* has a strong following among reporters who regard it as harder edged, freer swinging and less slick. *U.S. News & World Report,* once a poor third, is coming up fast as a thorough and intelligent digest of foreign news. Like every other branch of journalism, it all depends on who is on the ground and what the editors do.

The newsmagazines tread a careful line between presenting facts and drawing conclusions. More and more, they lean toward the latter. Chris Dickey, *Newsweek*'s Middle East specialist, who has filled in as foreign editor, explained, "A reporter used to file a huge pile of facts, including what he had for dinner, and editors put them into some structure. Now, with good communications, they can talk to a correspondent and shape a piece. Editors know newsmagazines can't be a recitation of the facts—on the one hand this, on the other hand that—ending with 'only time will tell.' They need a thesis. Not an ideology or point of view, as Henry Luce had with *Time,* but a thesis based on facts developed by the correspondent in the field."

*Newsweek*'s standard foreign news building block is a six-column spread, between 150 and 200 lines of type over two pages, with strong photos. Editors have found that to be the right length for the modern reader's attention span. Like television, the magazine might favor one story over another not for content but because the pictures are better. Other stories are fitted into the remaining space. Basic pieces are signed at the end, with small type naming the editor and reporters who contributed. But the magazine's signal for a more personalized view is "top byline," the writer's name in big letters under the headline.

In *Time,* where there once were no bylines, every article is signed. A news-in-brief section at the front catches up with the week's developments, and a mixed bag of material follows. Each piece sketches out the main points of the story and then draws a conclusion. The range is wide.

For the last *Time* of 1992, the editors commissioned William Shawcross to write a piece on Cambodia, "The U.N.'s Biggest Gamble." This was good journalism, well worth the price of anyone's magazine. In his 1979 book, *Sideshow,* Shawcross showed how the

United States had blundered into Cambodia and what price that neutral little nation had paid for it. Here, as an untested, new-style United Nations tried to put Humpty Dumpty back together again on a grand scale, he brought things up to date.

But in the same issue, *Time* cast doubts on correspondents everywhere with a two-page Press piece on Dusko Doder. With no news peg, it reported that in 1986 the FBI director told the *Washington Post*'s executive editor that a dubious KGB defector had relayed hearsay information that Doder had taken one thousand dollars from a KGB agent while he was the *Post*'s Moscow bureau chief. No evidence was found, and investigations petered out. The article's Washington-based author drew a moral, suggesting that especially good journalists were suspect because they might be too close to their sources. One wonders how he would know.

The article brought a stinging reply signed by almost every newspaper and magazine correspondent based in the Soviet bloc since the 1960s. Reporters tried hard to be close to sources, as a matter of course. Naturally, the KGB would want to use them or, if it suited a purpose, to suggest that they were somehow tainted. To anyone who knew Doder, the charge was particularly improbable. By passing along unfounded aspersions, the letter concluded, *Time* had impugned all correspondents, including its own.

*U.S. News,* with a looser approach, sometimes burrows in deeper and swings wider than its larger competitors. It is strong on economics, social undercurrents and the week's big stories. Michael Ruby, the co-editor, has helped bring circulation to 2.5 million, as compared with 3.2 million for *Newsweek* and 4 million for *Time.* "Can all three survive?" he reflected. "The question is, Can all three survive doing the same thing?"

*U.S. News* steers clear of *Newsweek*'s heavy point-of-view pieces or *Time*'s splashy and fragmented layout, aimed at a mass market. It ran a thick section on AIDS, exploring the economic impact in each of the worst-hit countries. An eight-page spread looked at refugees. But foreign news stays mostly inside. Ruby was about to do a cover on Russia when I spoke to him. "It won't sell," he said, "but we're doing it because it's the right thing to do." By late 1992, *U.S. News* had yet to do a Yugoslavia cover. The facts of life are that foreign covers sell 20 percent below average.

*Business Week* also covers world news but with a heavy emphasis on its specialty. Money is a good gauge for coming problems.

CNN editors watch the briefs in *Business Week* for clues on what crises may be in the wind.

Along with newsweeklies, or instead of them, daily newspapers which circulate nationally offer a strong dose of world news. The *New York Times* and the *Wall Street Journal* are obvious choices. Other major dailies are available far beyond their home cities. Pushed by television, big newspapers have moved into ground once left to newsmagazines. For major stories, they offer history, analysis, maps, graphics and profiles of the key players.

Despite all the changes in style, the distinction between fact and opinion is still a hallmark of American journalism. In news columns, readers should expect to find an attempt at objectivity. The principle is that given the viewpoints of different sides, people can make up their own minds. In practice, this can approach impossibility. In the former Yugoslavia, for example, reporters who quickly saw where to point fingers had to balance one group's atrocities against another's. Nuances which make up a clear picture get lost in the telling. In the end, everyone is right, and everyone is wrong. The reader has to dig deeper.

Editorial and op-ed pages should be approached with care. They carry such richness as the columnists William Pfaff and Richard Reeves and occasional offerings from writers like Richard Critchfield who used to visit remote villages for the *Christian Science Monitor* and stay for eleven months. Newsmakers and keen observers add new dimensions. But in little more than two months after Iraq invaded Kuwait, four papers alone carried 657 opinion pieces on the subject. That's thumbsucking.

The big papers have weekly background sections. In these, correspondents can unload their notebooks, and their souls. When Blaine Harden left Yugoslavia in early 1993 after three years in the region, he wrote a two-part piece for the *Washington Post* which swept aside the usual restraints of the daily news columns. "Serbia stands accused of igniting Europe's worst convulsion of destruction, cruelty and violent death since the fall of Nazi Germany," he began. "The chaos is far from over. Indeed, the worst may be yet to come." He described calculating, power-hungry leaders, who exploited legitimate Serbian fears, and the policy of ethnic cleansing they were carrying out. "The consequences of this policy for Croatia and Bosnia are horrible, but the long-term precedent for Europe could be worse," he wrote. "The 'Serbian solution' may well prove to be

irresistible for demagogues across the continent who are seeking
to attract voters and adjust borders."

A trimmed version of Harden's piece showed up in a daily com-
pendium of world news available just about anywhere, the *International Herald Tribune*. The *Trib* is edited in Paris by Americans who
know that their readers live in 160 countries. They try to project an
international view, with a global news focus and space for stories
from forgotten reaches of the world.

The *Trib*'s owners are the *New York Times* and the *Washington
Post;* their correspondents, and those of the *Los Angeles Times,* send
copies to Paris when they file to their own desks. The result is a
mix from seventy-five correspondents, as well as the AP, Reuters
and Agence France-Presse and stories from the paper's own reporters. An independent editorial page is rich in columns, commentary
from the owner papers and commissioned pieces.

Though edited in France, the paper's pages are sent by facsim-
ile to printing plants in fifteen cities around the world. After years
of reluctance, the *Times* agreed to sites in the United States, and
the *Trib* prints in New York and Miami.

For news junkies, another rich lode is the weekly *Guardian,*
which combines the best of its own daily pieces with those of *Le
Monde* and the *Washington Post.*

Obviously enough, there is no formula to follow. However complete a daily newspaper may be, newsweeklies add a different dimension. It's all a matter of taste and available time.


Whatever their strengths, newsmagazines are subject to con-
straints of length, format and style. Well-informed readers regard
newspapers, newsweeklies and broadcast news as little more than
a base from which to update a knowledge of the world built on other
sources. Correspondents are always in a hurry. Even if they don't
make a mistake, their sources might. Overall patterns are seldom
clear from day-to-day events. Even in fast-changing situations, the
best reporting is often done by those who take months to polish a
dispatch that will have to stand up for years.

Other sorts of magazines often have more room, literally and
philosophically, for writers who pose issues from a different point
of view. For example, there is Alexander Cockburn, who lurks in
the forests of northern California from where he hurls the odd thun-

derbolt. Not everyone agrees with him, to his relief, but fair minds have to respect the prodigious amount of historical trivia, grand theory and journalistic instinct that came with his upbringing. Cockburn's father was a cornerstone among Britain's quality papers. His brother is half of the team of Andrew and Leslie Cockburn, who rattle the cages in *Vanity Fair.*

Cockburn's media column in the *Nation* offers an object lesson for those who analyze a diverse world from a Judeo-Christian standpoint and wonder why things don't work out as expected. In one column, he excoriated the *Wall Street Journal* and *Time* for ridiculing the Church of Scientology after it had attacked the Eli Lilly antidepressant, Prozac. Lilly, he wrote, was close to the White House and media moguls. And the Scientologists got little sympathy because they were seen as a cult, which, as opposed to a religion, is fair game. He continued:

> By contrast, Bush, Quayle and many officers of Eli Lilly and indeed of the Dow Jones Company, which publishes the *Journal,* are adherents of the Christ cult, about which journalists are uniformly deferential. (The Christ cult anchors its belief system to the claims of a carpenter's wife nearly 2,000 years ago that she had been possessed by God, producing thereafter a child who demanded recognition as the "Son of God," claiming to have been sent to Earth to "save mankind." Celebrants of the Christ cult periodically eat a biscuit, claiming it is the flesh of the cult's founder. Many cult members have been convicted of sexual crimes and have killed in the name of their God.)

If a little blasphemous, this piece helps explain why Islamic zealots and other ideologues dispute our notion of an even-handed press. It does not matter whether they are right; what is important is being able to follow their line of thinking.

Jabbing at media bubbles is nothing new for Cockburn. Nearly twenty years ago, he aimed a shaft at C. L. Sulzberger of the *New York Times,* who has since retired. The essay, in *More* magazine, still applies to a lot of writers and editors who deal with world news: "C. L. has divined the central mystery of his craft, which is to fire volley after volley of cliché into the densely packed prejudices of his readers. There are no surprises in his work. NATO is always in crisis. There is and always has been an opening to the left in Italy. He never deviates into paradox. His work is a constant affirmation of received beliefs. . . . C. L. Sulzberger is much too experienced a hand to avoid the obvious when he has a chance to consort with it."

During the Gulf War euphoria, Cockburn was a counterbalance. He wrote: "Journalism annuls history, never more so than in war, where it promotes a depthless present, most tragicomically in television 'coverage,' the reporters—actors, in fact—having mostly as little relationship to reality as the Greek chorus in the *Agamemnon* debating among themselves what Clytemnestra is up to ('Is that a noise I hear?') as she hacks the King to death. Febrile discussion of the minutiae of war coverage—how much censorship in Riyadh, how much lying in the Pentagon briefing room—itself acts as a form of censorship, for it too avoids history."

A haunting historical parallel, Cockburn noted, was Winston Churchill's approval, in 1919, of using chemical weapons "against recalcitrant Arabs an as experiment." Churchill explained: "I do not understand the squeamishness about the use of gas. I am strongly in favor of using poisoned gas against uncivilized tribes. . . . It is not necessary to use only the most deadly gasses."

Cockburn's point was that journalists seldom have the time, space or inclination to sketch out the moral setting of hostilities. There is no such thing as a just war, only different points of view. "One could read with sympathy accounts by Israelis of the horror of sitting in sealed rooms wearing gas masks while Palestinians cheered," he wrote. "But few journalists and no Israelis quoted gave a thought for Palestinians closeted in their homes day after day under rigorous curfew, tear-gassed, tortured in prisons, their homes demolished by bulldozers with far greater efficiency and no public uproar."

The range is wide. T. D. Allman in *Vanity Fair* burrows under the skin of public figures, adding his own sardonic acid to their vital juices. The result occasionally produces words to live by. Chatting with Allman, Moammar Khadafy observed, "It is impossible to be straight in a crooked world."

In *Rolling Stone,* P. J. O'Rourke makes a point of not talking to official sources. The reader usually ends up knowing more about him than the place he is in, and he does not always slow down for the facts, but O'Rourke has a gift for cutting through the crap. From Bosnia, he wrote: "It was easy for Sonja to pretend to be a Serbian because Serbs and Croats are so much alike that the only way they can tell each other apart is by religion, and most of them aren't religious. So the difference between Serbs and Croats is that the Serbs don't go to Eastern Orthodox services and the Croats don't attend mass, and the difference between Serbs and Muslims is that five times a day the Muslims don't pray to Mecca."

Carefully done background articles help avoid misconceptions that come from the correspondent's inevitable shorthand. Terms like "left-wing" or "conservative" need a lot of explaining before they make any sense in distant societies. A letter to the *Manchester Guardian* in 1921 showed how tricky this can be. The writer was referring to England and France, two cultures which know one another well:

> Words, like money, are tokens of value. They represent meaning, therefore, and just as money, their representative value goes up and down. . . . Some nations constitutionally tend to understate, others to overstate. What the British Tommy called an unhealthy place could only be described by an Italian soldier by means of a rich vocabulary aided with exuberant mimicry. Nations that overstate suffer from inflation in their language. Expressions such as "a distinguished scholar," "a clever writer," must be translated in French as "a great savant," "an exquisite master." It is a mere matter of exchange, just as in France one pound pays 46 francs, and yet one knows that that does not increase its value at home. Englishmen reading the French press should endeavor to work out a mental operation similar to that of the banker who puts back francs into pounds, and not forget in doing so that while in normal times the change was 25 it is now 46 on account of the war. For there is a war fluctuation on word exchanges as well as on money exchanges.

A well-crafted magazine piece paints in the backdrop behind events which may seem simple enough in concise news dispatches. Walter Lippmann once observed that a grocer usually has very clear ideas about political conflict in Europe and Far East. He is less certain about groceries because he knows firsthand how complicated the subject can be.

Most magazines lean toward a certain type of article on foreign affairs. The *Atlantic* and the *New Republic* present a wide spread of fairly straightforward reportage. *Foreign Affairs* and *Foreign Policy* dig deep, scruffling away at the roots of problems with words of several syllables. The *New York Review of Books* enlightens on places that interest its editors, particularly Eastern Europe and the Middle East. *Vanity Fair* and the *New Yorker,* which often troll the same talent pool, seek impact with stories from abroad. Neither is comprehensive, but both do a good, and sometimes excellent, job. The *Nation, Rolling Stone, Harper's* and *Esquire* poke regularly at the world in unusual ways. *Playboy* and *Penthouse,* not always purchased for the punditry, can weigh in with something significant. There are a lot of others.

A problem with magazines is lead time. Articles are prepared months, even years, in advance. *National Geographic* did a piece on how the killing fields were silent in Cambodia. It was worth the read. But with the Khmer Rouge at it again, the silence had long since been broken. Another caution is that longer and later are not necessarily better. In Buenos Aires, I was amused to hear a *Reader's Digest* man explain how much more revealing magazines could be than superficial agency dispatches. This was while he rifled my files for old dispatches and asked Dick-and-Jane questions about Argentine politics.

Magazines often excerpt or review new books on foreign affairs. These days, foreign correspondents finish their assignments with engines racing and notebooks still full. The result has been some excellent books, and a few lousy ones, which wade into culture, politics, diplomacy and the sidelights of daily life. The best of these offer not only a second draft of recent history but also insight into events about to happen.

In these media-minded times, reading about magazine people is nearly as popular as reading what they put in their pages. Tina Brown's leap from *Vanity Fair* to the *New Yorker* was bigger news than a small South American coup d'état. The publisher of *Rolling Stone* is better known than the president of Romania. Gossip value aside, it helps to know who's who. And why.

When Warner took over *Time,* corporate fallout and layoffs left morale on the floor. Richard Clurman, a former editor on the magazine, reflected the mood in a book title: *To the End of Time.* Insiders studied the tea leaves and saw editorial power shift from the hands of Henry Muller, a former correspondent who understands the world and cares about depicting it accurately. Clearly, Warner's background in entertainment, glitz and cost consciousness would have some effect. The wise watched closely.

Mort Zuckerman bought the *Atlantic* in 1980 and, four years later, *U.S. News & World Report.* As a self-described hands-on publisher with a background in dealing real estate, he could hardly escape the extreme opinions expressed about him. Some would kill for him. Others prefer him to be the victim. Here was another case to follow. As 1993 opened, his magazines commanded respect. He had hired editors with the sense and confidence to know when to tell the hands-on publisher to keep his hands off.

Good magazines are usually extensions of someone's personality, and they change with the person. Who edits is usually more important than who pays. *Harper's* switched hands, but the man whose monthly essay put the world in focus was still Lewis Lapham. Yet budget restrictions, policy guidelines and subtle pressures all make their impact.

The most successful editors stick with their own feel, staying ahead of their readers instead of scrambling to keep up. Elise O'Shaughnessy, executive editor of *Vanity Fair,* put it: "It's a very dangerous area to get into when you start reading readership surveys. You have to see yourself as a reader. We look for what we think is going to be in the news." While television producers stick with what they think people definitely want to know, she said, a magazine ought to tell people what they would be interested in if anyone let them know about it. She doesn't worry much about what is domestic or foreign. "People like to read stories. They don't really care what they're about."

For readers whose main concern is the shape of the wider world, it is enough to know the magazine's broad lines and the writers' bylines. For the latter, at least, editors usually offer some guidance on a contributors' page. The Gore Vidals and Paul Therouxs present little problem. Some magazine contributors are working correspondents. When David Remnick of the *Washington Post* left Moscow, at the time of the coup, he wrote a profile of Mikhail Gorbachev for *Vanity Fair.* Others are unlikely authors, people from other fields with an unusual perspective. A strength of magazines is that there are fewer rules.

A few magazines go back regularly to the same stable of correspondents. *Vanity Fair* readers, for example, know the weedwhacker style of the ubiquitous Cockburns and the sly to smartass wisdom of T. D. Allman. When the Marxists finally fell in Ethiopia, fans of Alex Shoumatoff were able to relive the terror, war and starvation that had been reported piecemeal over seventeen years. He profiled Colonel Mengistu Haile Mariam, "the five-foot-four black Stalin who had brought about the death of hundreds of thousands, maybe millions, of the fellow Ethiopians."

Tina Brown let go some *New Yorker* regulars, preferring to leave the field open. Readers had gotten used to familiar names, she said, and she had done well by breaking other people's patterns. To explain the butchery in Bosnia, she offered a sensitive briefing from David Reiff. Not known as a foreign correspondent, Reiff had profiled Miami and Los Angeles in books that cut deeply. He stayed clear of Sarajevo and went to Banja Luka to explore the psychology of rifts that go back centuries. Brown also called on a German writer who did an unusually sympathetic piece on Erich Honecker, the dying ex-dictator of East Germany. Some readers would have liked to know that the writer was married to Honecker's lawyer.

"A magazine is supposed to come in when the newspaper reporter has turned off the lights and gone home," Bob Wallace said, sitting in *Rolling Stone*'s expanse of pricey real estate near Rockefeller Center. In twenty-five years, the magazine has climbed far beyond its warehouse by the tracks in San Francisco, and music was only part of it. Wallace, the editor, knows how news gathering ought to work.

As he sees it, too many people think they already know the story, and editors are often as hidebound as their readers. "The hardest thing to change is a first impression," he said. "Opinions evolve and get so rigid. News organizations are not doing better, in general. A reporter has to be very good, and editors are not picking their brains." Foreign news takes a backseat to copy that is closer to home, he said, but that is also seen in stereotype. "Even from Denver, how the *New York Times* reported the West, you saw this. For all the clichés, it might as well be Africa. . . . 'The nesting place of the forty-story crane,' that sort of thing."

His approach is to look at stories from the perspective of people rather than political science professors and civil servants. "There are so many outlets for the official voice," Wallace said. "Nothing is going to turn off Americans, our readers, like the predictable. Especially if it's a foreign story, they need to be grabbed viscerally. We're interested if a writer is dying to do a story. Unlike newspapers, the point is an emotional connection. This always gives a richness, a more passionate piece than you would normally get. Newspaper reporters contact us about stories they really want to do."

*Stone* editors listen to readers, but like O'Shaughnessy at *Vanity Fair,* they are not guided by focus groups. "The editor still has to drive the car," Wallace said. "We feel that if we give them what they want, we should also get to give them what we want." Maybe 20 percent of his readers might wade through a piece on Somalia, he figures, but that's good enough.

Wallace believes that people have to know why calamities like Somalia happen, why they repeat themselves and then worsen, but he contends that most news organizations don't go deeply enough into the real causes. As a result, most readers and viewers see re-action without understanding the action that triggered it. "Children starving is a story that must be put into a context," he said. "If you have starving children in Africa, the story is in Washington. The question is, Why are they starving?"

He was near the heart of the problem. In one way or another, Washington is part of almost every foreign story. How Americans react to events abroad helps shape their outcome. And if Americans choose not to take notice, the events will shape Washington's re-action when it inevitably comes. Reporters should be on top of this complex linkage between Washington and the rest of the world, but we're not. In terms of news theft, Beltway bandits are committing grand larceny.

Chapter 12

# Beltway Blindness: The Washington Filter

Back when the Bush administration decided to ignore war in Yugoslavia, in 1991, I went to see the Eagle. Dubrovnik was under siege. The European Community negotiated endless cease-fires which no one could enforce. And Lawrence Eagleburger, an old Yugoslavia hand who was acting secretary of state, knew what was coming next. Things would get much worse. Innocents would suffer in growing numbers. The Balkans were at risk, and Russia could get drawn in. Washington would do next to nothing. Correspondents were already saying these things, and I asked if their reports might influence U.S. policymakers to take action. "No," the Eagle replied.

In fact, he said, correspondents seldom make a difference in how Washington sees the world. "On a few issues, particularly if they are politically sensitive like China, there might be some impact," he said, "but by and large press reporting does not affect the way we conduct policy."

It seemed a curious response. Fifteen years earlier, I put the same question to Theodore H. White, the journalist-historian who made his fortune by explaining power in Washington. He leaped from a comfortable chair and did a brisk dance to emphasize his reply. "I would say the front page of the *New York Times,* what appears on it, is more important in policy-making than any CIA cable, or any State Department cable. And what appears in the *L. A.*

*Times* when it gets to those forty-three California congressmen, or what appeared in the *Chicago Daily News* when it had a foreign service, or what the AP lands on the front page in Cheyenne, Chillicothe or Denver—that is what shapes the mentality of Congress. And you can't get anything through without Congress, which explains the presidencies' attempts to manipulate the press. *Enormous, for Christ's sake.*"

But Teddy White has since died along with his era. His answer is still right, but so is Eagleburger's. The press, now the media, has enormous impact when a single issue coalesces to a critical mass, and it moves public opinion. In foreign affairs, this seldom occurs unless the government wants it that way.

Eagleburger knows that if cameras do not focus sustained attention on a story and newspapers do not hammer away, officials do what they want. The government tried to abandon the Kurds in Iraq and then had to change its agenda. But that was a rare instance. Reporters were already in the region, charged up to cover a war that had ended before they got going, and refugees starving in mountain passes was a natural. Yugoslavia was not such a popular story to cover.

"With the Kurds, they lost control of the picture," explained Dennis Murphy of NBC. "People could relate to those kids' eyes. If you cleaned them up, bought them some clothes at Penney's and gave them a haircut, they could have been at your kid's school. George Bush didn't have a chance." Still, when the cameras turned away, so did Washington.

The democracy theory is compelling. Elected leaders and hired hands devise a foreign policy based upon Americans' broader interests and moral values. Since this process is open to interpretation, the people are meant to keep track of what is being done in their name. When necessary, they send a collective message to the top. This is what, eventually, stopped the war in Vietnam.

In practice, the system is not all that hot. It took fifty-five thousand American lives, nearly a million Asian lives and ten years of anguish for people to realize that the first small band of correspondents in Vietnam had it right in the beginning. The war was unwinnable. Our good guys were hopelessly corrupt. Fancy weaponry helps, but you cannot root out ideologically committed guerrillas the way an Orkin man goes after termites.

With the nation barely recovered from Vietnam, a new set of policymakers did it again in Central America. They learned enough not to fight their war with American boys. But once again, they ignored what correspondents had reported from the field: The war we imagined was unwinnable. Our good guys were hopelessly corrupt. Fancy weaponry cost more than the government could spend, legally. Our proxy army and our allies, many of them trafficking drugs that were eroding our society, would bleed us white.

At every stage, reporters wrote what was happening. Their message never reached that critical mass, and Washington did what it wanted. When the Sandinista government in Nicaragua collapsed of its own weight or when Salvadoran guerrillas lost support because of their own brutality, the United States declared a victory and went home.

With Yugoslavia, the roles reversed. Washington strategists depicted the Serbs as fearsome warriors. A whiff of quagmire hung over the forests and mountains where Tito's partisans stopped Germans during World War II and kept Stalin at a distance. But careful correspondents had a different message. Serbs were not supermen. Mostly, the Germans had sidestepped them. In World War I, the Austrians chased them all the way past Albania. The Serbs had legitimate grievances but unreasonable demands. When they began shelling civilians, Western leaders determined to save lives had every option, from muscular diplomacy to smart bombs. NATO or the United Nations could have blunted aggression without taking sides.

All ethnic groups had reasons for fear and hatred. Croatian fascists massacred Serbs in death camps and in villages during World War II; Serbs murdered Croats; Bosnians were brutal all around. Under Tito's firm postwar rule, none was made to pay to the others' satisfaction. Croatia insisted on separation in 1991 and victimized Serbs in overlapping border areas. Serbia began to settle the score. At first, each side brutalized the other. Then the Serbs committed mass murder, raining artillery on Croatian cities. Later in Bosnia-Herzegovina, they did much worse.

Time after time, units of the Yugoslav federal army swung in behind Serb irregulars because no one called them on it. Towns were pounded to rubble. For months, late in 1991, Yugoslav gunboats lay unchallenged off Dubrovnik and shelled an Old World treasure as thrilling as Venice, not to speak of the hundred thousand souls living in its precincts.

A chorus of world figures urged the United States to take the lead, as it had in Iraq. But Bush had an excuse to hang back. This was a European problem, and a newly united European Community had said it would handle it. The twelve states were moving toward common political and defense policies. Here was the first test. U.S. strategists suspected the Europeans would fail, but that made little difference. This was a tar baby they did not need.

The picture quickly darkened. Europe proved incapable of stopping the Serbs. On the contrary, Slobodan Milosevic and his hard-line chieftains had read the situation right. They had carte blanche to bull their way toward a Greater Serbia. In Bosnia-Herzegovina, Radovan Karadzic, the Serbian leader, devised something very close to a final solution for Muslims in a republic that had always been their home. Called "Muslims," they were Serbs and Croats who had embraced Islam under the Turks. Only a missing foreskin made them different. No matter. With help from Serbia, Bosnian Serbs could have "ethnic cleansing."

By mid-July, reporters had painted a clear picture of what was happening. Roy Gutman of *Newsday* exposed the Serbs' concentration camps in Bosnia, where people were penned in cages, stacked four high. A British television crew showed prisoners near death. Evidence revealed a plan to annihilate Muslims and burn their homes. Serbian troops raped women by the tens of thousands to humiliate Muslims. U.N. teams watched, essentially helpless. Relief food arrived at the Serbs' pleasure. At one checkpoint, Serbian soldiers opened the back of a U.N. armed personnel carrier. Standing in a row, mocking and laughing, they pissed inside.

When Gutman wrote about the camps, he expressed surprise that Washington had not investigated. Others wondered the same thing. U.N. officers had known about them for a month. By then Bush had a new rationale: All sides were guilty. It wouldn't be prudent to interfere. This flew in the face of reality. Serbs had acted with vicious premeditation. Muslims, hardly blameless, had sought revenge. But their victims did not begin to approach the scores of thousands they were losing to genocide. The Serbs, well-armed before Yugoslavia collapsed, easily resupplied stocks by evading sanctions. The Muslims, who could not circumvent the sanctions, were barely able to defend themselves.

Thoughtful commentators said what should have been obvious. "Once again, as at Munich in 1938, the chief concern of Paris and London—and today Washington—is not to prevent or reverse aggression, but to find a face-saving way to avoid doing so," William Pfaff wrote in August. "The West still refuses to deliver arms to the

Bosnians and embargoes others from doing so." Stopping a war of conquest, religious purges and murder seems a simple enough principle to defend, he concluded. "Unfortunately, Washington, London and Paris seem unwilling to defend it, or even to admit that this is indeed the principle at stake."

Reporters in Sarajevo, including Pfaff at one point, laid out the facts in dramatic detail. In the 1990s, however, nothing is real if it is not on television. TV coverage was erratic, and conflicting reports blurred the picture. One evening, CBS showed someone's videotape of twenty-eight Serbs who had been mutilated by the enemies Karadzic had aroused. Narration from London said this was evidence that both sides were guilty. A Serb was shown condemning the butchery, tears in his eyes. It was Karadzic.

When Amnesty International released tape of Serbian atrocities, a State Department spokesman remarked, "This makes my stomach turn and my blood boil." No action was planned, he added. A CBS report from London explained that intervention would require hundreds of thousands of men—the Washington line. It was not explained how the reporter knew this, guessing from four countries away.

There was also incisive, poignant television reporting, and eventually Bosnia got to be a household word. But by the time the message had penetrated that the killing had to be stopped, the Pentagon said it was too late. Principles were principles, but the Serbs were too entrenched for the doctrine of overwhelming force. Generals preferred battles they could win without cost. Britain and France demurred. Hostilities would endanger their troops in the stopgap U.N. force that had been sent in the absence of stronger action. Allies agreed on a "no-fly zone," but they neglected to enforce it, encouraging the Serbs to resist.

Americans watched, swallowing their professed morality, while people who had survived ethnic cleansing died of exposure, one after another, in a freezing Sarajevo with no power, fuel, firewood, water or world powers to save them. All winter, shells landed on the city while the Serbs stalled for time in endless negotiation.

Warning voices grew louder. Former CIA director William Colby noted that analysts had exaggerated the Serbs' war record and neglected to factor in modern weaponry. Much more than persuasion was possible. "An inability to face down Serbs engaged in heinous war crimes would demoralize the West, and destroy the credibility of the United Nations," he said. "The very notion of sanctions would be discredited by failure." Next would be Kosovo and Macedonia, which might bring in Greece, Turkey, Albania and Bulgaria and force Russia to take sides.

Before leaving his job in January 1993, Eagleburger said the administration was convinced that the Serbs could not be defeated unless massive ground forces were committed. If air strikes did not work, then what? "I'm bothered by it on a personal level," he told reporters, "but I'm not as bothered by it professionally as I am sure you think I should be. If these people are intent on killing each other for what any sane American has to judge are totally irrational reasons, then the ability of the United States to cope with that, particularly alone, has to be recognized as limited." Unless allies forged an overpowering coalition, it was a problem "for which at this stage there is no answer that is within the realm of what any of the major powers are prepared to do."

In other words, it was too late for any of the other options that might have worked during the year and a half when people had watched it steadily worsen.

Bill Clinton criticized Bush on Bosnia and said he would do more. After three weeks in the White House, he came up with a plan: more negotiation. If there was peace, the United States would help keep it. Pressed to move, Clinton decided to send a message. U.S. C-130s dropped food from two miles up. They missed the target, and they also missed the point. The vaunted symbol of American concern was, in fact, confirmation to the Serbs that the world was afraid of them. As Western leaders talked of punishing war crimes without trying to stop them, one culprit snorted, "They'll never get me." Possibly not.


In November, a *Washington Monthly* article offered a rare insight into how these things work. It began, "The Bush administration pronouncements on the Yugoslav crisis between February and August exhibited the worst sort of hypocrisy. I know; I wrote them." It was by George Kenney, who resigned as the State Department desk officer. "My job was to make it appear as though the U.S. was active and concerned about the situation and, at the same time, give no one the impression that the U.S. was actually going to do something significant about it."

He wrote, "The trick in that instance was to ignore any facts—whether they pertained to atrocities, rumors of concentration camps, or starvation—that would complicate the policy goal of not getting involved. . . . Bosnia was an instance in which good policy does not make good politics, and Bush was committed to staying aloof for reasons that, as far as I could tell, had everything to do with cowardice, apparently fearing an election-year backlash for intervening abroad."

Reporters knew much more than diplomats, he said, because they could move around. When Gutman's camp stories appeared, he urged an investigation. Officials did nothing until shocking television footage brought public reaction. "Policy was media-driven, responding only when confronted by what the press had been able to find out, and then in ways that were entirely inadequate."

Officials were not prepared to believe press reports, but they did not seek information on their own. The State Department brass, Kenney said, were like children who block out the world by covering their ears and humming loudly. While declining to investigate, officials also withheld the information they had. At least five hundred incidents reported by the U.S. embassy in Belgrade were not forwarded to the United Nations.

At the State Department, policymakers decided that Sarajevo was not starving. "The [European] bureau judged from CNN pictures of Sarajevans running from mortar fire that there were still plenty of well-fed people," he said. "The front office was so committed to stasis that eventually it no longer believed reports of starvation from our embassy in Belgrade." Officials seized opportunities to find fault with Croatians and Bosnians, "denying the overwhelming preponderance of evidence that Serbia was responsible for the conflict."

In guidance for U.S. press officers, Kenney referred to Serbian shelling; the Serbs had a hundred heavy guns around Sarajevo, and the Muslims had fewer than a dozen. But senior officials pressed the briefers to blame "all sides." He concluded: "The system is there to make our country look good, as opposed to making it do good, and it is politicized from top to bottom. Currently, the only way to make an audible sound of protest is to resign."

If the sound was heard in Washington, it made little echo. Except for that flurry of interest when the camps were discovered, Americans did not seem to care. Well into the second year of siege, after Serbs grabbed three-quarters of Bosnia, Clinton was still only talking.

The reporting was there from the start, where anyone who looked could find it. From the first rumblings in Croatia and Slovenia early in 1991, through the Dubrovnik shelling, the AP never missed a day, fielding as many as a dozen people at a time. Tony Smith of the Vienna bureau weathered much of the Sarajevo siege, and others were there when he was not. Any newspaper could have followed developments in detail, and many did. Some sent their own people. CNN dug in; ABC tried hard. All networks and television stations had access to footage.

But the news that most viewers and readers got was sporadic and confusing. Dubrovnik was hardly noticed; weeks went by without a mention on the air. By the time the situation in Bosnia grew desperate, people were inoculated to the low-grade repetition of similar-sounding headlines. Reporting from the spot was diluted by Washington-dated news stories and commentary based on interviews with officials who stressed the dangers of getting involved.

Far from the bloodshed, for instance, Charles Krauthammer wrote in the *Washington Post:* "Bosnia interventionists strain mightily to produce some U.S. national interest. . . . These efforts have come to little." Later, he pronounced the Serbs' advance to be one civil war among many in the world. "The United States will not stand by if another people is dying and there is a way to save it," he wrote. But Bosnia was too much trouble. "This may not be the loftiest principle of humanitarian intervention, but it is better than the rest."

This view is obscene, countered William Pfaff, who had scrambled from the guns in Sarajevo. "It is very grave to invite the contempt of the enemies, as we are doing," he wrote in the *Los Angeles Times.* "As the amoral Machiavelli himself warned, the prince who invites contempt, by inaction or irresoluteness in defense of his interests, becomes known as a useless friend and a despicable enemy. After that, 'he will find himself utterly lost.' " Instead of seeing national interest in terms of Vietnam or Iraq, he said, Americans might think of Munich. Appeasing Hitler had brought "peace in our time" and the devastation of Europe.

Editorial pages were rich in enlightened comment. After leaving the State Department, Kenney wrote a column with Gen. Michael Dugan, the Air Force commander who had been fired for excessive frankness in the Gulf War. They explained how Americans could intervene at low risk—and what would happen if they didn't.

Margaret Thatcher, the former British prime minister, scalded governments on both sides of the Atlantic for ignoring their principles and rewarding aggression. Never mind the price, she said. Intervention was the right thing to do. When Secretary of State Warren Christopher called her remarks "emotional," she retorted, "I should hope so."

Another Briton, John le Carré, picked up this theme at a Boston speech urging the people who had beaten communism to rise to new heights of humanity. He mocked what he called the doubters' "same old sneering cry: 'We're being too emotional.' " He went on: "And, of course, they are right. Except. Except that, if there is one eternal truth of politics, it is that there are always a dozen good reasons for doing nothing. To do something, you've got to want to do it. Like, for instance, Desert Storm or the Falklands." Whatever happens, he concluded, "I don't think there's any way on earth the United States can escape the responsibility for repeated and risky foreign intervention in the coming decades."

Although delay had increased the risk, some wrote, innocents had to be shielded. Surely, our threshold for genocide had been reached. Elie Wiesel, borrowing from the Bible, made the point: "Thou shalt not stand idly by." If Americans do not shame others into action, William Safire wrote in the *New York Times,* hundreds of thousands will die. "And this time," he said, "thanks to new global communication, we would see the deadly result of our moral cowardice in vivid color."

At the crux, the question was whether this was civil war and, therefore, the world could excuse itself from responsibility. But reality was there for anyone who looked. From June, reporters and camera crews tracked the Serbs' advance, step by step. In August, *Newsweek's* war-hero military writer, David Hackworth, went for a look. Over forty years, he'd seen as much action as anyone. This was no civil war, he wrote. "This is indiscriminate violence and mindless slaughter." In another column, however, he warned of the q-word. This stank of quagmire.

By May 1993, correspondents agreed on a single point: Serbian leaders believed themselves to be unstoppable because no one was trying to stop them. A lot more real estate might fit into a Greater Serbia. And a Balkan war could lead anywhere if not circumscribed by diplomacy or force.

But in May, thirteen months after Serbs attacked, an NBC News–*Wall Street Journal* poll reported that 58 percent of respondents felt all sides were equally to blame and another 21 percent weren't sure. Only 16 percent blamed the Serbs. I spoke to a friend back home, a retired housewife who reads two papers a day and watches TV news faithfully. Intelligent and caring, she would break up a fight among alley cats if she saw one. "It's a civil war," she told me, "and we shouldn't get involved."

Government strategists knew it was hard enough to focus American attention on anything foreign, let alone someplace where people's names ended in itch. Washington invented its own, more convenient Yugoslavia. The press—the media, now—did not keep reality in plain view the way Teddy White would have expected. That critical mass never formed. Someone had stolen the news.

Americans have a national interest in everything that disturbs the planet, even if the connection is less obvious than oilfields. But war, once aflame, is hard to stop and harder to keep stopped. The time to act was during the siege of Dubrovik, not that of Sarajevo. Napoleon made the point when a cornered general asked for advice. The solution, he said, is not to get into such a mess in the first place. Napoleon insisted on receiving dependable dispatches, and he read them. In the end, America shut its eyes and stepped aside.

It seems likely that the American people, had they been better informed in a way that touched them, would have pressed for action in time. Perhaps not. We will never know. Instead, it was as Eagleburger said. Policy was left to professionals.

The gulf has always been wide between foreign bureaus and Washington offices. In some ways, it is narrowing. Many Washington reporters, correspondents who have come home, know the pitfalls of seeing other cultures through their own optic. Some coordination is improving. At the *New York Times* and the *Los Angeles Times,* Washington stories on world affairs are handled by the foreign desk. In the past, both papers occasionally ran two separate stories side by side on the same event, one from up close and the other from Washington; they did not always match.

But Beltway blindness may be incurable. Too often foreign dispatches are received at home as so much junk mail to be stuffed in crevices Washington does not fill. The State Department's noon briefing is an institution. Each day, press officers gather early to scour the papers. During the morning, they huddle with desk officers and their bosses to make up a briefing book. By 12:30, they have defined the world. Answers are ready to all likely questions. They are rarely surprised. If there is something to sell in a policy announcement, this is the time. It might be Panama's turn. Or Germany's. The briefer sketches situations as the administration sees them. Intended or not, the spin is always there. No one attends from other countries to give their versions.

Something similar happens at the White House and the Pentagon. On Capitol Hill, legislators have their own views to pitch. Reporters canvass diplomats, lobbyists, think tank types and eminent has-beens. Their stories should add to a larger picture. But frequently they *are* the larger picture. Dispatches from the field are shunted aside, if they are available at all. However astute a journalist may be, covering foreign events from a domestic capital is second-hand reporting. It may be valuable, but it is never enough. There is no substitute for being on the spot.

In news by briefing, history often begins when the source enters the room. When Saddam Hussein was suddenly reviled as a Hitler who was endangering the American way of life, not many reporters noted that during the previous year Iraq was second only to Mexico in receiving U.S. Department of Agriculture credits. (Fewer still suspected that American agents knew Saddam had used some of them to develop a nuclear arsenal.)

Logically, foreign staffs and Washington bureaus would pool ideas and information. It seldom works that way. When the Vietnam War was raging full blast, Singapore devised a Southeast Asian diplomatic framework that eventually helped the Americans to leave. Had it been nurtured at the start, this breakthrough might have spared us years of war. Some Washington colleagues came to Singapore with a secretary of state, and we correspondents based there tried to brief them over lunch. The topic never veered from who would run for vice president back home three years hence.

I mentioned this years later to the Washington bureau chief of a major news organization. "That's the way it should be," he snapped. He mentioned a story he had seen from Paris about U.S.-French relations that gave François Mitterrand's point of view. "Who cares?" he concluded. "It's Reagan who counts." He may be right. But that is why generals are surprised when pilots have to fly via the Azores to bomb Libya from Britain.

If more editors are now at least trying to weed out inconsistencies, the gulf remains. Inevitable human conflicts intervene. During the pivotal Mikhail Gorbachev period, one television network's Moscow correspondent ran mysteriously afoul of a New York editor. He was an excellent reporter, a Russian speaker who knew Moscow well. But his work was repeatedly pushed aside in favor of reports on the Soviet Union from the White House correspondent in Washington. Finally, he moved on.

Not only reporters but also editors have their sources in Washington. As Iraq girded for a showdown in the Gulf, one newsweekly's Middle East correspondent received a guidance cable from his chief. "Our best sources say that Saddam is only posturing," it declared. He knew better; he also knew this perception would affect how editors handled the story that week.

It is the natural order of things for Washington journalists to put faith in their sources. With all the exceptions that exist, many of them relish their proximity to power or simply fall unwittingly into line. They pamper their favorite insiders. As Noam Chomsky puts it, more or less, their thinking is limited to a narrow band width. During Vietnam, young realists in the field were chastised for not being part of "the team." The Washington dissenters are remembered still, reporters at the edge like the late I. F. Stone, who was viewed by the team captains with the amused tolerance allotted to lovable loonies.

Over years of close proximity, the community of Washington reporters interested in foreign affairs has evolved into a closed society that might have confused the doges of Venice. Grand old-timers set the tone, and younger hopefuls hover at their elbows. Some of these are excellent reporters, with distinguished records abroad. But with very little comparing of notes, an accepted wisdom soon emerges on each major issue. Only the very secure, the iconoclasts or the foolishly reckless strike out alone.

Stephen Hess, a media analyst at the Brookings Institution, has taken the measure of this inner circle. The most satisfied, with the highest prestige and therefore the heaviest clout, are the diplomatic reporters. Then come the White House reporters.

Foreign correspondents enter town as country cousins, possibly skilled in their own specialties but ignorant of the court language of power. This applies when Washington takes to the road. At a conference on chemical weapons in Paris, I phoned New York to interview an expert who had just left a senior Defense Department job. Hours after my dispatch moved on the wire, a Washington duke from a large paper stopped me. "I see you quoted ———," he said, naming the man. His smirk added tacitly, "Don't you know he's not on our list?"

Tracing official links to drug smuggling, I spent hours at the Christic Institute, a flaky haven of public-interest activists. Their credibility was low, but their files were terrific. Cabinets bulged with documents, phone lists, clippings and background reports. Press officers were anxious to help. And few Washington reporters would be caught dead within blocks of the place. This might be reasonable if they had better sources. But the drug connection was pinned down only at the edges: in *Vanity Fair* and the *Nation,* in a few books, in public television documentaries, among other places. The "major media" sometimes got close to it but then backed off.

(Cautionary interjection: Beware, here and elsewhere, of generality. There are exceptions, and these judgments hardly cover everyone. A lot of broad-viewed Washington reporters have helped me over the years. Some vital aspects of foreign stories come out of Washington. But this is the pattern.)

This self-assuredness extends to long-distance reporting from Washington. The same man who smirked at my use of an unclean defense source wrote about a secret U.S. government report on humanitarian aid to Bosnia. A quarter of food relief went to Serbs, he said. He did not mention that Serbs made up a quarter of the people around Sarajevo. "I wish they had given the story to someone who had been there," remarked Sylvana Foa, spokeswoman of the U.N. High Commissioner for Refugees and a former UPI foreign editor. "Either someone leaked to him only a small part and he bought it, or he chose to focus on a detail. The real point of the report was to show why the United States should intervene."

In Washington, official dissent comes from another community of all-purpose free-floating foreign analysts. These include former diplomats who now teach, magazine writers with time on their hands and bona fide foreigners who have settled in the United States. Television sanctifies them because of its constant need to fill the screen. When big stories break, producers rush to their Rolodexes to put on their air what Ed Cody of the *Post* calls the washing machine. "They just tumble around ideas, over and over," he explains. "People think it is news to have two experts argue over some event. In the end it's only two professors shouting at each other. That's not news."

Washington and foreign correspondents often meet in the field. The world at large offers a handy backdrop for politicians and officials who need to beef up their credentials. During the Bush years, the White House sent Dan Quayle to forgotten blotches of the globe to broaden his horizons and take care of minor business. Sometimes, it was his wife, Marilyn, who went.

During the Bangladesh cyclone of 1991, when a U.S. amphibious force was sent to help deliver emergency food, Mrs. Quayle went for reasons which were not clear. For days, the helicopter airlift was paralyzed. Choppers that were not assigned to ferry around her official party stood by as backup. At each stop, an aide set up spontaneous pictures as photographers waited patiently for him to finish. He rounded up skinny kids and shooed away those who looked too well fed. Once, as U.S. Marines humped 123-pound sacks of grain, Mrs. Quayle posed in the line as though she was carrying one of the bags. When it was over, a Marine dispatcher calculated that for each seat occupied by the official entourage and press corps, he could have sent a family of six enough food for a month.

More often the visits are "codels," congressional delegations meant to give legislators a close-up look at situations they talk about in committee. The idea is sound; hobnobbing with the players and seeing the terrain beats reading someone else's assessment. Correspondents have a chance to learn something about policy and perceptions from Washington insiders. In practice, however, codels usually end up reconfirming the reporters' worst fears about Washington.

As Armenians fought Azeris late in 1991, I heard in Moscow that a congresswoman from a Western state would visit Nagorno-Karabakh, the Armenian enclave in Azerbaijan. This took guts, I thought, and I went to join her. In Armenia, the trip was called off. Someone told her it would be dangerous. Instead, she would see victims of a past earthquake. Refugees are refugees. Her party, burning scarce fuel in a dozen cars, climbed the mountain to Kirovakan. The mayor smiled bravely when we invited ourselves to dinner. Hospitality is a sacred trust among Armenians, even when they have nothing. At dusk, we drove miles more to a house where someone was roasting a cherished goat in our honor. But there was no running water. Someone explained to the visitor that water had been cut since the earthquake; they'd worked out hygiene. Too risky, she said. Hepatitis. We would go immediately. She offered to pay, compounding the insult into grave offense.

The woman meant well. She was no dud; the next year she took a step up in politics. She just did not understand the cultural gulf. It was sobering. She was at the high end of the people who make laws on international issues and appropriate funds for foreign policy. I found myself wondering what legislators read before setting out to define a world they did not fathom.

Peter Arnett must have wondered this when he heard Sen. Alan Simpson of Wyoming pile on to vilify Saddam. Simpson suggested that Arnett had comforted the enemy in Baghdad because, by some McCarthyist misreading of facts, he had a Vietnamese Communist in his family. The year before, Simpson touched his forelock to Saddam, in Baghdad, and advised him that the only problem he had was "the Western media."

After the 1992 elections brought a surge of new blood into Congress, there was cause for hope. That is, until *Spy* magazine brought us back to reality. Posing as a radio talk-show host, a *Spy* ringer called a selection of new members of Congress to ask about policy toward Freedonia. Most answered in learned detail, urging decisive action or warning that involvement could mean a quagmire that lasted ten years. Freedonia, of course, existed only in Groucho Marx's head, in the film *Duck Soup*.

I talked about this with an old source I had grown to respect. Jack Blum, a lawyer with legs, was chief investigator for Senator John Kerry's campaign against drug trafficking for the Senate Foreign Relations Committee. Blum turned over rocks and watched the bugs scurry to cover. He associated with the Senate's best and brightest, and he squared off against damage control experts in the State Department and the Attorney General's office. When most of his findings were blocked in committee, he left government, disgusted, to do well as an international consultant.

"The best, more knowledgeable Americans have cartoon knowledge of the world," he said, "and in trying to get into the details, you lose them. The Russians understand this. They're learning all about spin control. They've hired PR firms which taught them all the buzz words." And in Washington, he said, buzz words are usually enough. The main one is democracy. "This is ridiculous,"

Blum said. "Without justice, democracy is worthless. Without a semblance of fairness, democracy is simply a contest among the crooks over who gets the power to steal."

Unburdened by the actual facts, he said, American officials determine foreign policy and then implement it beneath the surface. "We have lost the concept of correctness in foreign policy, of any investment in overt policy," he explained. "You take biggest bully on the block, and let him do it for you, and you have normal relations on the surface. The public can't debate this, can't bring it out. We destroy the credibility of people who want to speak out. It is much harder to do overt foreign policy. You have to educate people and hold public forums."

Blum ticked off examples from all over the globe. "Look at all the garbage governments we've created without public discussion. Now it is coming home to us." Having just returned from Somalia, I could see his point. "Politicians lie, it gives them the freedom to do what they want. If not knowingly to the public, then they lie to themselves. Then they can go off and do anything they want."

Because the press neither sounds the alarm nor keeps the record, Blum said, the way is clear. "There is nothing to connect liars to the truth. The Soviets cruised on empty for ten years. Saddam was never the threat he was painted as being. In the United Nations, it is one lie after another. The government has lied so much that it can't figure out what the truth really is. Now the question is, Can anyone in government speak the truth and survive anymore?"

He had seen a Defense Department assessment which warned that the Soviet economy might outstrip the American economy by 2000; it was pulled back before distribution just as the Soviet Union began to collapse. Blum sees this sort of thing often in Washington. "If bureaucracies can operate without restraint," he concluded, "somewhere there has to be a reality connection."


The reality connection is supposed to be built into the American way of doing things. When government policy slips below the surface, reporters are expected to dig down and have a look. But if their main sources are the officials and legislators behind the policies, the record cannot be kept straight in Washington alone. A young AP colleague who tried to make sense of the early years in El Salvador, observed, "You realized when you read the stories out of Washington that they were totally clueless, outright lying, about what was going on."

For a check on reality, it is up to foreign correspondents to report what they see and hear on the spot. But often they can't. Reason and definition originate within the Beltway. From this optical base, policymakers and newspeople of influence see the hinterlands, in eastern Maryland or the Middle East. After the Gulf War, a familiar voice wrapped this up during a seminar at the University of California at Berkeley. Ed Cody put it:

> A really important problem, one that we saw demonstrated to an extraordinary degree in the Gulf conflict, is the concentration in Washington of how things are conceived and issues defined. It's a problem that I have faced over the years, and I think there's an evolution in the wrong direction with the definition of the story increasingly happening in Washington. Great newspapers spend ... $450,000 a year for a correspondent, and then they allow the problem to be defined in Washington more and more.
>
> An avalanche of information comes out of the U.S. government. They do it with such intensity and such volume that almost automatically it becomes the definition of what's happening. Anyone in Saudi Arabia, in Kuwait, in Baghdad, who has the temerity to approach the problem from a different angle, to say wait a minute, this is the situation, I'm here, I'm talking to this person Mohammed and he tells me that's the way it looks from his point of view—that voice is not rejected, it's simply ignored or its volume is not at a level that can compete with the volume of information coming out of what is essentially the U.S. government and its agenda.

That, of course, explains the contradiction between Eagleburger and Teddy White. Although White's reading is still correct in theory, sometimes even in practice, government has figured out how the system works. Press reports from abroad amount to a low-volume cacophony, as complex as the world they reflect. An official master of ceremony has only to pick among the sounds and then walk over with the microphone. The "media," with their own mikes and spotlights, could aim elsewere. But Cody is right. They seldom do.

Chapter 13

# How Others
# See It

A Japanese journalist, poking around North Carolina for a retro-
spective article on Pearl Harbor, asked a high school student to say
the first thing that came into her mind at the mention of Japan. She
replied, "Tiananmen Square." This was no surprise to Hiroko Kobayashi, a metro reporter from Kyoto on a graduate studies program
in Chapel Hill. Asked what Americans knew about Japan, she gave
an apologetic giggle at uncharacteristic bluntness. "Nearly nothing,"
she said. "I was amazed."

Kobayashi was in North Carolina during what one national poll
of newspaper editors later judged to be one of the most important
world events of 1991. A Japanese official called American workers
lazy. That was Yoshio Sakurauchi, speaker of the lower house of
Parliament. Soon afterward, the prime minister was quoted as having said something similiar. Resulting outrage bordered on cultural
holy war, endangering Chinese Americans all over the country.

It seemed amazing enough that foreign politicians could touch
off such sensitivity by expressing an opinion; Americans were free
enough with their own cultural stereotypes. More amazing, Koba-
ashi found, was that the furor was all the result of a misunderstanding. The remarks, pulled out of context and exaggerated in translation and retelling, were enough to trigger retaliation.

When she saw an article in the *Durham Herald-Sun* that began, "Japanese Prime Minister Kiichi Miyazawa fired a stinging shot Monday in the escalating war of words with the United States," she went back to the original Japanese and the circumstances. In remarks to a Liberal Democratic Party leader, she found, Miyazawa said Japan's economic bubble seemed to have burst. Then he expounded: "Looking at what things have come to over the past ten years, we might say the interpretation of producing things or creating value has become very loose. After this bubble, both countries now have a lot to clean up in the aftermath, and all of our people learned a lot from this. It is very important to build things of value with the sweat of our brow."

This might have been Lee Iacocca or any American economist drawing conclusions from the Michael Milken trial. Miyazawa, like the legislator earlier, was saying that workers in the United States and in Japan were losing the work ethic. If the two linked giant economies did not concentrate more on goods rather than financial operations and nonproductive services, the world could be headed for serious hard times. But some American readers might have missed Kobayashi's commentary on page eleven of the March 4, 1992, edition of the *Herald-Sun:*

> While writing about the increase in Japanese land prices and the stock market for my newspaper, I watched investors pour huge amounts of money into real estate and money markets and reap big profits without working. I've recently heard Japanese parents accuse their children of lacking ambition and dedication. And I have witnessed college graduates, even in scientific fields, gravitating toward high-paying jobs with banks and securities companies instead of those in manufacturing.
>
> This is what Miyazawa meant. . . . [He] did criticize American workers. But the sad thing is that the news media made things worse. News reports seemed to create negative images of Japan and cause misunderstandings.

She wondered at the philosophy of aiming a "Buy American" campaign at avoiding Japanese products. Wouldn't it make more sense to buy American in order to strengthen U.S. domestic industries? In any case, she said, by operating in ignorance, consumers cannot tell which is which. Kobayashi drove a Ford in Japan; it was made by Mazda. In America, she drives a Mercury, built mostly of Mazda parts. Both, she said, run about the same. Japanese stores are filled with Campbell's Soup and Budweiser.

"What makes me worry," she concluded, "is the feeling of *kembei,* or resentment of America, that has recently arisen among Japanese. Some feel the United States has pushed Japan too much to change its business systems, and that American criticisms fly in the face of reason. . . . People in both countries should try harder to understand one another rather than merely criticizing and trying to impose their own ideologies. Fifty years have passed since Pearl Harbor. . . . Japan should not remain a mysterious and Far East country in the minds of Americans, and Americans should not be enemies in the eyes of the Japanese."

What Kobayashi did not say is that Japanese tend to know much more about the United States than Americans know about Japan. Japanese may have strong feelings, for or against, but these are likely to be based on some familiarity. When they see Americans react viscerally, even sympathetic feelings are put to a test. By and large, this applies to foreign cultures across the board. We understand others less than they understand us. Some people are hurt; others are hostile.

This knowledge is impossible to measure. But there is the old reporter's tool: feel. The readings are unmistakable. Whenever I speak to foreign residents in the United States, especially journalism students at universities, I ask what they have read or seen about their country since leaving home. The most common response, from Swazis to Swedes, is a disgusted snort. When I travel, from Swaziland to Sweden, I check out what is reported about the United States. It is often quirky and sometimes inaccurate, but it is plentiful enough to create a fair picture.

Newspapers and television in almost every sizable country pay more attention to international news than the American media. Partly this is because of the shadow principle. Tall objects cast shadows on shorter ones, in a decreasing effect. The United States, the only remaining superpower with the world's largest economy, throws its symbolic shadow over other countries. Costa Ricans, in their own interest, need to know more about the United States than Americans do about Costa Rica. That is the theory. But over and over, we learn the hard way about some new backwater we should have better understood, such as Vietnam, Nicaragua or Iraq.

Today, no one casts that much of a shadow. According to Lester Thurow's head-to-head premise, economies no longer have secure niches in the world. Countries have comparative advantages, such as long experience or raw material deposits. But, in the broad sense, everyone competes in an open market. Each country shapes its own industries, trade policies and import legislation. The winners are those who best understand the customers, and the competition.

A few courageous academics have tried to put numbers to comparative coverage of foreign news, but the literature, as academics say, is sparse. One study published in 1981 looked at sixty newspapers from nine countries over a single week in 1970. Though far out of date, the trends still apply. Counting up inches is of dubious value. Soviet bloc papers used the most foreign news. That is because only 2 percent of their space went to advertising, and good domestic news was in short supply. The more important question is what the foreign news said.

But for their survey, in the *Journal of Communications,* George Gerbner of the University of Pennsylvania and George Marvanyi of Hungarian Television did a lot of work. When they compared oranges with oranges, a picture emerged. Among the capitalist press, Germany's *Die Welt* devoted 44 percent of its news hole to foreign news; its name means "The World." The *Times of India* used 25 percent of its space for overseas stories. The *Times* of London's figure was 22 percent. For the *New York Times,* it was 16 percent. And the New York *Daily News'* percentage was 7. A similar study in 1951 showed almost the same numbers for the London *Times* and the *New York Times.*

Any correspondent can offer anecdotal evidence to suggest even bigger differences just by looking at who is standing nearby when the swarm gathers. However many inches end up in print or what gets on the air, there is no doubt about who are taking the trouble to see things for themselves.

In terms of proportionate size, the United States lags far behind most European countries in overseas coverage. *El Pais* of Madrid has almost as many foreign correspondents as the *Washington Post,* and *El Mundo* is not far behind. On a typical day in 1993, *El Pais* carried thirteen bylines from reporters abroad. One dispatch from Tajikistan covered an entire page, explaining the impact of a largely ignored rebellion on any new world order. *La Vanguardia* of Barcelona, in Spain's second city, has a permanent staff on the move. At news conferences in far-flung places, the forest of microphones were once marked CBS, NBC and ABC. Now they bear symbols for Portuguese television or France's third channel.

Tokyo's *Yomiuri Shimbun* and *Asahi Shimbun* each has nearly sixty correspondents abroad, twice as many as the the *New York Times*. *Mainichi Shimbun* has thirty-two. The Japanese state television network, NHK, keeps fifty-two people overseas, more than ABC, NBC and CBS combined. And four private Japanese networks each has a larger foreign staff than CNN's.

On big stories, correspondents are likely to turn up from India, or Venezuela. Quality varies widely, not only from country to country but also within each national system of news gathering. The French, who on occasion consider themselves the inventors of modern journalism, are worth a close look.

Albert Londres, the great French reporter of generations back, set a tone that inspires his successors. "Londres is less concerned with exactness than with truth," his editor once remarked. This sounds suspiciously like what some other editors might call sloppiness with the facts. But it is the main difference between the French approach and what we learn in the first hour in Journalism 101. Reporting American style is to isolate facts as building blocks toward a story. In the Londres school, facts are only facts. They do not necessarily add up to reality. "I am neither a historian nor a futurist," Londres wrote. "I deal with the present."

This style, which predates Victor Hugo, carries into television. When correspondents go out to cover the news, they look for *un sujet,* a subject which reflects the news itself in allegory. But there is air time for coverage. France's three networks can be far more aggressive, though not necessarily more skilled, than the over-the-air American networks. Major world stories might fill up to half of the evening newscasts, and each network has at least three major news shows. Some crews tend to get overcreative. During a terrorist scare, a TF1 correspondent sent a phony bomb through security at Kennedy Airport to film the reaction of authorities. They arrested him.

A good French reporter can take a reader to the heart of a story, describing not only sights and sounds but also the human nuances many Americans miss. But a bad one is prone to shoot from the hip, blowing barroom talk into news analysis with a marked shortage of legwork and facts. Since literary style is so important to French journalism, it can be hard to tell one from the other. Even when French reporting is good, it helps to know each paper's tendency, just as readers once had to know a lot about Henry Luce to read *Time.*

*Libération* is by far the most lively French paper. It was started by grown-up leftist rock throwers who edged toward the center, and it has evolved into a thorough and thoughtful tabloid that works hard to cover the news. *Libé* reporters try to get things right, and they try even harder to reflect the flavor of a story. *Le Figaro* sells well, holding fast to a conservative viewpoint. But *Le Monde* remains the cornerstone.

*Le Monde,* started with help from Charles de Gaulle after World War II, soon earned one of the most solid reputations in international journalism. It was liberal, leaning toward left-wing, in the direction of the intellectuals it served. The style could be arcane. *Le Monde* legend tells of an editor complaining to a reporter that he could not understand the man's story on some political intrigue. "This article was written for three people," the reporter is said to have replied, "and you're not one of them."

When the Middle East suddenly loomed as a story in the mid-1970s, *Le Monde* explained its undercurrents. Reporters in Latin America saw the links between leftist terrorism and similar trends around the world. But there was that penchant to sit in Paris and pontificate. As the Khmer Rouge emerged, the paper offered a long and learned analysis about two different leaders who were fighting for control. It explored the strengths and foibles of each. As it turned out, the two were the same man, with a very long name. The writer had simply made a little mistake.

*Le Nouvel Observateur,* in 1992, published a fat section entitled "Do Journalists Lie?" It recounted how, in 1970, a French diplomat in what is now Bangladesh was about to report that tens of thousands had died in a devastating cyclone. When he heard that Lucien Bodard of *France Soir* was on his way, he raised his estimate to 500,000. "I can't report less than Bodard," he was quoted as saying. "Now I'm covered." The articles were meant as an exposé of journalists' mistakes, but they made a number of their own. They cited how "Colonel Azikwe, who had himself called the Black Scorpion," had organized executions in Biafra for cameramen in a hurry for pictures. I knew the Black Scorpion well; his name was Adekunle. Azikwe was a peace-minded politician. Adekunle was in Nigeria, not Biafra. And I never saw him stage an execution. But he was a killer, all right.

Albert Camus, who shifted between journalism and fiction without always remembering which was which, once sought to codify bias. A sharp observer, he knew that any writer's own optics inevitably colored his or her view. He wanted to publish a readers' directory which measured every newspaper's slant: its political orientation, its social attitudes, its financial pressures. Each writer would be profiled and graded to help readers restore balance for themselves. He never got around to it, which is just as well. The idea had a fatal flaw: Who would define Camus?

Britain's the *Independent,* the *Times,* the *Guardian,* and the *Financial Times* offer solid supplemental reading for Americans who are curious about other points of view. Their style is to pick a point of entry, an anecdote or an incident, and burrow deeply into a story. If done well, this method shows the layers of complexity which explain the bigger news. British reporters are seldom afraid to populate their dispatches with a full cast of characters and pertinent history. Their readers have the patience for it.

But Fleet Street also gave birth to the sensationalist tabloids, which seize on sidelight details and reduce complexity to cliche. One debonair correspondent of the *Daily Mirror,* a David Niven look-alike of immense culture, used to amuse colleagues by announcing, "It is time for me to go write my two hundred words for people who move their lips when they read."

If BBC Television is not the most lively news source, no one approaches it for consistent, measured and serious-minded coverage of world affairs. Rather than flashy anchors, it has "news readers." One story follows another, often with only backdrop photographs if no video is available. The result is a solid briefing from a range of places.

But if not quite as brutally as in the United States, BBC and private networks fight for ratings. Entertainment value elbows its way into the mix. Rupert Murdoch's Sky TV was fighting for an audience during the 1989 uprising against Nicolae Ceausescu. As it happened, I was in the telex room at the Bucharest Intercontinental where any unscrupulous correspondent, that is, all of us, could read someone else's mail. My eye fell on a message that referred to "Chow Chow." Being slightly offended at such familiarity from a person in London who had not been introduced to the fallen tyrant, I decided to read on. From Sky, it said (this is close, from memory): "Let's squeeze this story for all it's worth and keep it going as long as we can."

Anyone with a serious itch to understand the wider world is bound to be curious about how others report it. CNN offers a sampling with its "World Report," a regular feature in which television crews from other countries cover features from their own point of view. Viewers must keep in mind what they are getting. Contributions from government-run stations can offer a one-sided view on a touchy issue. One piece from Chinese television explained how life was rosy in Tibet, infuriating those who knew better. Before an international meeting on the ivory trade, Zimbabwe Broadcasting did a report on how elephants were overrunning farmers' fields, causing famine. The piece made a case for selling ivory. The East Africans' view, backed by a clear majority, was that sales should be banned. But "World Report" is a painless way to see full-blown reporting pieces and commentaries from some fine correspondents abroad, who don't happen to be American.

Some newspapers are experimenting with an exchange of reporting assignments. The *Dallas Morning News,* for example, might ask *Asahi Shimbun* to cover a country-and-western craze, or something more substantial, in Japan. *Asahi* could cover Texas with correspondents from Dallas. "We have the technology and the language translation capabilities," said Burl Osborne, publisher of *News.* "Why not? I think we'll be seeing a lot of this in the future." Obvious drawbacks suggest themselves. How many Japanese have seen an armadillo up close? But a reporter from Tokyo can tell Texans a lot about Japan, without an American cultural bias.

To delve deeply into foreign points of view, there is the redoubtable *World Press Review,* a monthly published in New York. Its editors scour the planet for commentary, short pieces of reportage and cartoons to reflect how other societies see the world. It is a good mix, well-presented, and an eye-opener to Americans who thought their own press was comprehensive.

Each year, the *Review* carries its poll of top ten stories. It reprints the AP's list, based on 153 American newspaper editors' responses, and also UPI's, with 72 responses. For comparison, there is the AP's international poll, a survey of 90 editors in forty-two countries. Five more lists show the judgment of news organizations in Britain, Hong Kong, Bangladesh, Costa Rica and Peru. As might be expected, disagreement is vast.

For 1991, the AP and UPI lists were remarkably similar. More or less in agreement, the first nine were these: Gulf War; Soviet collapse; Clarence Thomas hearings; Middle East hostage releases; U.S. economy; end of the Cold War; AIDS in America (and Magic Johnson); Jeffrey Dahmer's mass killings; and Middle East peace talks. The AP's tenth was Los Angeles police officers' beating of Rodney King. UPI's was a massacre of twenty-three in Killeen, Texas. None mentioned Yugoslavia, although Croatia and Slovenia had each fought wars for independence.

The AP international list read:

1.  The Gulf War.
2.  The Soviet coup attempt.
3.  Yugoslavia's civil war.
4.  Middle East peace talks.
5.  The end of the Cold War.
6.  South Africa dismantles apartheid.
7.  The European Community wrangles over closer integration.
8.  AIDS in the world.
9.  Cambodian peace settlement.
10. Rajiv Gandhi's assassination.

Of the five other lists, four ranked the breakup of the Soviet Union as a bigger story than the Gulf War. This was a reasonable enough view. Since those ten days that shook the world in 1917, the Soviet Union had cast a large shadow. These were the people who gave us Stalin, sputnik, the Berlin Wall and the "We will bury you" speech. Suddenly, they were a collection of banana republics and a destitute but aggressive Russia. The Gulf War was only a bunch of soldiers beating back a megalomaniac who was flexing his ego. But hardly anyone who had watched our collective coverage of the war could think anything else was more important.

Only two U.S. stories showed up on the five lists. Eduardo Ulibarri, editor of *La Nación* in Costa Rica, put the U.S. recession as No. 9, after the renewed role of the United Nations. Enrique Zileri, editor of the Peruvian weekly *Caretas,* ended his list with "Global titillation with the Thomas hearings and the William Kennedy Smith trial." Only *Dialogue* of Bangladesh failed to mention Yugoslavia. Its list included three stories from the Indian subcontinent, plus South Africa's return to sports, a major issue in that region. Geography flavored other judgments. *Asiaweek* of Hong Kong listed Thailand's military coup. And Zileri, a Peruvian, put the Middle East hostages release in a different light: "Freed hostages add luster to Secretary-General Javier Pérez de Cuéllar's farewell to the U.N."

The 1992 lists, like those in earlier years, made the same points. No one can define news, and universal news judgment is impossible. To understand how other societies think or to sense how they might react to events, it helps to look at their own media. If that's not possible, look for commentators like Hiroko Kobayashi to see what has been lost in translation.

Chapter 14

# War and Mayhem

For American correspondents, modern wars fall into two categories: those in which U.S. forces take part and the other kind. It is only natural that one would be covered more thoroughly than the other. What is amazing, however, is the distance between the extremes.

At any given time, anywhere from a dozen to half a hundred wars are percolating around the globe. In southern Sudan, the same war has gone on since the 1960s. The endless Angola war was declared over in 1992, but it wasn't over. Burmese insurgents, who went to the jungles before Americans fought in Vietnam, have not given up yet. These conflicts are all but ignored.

In *Scoop,* Lord Copper sums it up nicely: "What the British public wants first, last and all the time is News. Remember that the Patriots are in the right and are going to win. The *Beast* stands by them four-square. But they must win quickly. The British public has no interest in a war which drags on indecisively. A few sharp victories, some conspicuous acts of bravery on the Patriot side, and a colorful entry into the capital. That is the *Beast* policy for war."

Attitudes have hardly changed. Small wars in obscure places drop quickly in priority when they look as if they may drag on forever. Larger ones depend on the swarm's erratic attention, which sometimes seems directed by Lord Copper's ghost. Lebanon commanded serious coverage because of where it was and what it meant. Afghanistan, equally important, dropped off the map.

One obstacle to covering armed conflict is that there are few people to do it. For reasons which reporters who cover war find mystifying, a lot of people see glamor in the idea of being a war correspondent. In fact, there is no such thing. Editors cannot afford to keep specialists hanging around waiting for hostilities to begin. A correspondent does economic summits, plane wrecks, elections and cats up a tree. If shooting starts somewhere, available hands are called into action. Then most of them go happily back to their real work. War, in case anyone has forgotten, is hell.

Some veteran correspondents like a challenging, nasty war. But editors use their old hands judiciously. For the long haul, they prefer to send young reporters, often on their first assignment. But young or old, any staff correspondent means salary, expenses, home leave, the works. The war had better be worth it.

There is an alternative. An ample supply of hungry stringers, known as runners and gunners, volunteer with every conflict. Anxious to make their name, they are happy to take chances that wily old survivors might wish to avoid. Peter Arnett, among a lot of others, started that way. Wars also attract a whole cuckoo's nest of con men, punks and druggies for whom press credentials would be a ticket to ringside. Distant editors have to determine who is who.

The Afghanistan War brought home the dilemma. Presses stopped when Soviet troops invaded in 1979. No one missed the significance. President Jimmy Carter, seizing a chance to show backbone, declared a Cold War standoff. It was a fight to the death between Islam and godless communism. Soviet troops were largely Central Asian Muslims. Where would that lead? U.S. Stinger missiles went to rebels of dubious principles. How long before Iranian fanatics had them? By the time the last Kabul government fell in 1992, well over a million people had died. As some analysts divined at the outset, Moscow's Vietnam was instrumental in the collapse of the Soviet Union. But soon after the war started, attention wandered. Not many correspondents were interested. Editors did not push. Readers did not seem to care.

In a near vacuum, a small band of irregulars covered Afghanistan, reporters willing to disappear in the mountains for weeks on end with rebels they did not trust as far they could dropkick them. Others tried to follow events from the Pakistan side of the Khyber

Pass, a modern-day equivalent to watching the world from reflections on Plato's cave wall.

During this hit-or-miss early coverage, Dan Rather and CBS News seized on the story. Rather himself flew to Peshawar, slipped across the border with a schmatte on his head and earned the nickname "Gunga Dan." He was in Afghan costume, but we never learned the disguises of his crew and camera. The CBS "Evening News" had up to three times as much air time on the war as its two main competitors. But even CBS interest waned. Meantime, the "Evening News" shifted its emphasis away from world news. When President Mohammed Najibullah finally fell in 1992, Rather was able to squeeze only a few words into the broadcast. The words did not include Najibullah's name. It was too big a mouthful for an unprepared audience.

From start to finish, CBS and a lot of other organizations depended heavily on stringers. Some were excellent. Early on, a young reporter named Ed Girardet showed up at the *International Herald Tribune* while I was editor. He had experience with UPI. His clips were solid, and his references were enthusiastic. We had nowhere near enough good copy from the war. I gave him the weasely answer of budget-tight editors everywhere: Sure, kid. Get yourself there and if you send us something useful, we'll buy it. Others said the same thing, and he went. Later, the *Christian Science Monitor* gave him a real job. Without him, all of us would know much less about that crucial conflict. Some others were of lesser quality.

One staff correspondent smitten by the story, Mary Williams Walsh of the *Wall Street Journal,* decided to write an article about Kurt Lohbeck, a regular CBS stringer, who she said had distorted coverage for his own purposes. She also wrote about Mike Hoover, a contract CBS cameraman, who Afghans said had faked videotape. For a while, the hostilities that this triggered far outplayed the real war.

Lohbeck, who had served time in the United States for passing bad checks, was running a dubious charity in Peshawar, Walsh reported. Worse, she said, he was working hard to promote one rebel faction leader and play down the others. And, Walsh added, he was seeking to mislead and intimidate the small Afghan War press corps. When the *Journal* killed the piece, Walsh accused her editors of cowardice. She quit to join the *Los Angeles Times.* The *Columbia Journalism Review* published her material, although Walsh said the journalism dean had censored part of it.

Hoover, meanwhile, was splashed on page one of the *New York Post.* The article said he had had rebels blow up a power pylon because he had arrived too late for the real thing. Then, it said, he had others stage a battle which ended up causing casualties. John Simpson, BBC Television's foreign editor, would not show the footage.

CBS denied any wrongdoing by Lohbeck. Network officials waited for the storm to subside before quietly cutting him loose. Hoover got a similar clean bill of health. Network officials said they had examined footage and determined that nothing on the air had been faked. CBS News president David Burke defended his network, calling its Afghan coverage "fantastic."

Long after the fact, I asked Rather about the incidents. Both men showed bravery in dangerous situations, he said, and do not deserve slurs. A CBS insider, who spoke frankly on the assurance of anonymity, criticized Walsh's manner but confirmed her judgment on Lohbeck. Hoover, the insider said, was a filmmaker, and sometimes filmmakers set up their shots.

Hoover had gone to Afghanistan with the reputation of a man with an imagination. In a mountain film shot in South America, colleagues say, he placed a rubber snake on a ledge so a climber could enliven the footage by acting startled and flinging the reptile into space. Afterward, I spoke to Girardet, who strings for the "MacNeil-Lehrer Newshour," and has spent at least two years on the ground in Afghanistan over a ten-year period. He was incensed at the defense of Hoover.

"Cameramen go in and risk their lives for eight weeks and sometimes come back with nothing," he said. "That is how it is in Afghanistan. Hoover went in for a few days and came back with perfect stuff." Suspicious, Girardet studied the tape with Pakistani intelligence experts, who, he said, burst into laughter. Pakistani jets are identified as Afghan MiGs. In the same sequence, the terrain shifts from mountain to flat desert and back again. Girardet recognized an Afghani training camp in Pakistan that he had seen a dozen times. And so on. "CBS used faked film, and they are trying to cover it up to protect their reputation," Girardet said. "That is not right."

BBC's Simpson, a respected old hand, went further in *The Spectator.* He explained how Afghanistan had attracted "adventurers and crooks" who produced footage for television. "Newspapers and television organizations have often bought faked pictures without realizing it," he wrote. At the American Club in Peshawar, he added, the hard core of regulars "knew all about the various hoaxes that were perpetrated, and who was behind them." Sometimes the motives were political, such as pictures that confirmed the charge that Soviet troops had sown mines disguised as children's toys.

No professionals believe that CBS wanted to present a misleading view, Simpson said, but many think that it was overly credulous in its enthusiasm for good pictures. American news organizations, he added, "show few signs of understanding what is genuine, and what is false, out of Afghanistan."

Though a sideshow, the incident was troubling. Had news organizations paid more attention to Afghanistan, coverage would have been in the hands of known quantities. If shadowy characters lurked at the edges, more colleagues would have exposed them. In war coverage, or any other kind, credibility is the correspondent's only capital. Any editor can make a mistake and hire the wrong person. The test is what happens when mistakes come to light. The lingering impression is that CBS executives sought to defend their good name by damage control. Perhaps not. If they were right, they protected two men who had been wronged. If not, they damaged us all, correspondents, editors and the people who count on us.


Every war presents its own obstacles to coverage. Where Americans are not involved, restrictions on reporting tend to be ad hoc and haphazard. Unlike the Pentagon, with its solicitous concern for safety, other military authorities often let journalists take their chances. As often as not, reporters can travel with frontline units who are happy to have someone along to explain their cause to a largely indifferent world. In Lebanon and the collapsing Yugoslavia, no one made rules. Each faction's roadblocks usually allowed through anyone who the guards thought was a journalist not committed to a particular enemy. Correspondents had to trust their luck; the alternative could be a bullet.

When access is denied, as it was during the Falklands War, resourcefulness is stretched to its limits. Only one reporter, an NBC correspondent, sneaked into the Falklands' capital, Port Stanley, under the British blackout. He was caught after twelve hours. No one witnessed any action until the generals decided it was time. The Pentagon went green with envy.

The Iran-Iraq War was frustrating from both sides. Neither country has much use for journalists, especially when facing military embarrassment. Iraqis organized tightly controlled press trips, which seldom approached the front. On one, John Kifner of the *New York Times* got stuck in a bus with piercing Arabic music at full blast on the cassette deck. He sneaked in a Waylon Jennings tape, creating havoc with the minders.

When it suited their purpose, the Iranians took reporters close to the fighting, sending along Information Ministry escorts. Najmul Hassan, a veteran Reuters man from New Delhi, was killed by a land mine that his minder had failed to notice.

Censorship is seldom an insurmountable problem. One correspondent tried to send a dispatch from the Iraqi front which referred to Saddam Hussein as "the Iraqi strong man." A censor stopped it. He instructed the reporter to write, "the Iraqi strongest man." But learning anything substantial, or reliable, is always difficult. Few military officials tell the unvarnished truth, or at least all of it, and often there are no alternative sources. Bill Drozdiak of the *Washington Post* came upon one fanciful communiqué that said something like "Heroic Iraqi troops overcame cowardly Iranian forces hiding behind a wall and seized 300 helicopters, 400 tanks, 350 artillery pieces and two shovels." The writer meant road-building steam shovels, but that part of the communiqué was no more ridiculous than the rest.

When America goes to war, the problem is too much interest. Each time a major unit is mobilized, every substantial television station within a day's drive of its base dispatches a crew to do home-town stories. Newspaper editors with a few extra bucks in the budget send a reporter or two, a reward for noble services rendered closer to home. Columnists, commentators, even publishers join the usual swarm of correspondents. And since coverage will be scrutinized and ratings and circulations are at stake, the large organizations pull out every stop.

On its side, the Defense Department works out an elaborate strategy to handle the crush. Public affairs officers are as numerous as artillerymen. As U.S. Navy Seals slipped ashore in Mogadishu, under the glare of television lights, a wet and miserable officer paddled through the surf in his own rubber dinghy. "Gather round," he yelled to reporters who were already racing off the send what they had seen. "I'm here to brief the press."

All of this coverage and public relations work do not necessarily give the public back home a clear idea of what is happening with their blood and treasure. More often, it confounds reality. In the Gulf War, we "media personnel" took as fact the Bush administration's outrageously skewed idea of the military threat. And, like the U.S. government, we underestimated the politics of it all. And few of us learned from the experience. This is partly because U.S. officials have learned how to direct the swarm and discredit the loners who point out the failings. Even more, however, reporters and editors too often miss the point.

Our system of news gathering falls down when suddenly spurred to a faster speed. All available hands are called into action, from home base and abroad. If the conflict is good-sized, a gang of regulars is likely to turn up. Mal Browne leaves his science beat at the *New York Times* and returns to a specialty at which he has excelled since the first days of Vietnam. Tony Clifton of *Newsweek* won't miss a good fight. Each television network has its bang-bang veterans. The gang is ill-defined, but it probably numbers no more than a score. Another group of newcomers learns fast on the job. Others find themselves in over their heads.

The work, if done right, is hard and dangerous. Even the most seasoned reporters must start from scratch, finding sources, learning the terrain, plotting logistics. They have to gamble, not only with their lives but also with their time. Is it worth going up the road? Is there more to be learned at a headquarters camp? Experienced people know handy basics, such as the difference between incoming and outgoing artillery. They recognize weapons, units and tactics. And they know how to talk to troops, earning the confidence they need to worm their way in close and get straight answers to questions.

As American troops psyched themselves up for the Gulf War, I went on a minipool trip to visit Marine tankers who were sighting their guns. They were a reserve unit, just called up, but the gunnery sergeant was a tough old leatherneck with a bullet head and a face like beef jerky. If he decided to open up, he would have a lot to say. But he scowled when a busload of reporters showed up, and he did his best to ignore us.

While my colleagues climbed over the tanks, I circled around the gunny to wait for an opening. He snapped orders and studied charts as if I wasn't there. After a while, he warmed a little, and I started to move in. Just then, a reporter from New York walked up, making her round of reservists. In a half-amused, slightly snotty voice, she asked, "What do you do in real life?"

The gunny spat on the ground. "This is real life," he said, the last words he had for us that day.

In an overcovered war, good reporting is often masked by the other kind. In televised briefings, too few hard-minded pros keep hammering at the right questions. When they do, they stand out as crude, even unpatriotic. Goading a briefer for an answer can be a useful tactic. A better one is wearing him down with patient persistence. Neither is presentable on camera.

Experienced correspondents know how to use a briefing. In Vietnam, U.S. commanders fumed in frustration when, day after day, the AP's George Esper accurately reported how many B-52 strikes had hit Laos and Cambodia after they started their secret air war. They were his unwitting source. Esper, who spent a decade in Vietnam, knew how things worked. Briefers gave only the daily number of missions over North Vietnam. But George knew the past average. If the number fell short, he concluded the rest had been diverted to Laos and Cambodia. With that, confirmation was easy. He bluffed about what he already knew, and a helpful officer added details.

Then again, there is only one George Esper. Using similar simple arithmetic, he once figured out that President Lyndon Johnson had made a secret stop at Cam Ranh Bay to visit troops on his way home from Saigon. Comparing the president's departure time from Saigon and his scheduled arrival in Hawaii, George found an extra few hours. He traced the route on a map and came across the huge naval base. A master of the Tiger military phone system, he rang the switchboard. "This is (cough, cough) Esper," he said. No liar, George could make a cough sound like anything from major to field marshal. Johnson had just left, the operator said, adding a rundown of the visit.

After one nasty incident, Esper heard that a wounded soldier had been taken to a base hospital. He rang up with his useful cough and said something like, "Put me through to that new burn victim. McGillicudy, isn't it?" No, sir, the man said. It's Smith. "Right, I always get confused. Put me through." A weak voice was soon on the line. Smith gave details and suddenly stopped. A stronger voice continued. "He has passed out, sir." Esper, only halfway into the story, yelled, "Well, wake him up."

However skilled, no one can accurately report conflict from a distance. Since the Crimean War, when correspondents began covering battles in earnest, the challenge has been to get close to the action. Dozens of reporters and photographers have gotten too close over the years, dying along with the soldiers they followed. Through the Vietnam War, a journalist's nerve was about the only limitation. Anyone crazy enough to camp in a firebase about to be overrun was welcome company.

Up close, the view is always different. In January 1973, reporters in tiger camouflage clustered around a radio on Highway 1 west of Saigon listening to President Nixon tell the world the that Vietnam War was over. It was eight o'clock sharp, the moment at which all sides had agreed to cease firing while they settled on a permanent accord. Nixon was saying, ". . . the beginning of an era of peace for all mankind," but he was hardly audible. South Vietnamese jets, which had burst from the clouds to drop five-hundred-pound bombs on North Vietnamese positions, were making too much noise.

This was no surprise for correspondents and photographers who had watched military commanders grossly underestimate the threat against them while exaggerating their own impact. They understood the war and the politics behind it, and they showed both in vignettes to Americans back home: a police chief shooting a prisoner through the head, a Buddhist monk immolating himself, children engulfed in napalm flames.

In the thick of the war, Morley Safer of CBS turned a camera on a well-brushed American marine, straight off a recruiting poster, as he ignored a weeping old woman who was pleading to keep her home. As the marine touched his Zippo lighter to the thatched roof, Safer delivered his message to people back home: This is the war in Vietnam.

Decades later, the Vietnam War is seen as a benchmark for open reporting, the last instance when the press roamed free, with little interference from military minders. Even then, in fact, field correspondents fought for space with Washington reporters, short-time visitors and columnists who echoed the U.S. command's optimistic view. In Saigon, up to six hundred newspeople contradicted one another, sometimes missing major news to play up isolated events. News agencies and newspapers often fixated on fragments: B-52 strikes, body counts, firebases won and lost. By the time Americans realized there was no light at the end of the tunnel—the war had been lost from the beginning, just as those first reporters had said it was—the price had been paid.

War correspondents learned on the job. The bang-bang was the easy part. They found out how hard it is to get close enough to the story to feel it but stay far enough away not to be drawn into it. This applies to every sort of reporting; in war, it is paramount. The impact of death and pain makes it next to impossible for journalists to keep passion from shading an objective view. If they detach themselves enough to block out emotion, they are left with little more than casualty figures and disjointed bits of description. But if they let themselves share the anguish of an 18-year-old corporal cradling the entrails of a platoon leader he must succeed, they are not likely to see the fuckers on the other side as someone else's enemy. A minor skirmish can seem like D-Day to a correspondent pinned down all day by artillery.

The wider lessons, fallout of something called a Vietnam Syndrome, were evoked daily during the Gulf War. Frequently, they were misunderstood. Vietnam coverage must be seen in the context of the history that shaped it.

Back when Pulitzer was not a prize but a publisher fighting a war waged with yellow ink, correspondents had the status of field commanders. During the Spanish-American War, in 1898, they called themselves "special commissioners." In *The Yellow Kids,* Joyce Milton describes the day Spain surrendered to U.S. forces in Cuba. An honor guard prepared to raise the flag. Sylvester Scovel of the *New York World* muscled forward and grabbed the halyard. He had played such a crucial role, he figured, it was his place to run up the colors. When the American general brushed him aside, Milton recounts, Scovel belted him in the chops.

Shades of Sylvester Scovel hang over the system. Military men may have caught on that the pen is not mightier than the sword, but they are not so sure about the Handicam. Print reporters in Saudi Arabia, known collectively as "pencils," watched amazed as colonels carried the bags of one "media personnel" individual and followed him around saying, "Yes, Mr. Donaldson." One television correspondent tried to insist that a crucial part of the surprise invasion be delayed until his crew was ready.

But the special commissioners' role has evolved over the years. The crucial difference is that back then war dispatches were widely read. There were not very many of them. Fewer diversions competed for their readers' attention. A Richard Harding Davis was Mal Browne, Vanna White and a spectrum of cable channels rolled into one. Policymakers had to think about the newspapers, however crazed. It is questionable whether William Randolph Hearst really cabled Frederic Remington, "You furnish the pictures, and I'll furnish the war," but he might have. When his paper howled for blood, a lot of it spilled.

World War I happened without any newspaper's help. It forced on hit-and-run editors the challenge of finding reporters to suffer up front with the troops and send back infrequent dispatches when faulty communications allowed it. America came in late to someone else's war. Closer to the action than the politics behind it, correspondents focused on the drama of men at war, developing a style that has inspired every generation since.

In World War II, no one wondered about where patriotic duty fit in with an abstract idea like objectivity. With the help of newsreels and radio, Americans saw their enemy, a rug-chewing German lunatic and squinting little yellow deviants. The most famous correspondent, Ernie Pyle, perfected the style of focusing on soldiers. He described a wider war through their eyes, often one soldier at a time. He and the others wore uniforms, had their own military jeeps and lived the same life as the men they covered.

"It depends on the war," Homer Bigart remarked, soon after retiring from the *New York Times* in the 1960s. He did not miss a major conflict in thirty years. "In World War II, you were on the right side, and there was no question about it." He remembered a time when German troops voluntarily held their fire to let an ambulance convoy pass. "I was surprised that they were capable of that," he said. "But I never wrote it. To my knowledge, no one did." The politics and societies of warring nations were useless garnish, pushed to the edge of plate.

Korea was also reported essentially as us-against-them. Correspondents were assigned jeeps and had free run of the war. Not much was made of censorship rules. Each reporter knew the limits, and most stopped well short of them. It was in Vietnam that the style changed drastically, and that caught a lot of people off guard.

Vietnam started as just another troublesome story in the nether zone that later came to be called the Third World. France had lost a terrible war to hold on to its Southeast Asian colony. A tenuous government was struggling to keep power in the face of a new phenomenon, shadowy bands of jungle fighters fielded by warlord philosophers committed to their particular reading of Marx and Lenin. Their struggle was partly ideological. Mostly, it was a cultural and ethnic battle with roots going back a thousand years.

The first U.S. agents, like Graham Greene's *The Quiet American,* learned the hard way what a complex skein they were hoping to unravel. By the time U.S. advisers edged into a military role, the young reporters who were covering Vietnam knew far more than the military did about their allies and the enemy. David Halberstam of the *New York Times* had covered politics in New Jersey; he placed himself in the middle and saw the whole picture. Mal Browne of the AP, trained as a chemist, weighed all sides and made no assumptions. Arnett, who worked with him, wrote what he saw. Neil Sheehan of UPI, like the others, did not think in terms of friend or foe. But that was the early stage, in the early 1960s, well before any sort of critical mass even began to jell. As a story, Vietnam had barely risen above the level of also-ran.

The first major influx of American forces also brought reporters of the old school. One was Richard Tregaskis, who by the age of twenty-six had written himself into history. His best-selling book, *Guadalcanal Diary,* was made into a hit movie. His dispatches helped set the standard for covering World War II. When he came to Saigon in 1963, the generals were thrilled. They had just been humiliated by the debacle of Ap Bac and were blaming hungry, inexperienced reporters for making too much of it. Here was a veteran who would look past the political underbrush to the objective at hand, a war the Americans had to win.

Halberstam, then twenty-eight, had hopes for his old hero, according to an account by author William Prochnau, who studied that period. Tregaskis wrote soon after landing, "It may turn out that the guerrilla-type operation in this critical struggle with communism will be more important to our history and our future than even World War II." Halberstam invited Tregaskis for a look around to see what the future might bring.

The two drove through the disputed delta ricefields south of Saigon. There would probably be no action, Halberstam said, but he wanted his colleague to meet some of his sources. They saw the majors and colonels who watched the war up close, unfiltered by the military command in Saigon. Each told of corrupt South Vietnam officers and tax collectors, heavy American vehicles that bogged down in the mud, hapless South Vietnamese troops whose disasters on the battlefield turned to victories in official reports, body counts that were multipled up to ten times as they rose to the top command levels.

They drove home at dusk, past lonely security points that would signify the government's nighttime presence in a countryside that would change hands at dark. Tregaskis was quiet until they neared Saigon. "If I were doing what you are doing," he told Halberstam, "I'd be ashamed of myself." With that, Prochnau concluded his account, "The two reporters rode the rest of the way in stony silence, skipping dinner."

As the war went on, Vietnam coverage followed patterns shaped by the young pioneers, but old habits died hard. Reporters sometimes referred to the Viet Cong as "the enemy." One news agency desk editor told a correspondent in Saigon to stop harping on how courageous and tenacious the other side seemed to be. Once when Arnett reported that he had seen American troops looting, a top AP executive tried to kill the story. The boss, who had been a correspondent in World War II, declared, "American troops don't loot." He backed down when editors protested.

One lesson we learned was what Browne concluded after the Gulf War: "No uniformed fact-suppressor will ever equal the persistence and determination of a resourceful reporter." By attempting, the Pentagon can only blacken its own image. But the other lesson was that, assuming we are a collective called the media, it is not necessary for the military to blur our clear vision. If we're not careful, we can do that ourselves.

Like all wars in the past, the conflicts since Vietnam have been political. And, since then, we have covered them that way. That era, in fact, inspired a new generation of reporters who set out with a mission to spare the world another stupid morass. A lot of them ended up covering political war in Central America.

In an essay for the Freedom Forum Media Studies Center, Clifford Krauss detailed the coming of age of a press corps made up largely of first-assignment reporters who came down expecting to find nobility on the left. "There is a socialization process in journalism, just as in all professions," he wrote. "There are codes, ethics and an ethos of critical nonpartisanship to be learned and upheld. The same young reporters who came down to Central America to prove that the Contras commit atrocities (which they do) and that Washington still lies (which it does), found out that the FMLN guerrillas [in El Salvador] also murder innocent civilians and that the Sandinista comandantes can lie with the best of them." But this, he adds, took a while.

Krauss got himself to Peru as a freelancer straight out of school and then signed on with UPI in Mexico City. In 1977, he headed toward Managua to cover the first Sandinista offensives that would turn out Anastasio Somoza Debayle two years later. Later, he joined the *Wall Street Journal.* Many of his colleagues were remarkably similar in background or point of view.

"We brought to this newest foreign adventure, one that early on resonated with Vietnam parallels, new and critical assumptions that the vast majority of our older colleagues would have found unacceptable," he wrote. "We had grown up with the Kennedy and King assassinations, the Tonkin Gulf incident, the secret bombing of Cambodia and finally Watergate. Our first assumption was to doubt the word of U.S. officials and the justice of the American cause."

In Nicaragua, he wrote, "For the first few years of the Sandinista government I reported what I wanted to see and discounted the repression." Later in El Salvador, he recalled, he refused to believe horror stories of peasant families, mostly loyal to the right wing, that guerrillas had burned their homes and taken their land.

Gradually, Krauss concluded, he and others drifted to the center. Some moved faster than others. The frankness is refreshing and bespeaks a fair mind. But it is troubling, nonetheless. Readers at the other end cannot be aware of this education process. Leftists and rightists, they go to the same source of daily news for raw data on which to base their own assumptions. They can't wait for those six months, or two years.

But there was also a balancing mechanism. Reporters of different backgrounds and other levels of experience were also reporting from Central America. Whatever Krauss' generation might have missed, they moved fast, often bravely, to report facts as they saw them. If their early assumptions led to blind spots, they warned readers from the start that Washington was lying. The next generation, those who cut their teeth on the Gulf War, might have taken note.

The main lesson is for the reader and viewer. War coverage, political or military, brings out the human being in reporters. This is a drawback for those who expect too much, but it can be a strength for those who want the full flavor. The triangulation of sources that is so useful in all news stories is absolutely essential in war. No one sees it all. And certainly no one understands it all.


Bias, inadvertent or otherwise, is difficult to excise from war reporting. Even now, with all of the talk about objectivity, American television anchors sometimes refer to "our troops." What is supposed to be the opposing force, seen from the center, is still "the enemy." A certain cheerleading quality suggests a clear situation of us against them.

Unconscious bias creeps into copy and narration. The good guys make driving advances and well-planned ambushes; the bad guys counter with brutal onslaughts and sneak attacks. One side questions villagers, while the other side terrorizes them. A reporter who is unwittingly involved is more apt to believe intelligence reports that the enemy has morale and supply problems against evidence that it is doing fine. Conversely, if friendly generals insist that the threat can be met only with maximum force, their word is likely to be accepted.

Even when there are no patriotic considerations, reporters often tend to lean to one side. This can be sympathy for the underdog or a desire to be on the winning side. There is no fixed pattern, but natural tendencies influence the best correspondents. Reporters who travel with one army, sharing rations and watching familiar faces sudddenly go slack, find it hard to separate themselves from the troops around them. Air raids threaten not just the army around them. Particularly if they share cultural values with one side, they can understand why it is fighting. It is not so easy to see why the other side is resisting so unreasonably.

In general, when whites battle blacks, yellows, reds or browns, American reporting leans at least slightly in their favor. This is not so much a racial response as simple practicality. European armies, even white mercenaries, are more likely to take along reporters to write with relative freedom. They are, in any case, easier to reach and better equipped with telephones and field hospitals.

Inadvertent bias is magnified if readers and viewers add their own distortions. Few people back home can accept the abstract idea that anyone killing their sons and husbands is just of one the combatants in a multisided war. Logically, a person's attitude toward Arabs, Jews, Africans or Cubans will affect reactions to any conflict involving them. From far away, it is hard enough to follow a war, even one that is reported with pristine objectivity. If elements of bias are added, serious misunderstanding is inevitable.

War reporting is improved when the same correspondents can work from both sides, alternating back and forth. This sort of thing can get a reporter shot as a spy. Commanders are chary about observers straddling front lines. But it happens. Some people who covered the Gulf War from Saudi Arabia also did a stint in Baghdad. Reporters who traveled with Afghan rebels could also get visas to see things from the government side.

Sensible editors know that if war corresponding is no longer a profession, it ought to be. Experts who can look at the elements of war are less likely to take sides. At the very least, they know what they're talking about. *Newsweek* started a trend by making a contributing editor of David Hackworth, a retired commander who had covered himself with glory on the battlefield. In the Gulf War and Somalia, he acquitted himself well at journalism. Hackworth's cool assessments pointed out absurdities in military logic that amateurs looked past without seeing.

Too often, editors had to settle for the opposite, reporters who saw the war as an opportunity rather than a challenge. When the Gulf War ended, I was sitting with colleagues at Riyadh airport waiting for a plane. A television correspondent, fluffing his hair, grumbled, "These guys think we're only doing this to get on the air and advance our own careers." A battered old radio reporter looked up and snorted. "Now where," he asked, "would they ever get an idea like that?"

Experienced reporters have a better chance of staying alive. No one's rulebook is much help. Reuters has a set of guidelines, which it takes seriously. When one Reuters man was captured by Iraqi guards, a top executive roasted him for endangering a company resource—himself—and wasting the valuable time of managers who had to get him freed. BBC Radio's news editor, Larry Hodgson, argues that conditions vary so much that rules written in London seldom apply. He knows reporters would ignore them, anyway. "In short," he said, "selecting the right person is more important than laying down principles that probably can't be adhered to."

A few simple things make sense. Wise reporters don't draw circles on maps; they look too much like targets. They carry a white flag and check their gear carefully. One Canadian reporter at a Salvadoran roadblock had to explain away the M-16 cartridges someone had left in the glove box of his rented car. When soldiers later found some scathing dispatches he had written about the government, they asked him to translate. He forgot his Spanish.

Land mines are often a problem, and it helps to know how to follow tire tracks and avoid booby traps. On a parked Saudi press bus in Kuwait, two American colleagues spotted a friend in a nearby jeep. They grabbed their gear and leaped off quickly before anyone could ask to join them. One of them planted her left foot six inches from an anti-tank mine.

Seasoned correspondents are crucial to the reader. In war, a reporter's courage is perhaps the best gauge of reliability; courage suggests commitment to the story and to basic principles. The finest of lines separates courage from stupidity. After covering Central American wars, Lydia Chavez of the *New York Times* recalled Starbuck's rule in *Moby Dick:* "I'll have no man in my boat who is not afraid of the whale." But a reporter has to be willing to go up the road.

When I talked to Arnett for *Coups and Earthquakes,* he remarked: "I'm one of those who subscribes to the belief that some stories are worth dying for. A reporter should be able to determine his own destiny, but it his responsibility to cover his story. That's why I stayed in Saigon after the North Vietnamese took the city. If at a forward position a company or a battalion was under fire and taking casualties, I felt it binding upon me to go. I never went out on the point or crawled out to machine-gun posts. But there are times when you have to get out—you have to risk your life."

When he returned from Baghdad, I asked if he still subscribed to that belief. "Since I made that statement, dozens of journalists have died," he replied. "To say a story is not worth dying for is to deny the commitment of all those people."

# Chapter 15

# Covering Economics

Correspondents' T-shirt chic featured a new creation for the '90s, alongside stalwarts like "Beirut Ceasefire XIV" and the El Salvador favorite, "*Periodista. No Tira!* (Journalist. Don't Shoot!)." The new one read, "1992 Economic Summit of the Industrialized Nations."

It is a little hard to picture Bogart in his trenchcoat, rumbling over a scratchy transatlantic phone line, "Hold the page, chief, I've got something big on GATT." Many of us can hardly add up our expense accounts without help, let alone sort out the trigonometry of trade. But, like it or not, money is big news. If people are interested most in foreign stories that affect them directly, nothing but a war they must fight hits them so hard. Economic reporting, which lived at the back of the book, has muscled its way to the front page.

This is not exactly new. The economy made headlines in 1971 when Richard Nixon took the dollar off the gold standard and let it find its level in the world. Americans realized that their currency and economy were linked to everyone else's. Two years later, economy dominated the news for months on end. Arab states, angered at Western support for Israel, made a political point with economics. They turned off the oil taps. Overnight, people who had never heard of Oobie Doobie or Kuwhat were fuming in endless gas lines, radiators bubbling over, and listening to their radios for clues about what had happened to them.

The oil embargo caught most news organizations completely off guard. Correspondents, by and large, were police reporters far from home. They covered events or places or foibles of the human condition. Without warning, they were called upon to understand spot markets, grades of crude, commodity barters and the dizzying vagaries of currency exchange. It mattered to know whose money was deposited where and how it moved.

Oil producers got together in the Organization of Petroleum Exporting Countries. Other states with valuable mineral exports formed their own groupings. Agricultural producers tried to fight back by running up the price of food. Reporters, better prepared, began to see links. By the worldwide recession of 1981 and 1982, few doubters remained; economic news was a permanent fixture. Since then, almost every major political or social story has had an economic element to it.

It was a big challenge. With a little work, most reporters mastered the basics of international economics. The trick was to get it across to only mildly interested readers with a limited experience in the bizarre climates in which economic news happened. An Oklahoma car dealer who panics when annual inflation nears 7 percent does not easily picture an African economy with inflation spurting up at a rate of 50,000 percent a year.

Once in a story from Argentina, I mentioned that the cost of a small sedan had risen by ten times in a year. My editor wanted to know sticker prices, before and after, in dollars. Argentines spent pesos, not dollars, I tried to explain. Sharp devaluations canceled out the inflation in dollar terms. He insisted. The story explained that a car costing $4,000 had gone up in price ten times to $4,000.

Television has had a tough time catching up with the new twist. Graphs and pie charts make dull visuals, but it is hard to get much else on camera. In the 1960s, when West European nations began linking together in an economic community, John Chancellor persuaded NBC to set up a Brussels bureau to follow vital economic changes. It was, he remembers, the hardest job he ever had. After a while, the network gave it up.

Even now, fundamental economic sea changes are often shown by their simplest symptoms. During 1992, Germany let the Deutsche mark flex its new muscle. Largely because the dollar stayed home, the DM emerged as the currency of choice throughout the former Soviet empire. The currency, backed by an aggressive Bundesbank which refused to lower interest rates, tipped the delicate balance of the European Community. At the same time, uncertainty in the United States caused the dollar to fall against all European currencies. CBS showed the effect of all this by interviewing an American tourist in London who complained about the price of a Big Mac. The wider impact, on trade balances and industrial investment, was not mentioned.

Soon after, the British pound and the Italian lira were devalued, throwing into question a monetary system the European Community hoped to put in place. This raised doubts about a unified Europe, a trading bloc of 350 million people. Too complicated for a bite of sound, or of hamburger, it went mostly unnoticed on American television.

At the end of the year, the first step was taken toward Europe's dream of a single market. People could cross borders to buy whatever they want for personal consumption: truckloads of liquor, groceries, electronic gadgetry or whatever they could find cheaper elsewhere and carry home. A complex set of rules kicked in, allowing Danish dentists to pull teeth in Provence, Greeks to retire in Ireland and companies to market their products without restraint, but only more or less, in twelve countries. A CBS correspondent showed that this was still no United States in Europe by holding up the different electrical plugs still in use.

Newspapers and magazines also had a hard time of it. During the mid-1970s, Phil Revzin had to explain to a copy editor at the *Wall Street Journal* that the dollar's value fluctuated against that of other currencies and that this was important enough to write about. American journalists do better now, but many still fall short in explaining foreign economies.

For the society as a whole, this is a problem. Nations which do best economically are those which understand the market, and the competition. Americans are not necessarily among them. Anyone who wants serious, complete economic coverage must seek it out. It is there, but it is not always in the usual places.

A fourth of all correspondents aboard work for business news organizations, according to Ohio University's Ralph Kliesch. These include the *Wall Street Journal,* which is a good place to start. The *Journal*'s two feature article positions on the front page offer insights into the economic state of countries, companies and fields of endeavor. The righthand lead story is usually a hard, close look at some aspect of doing business in the world. Despite a forbidding layout, with railroad tracks of photoless type, the paper is a good read.

Revzin is now editor of the *Journal*'s European edition. "The best economic reporters know that in the presentation of their reporting they must include sharp, fresh examples, lots of explanation of jargon and complicated concepts," he said. "Above all, they try to relate abstract concepts to concrete things. The one and only trick I use is to remind myself constantly that essentially anything that's interesting to me has a business angle." Breakfast, for example.

When Revzin first arrived in France, he noticed that his box of Kellogg's Corn Flakes came with instructions: 1. Add milk (preferably cold). 2. Add sugar to taste. 3. Dig in! With a few phone calls and a visit to Kellogg's Paris headquarters, he learned that research showed most French people were still eating yesterday's leftover bread and butter for breakfast. Many didn't know you were supposed to put milk on corn flakes. If they did, it was usually hot milk left over from *café au lait,* resulting in a soggy and unappetizing mass. So Kellogg's directed its advertising and marketing toward educating Frenchmen in breakfast.

The point, Revzin says, is that economic and financial reporting from abroad is just plain reporting. Certainly the dividing lines are blurred. When reporters went after the Bank of Credit & Commerce International (BCCI), it was essentially a financial story. By the time all the pieces had fallen, it was about drugs, CIA operations, bribery in high places, scandal in the Democratic Party, Washington cover-ups, Middle East power politics and every sort of wrongdoing that produces cash to be laundered.

"There are many more correspondents who know and care about business and finance [than previously]," Revzin said. "Because globalization now affects everything from drive-ins to disk drives, even general reporters find themselves inevitably writing more business and finance stories, even if they don't realize it. I'd even argue the Gulf War was an economic story because of the oil angle."

Tony Horwitz, who covered the war with skill for the *Journal,* uses the same techiques for economics. To depict hard times in Britain, he went to Hartlepool to hobnob with Andy Capp working-men. Fifteen-year-old Paul Dawes humped coal with his father, shoveling in a black slush of seaweed and slag on a frigid winter's night. When they keep at it, three tons of the cheap fuel is worth forty dollars. At the Boilermakers' Club, an unemployed shipbuilder named Arthur Tuncliffe drank Strongarm beer and declared, "The working class will always be here—even if it isn't working." Facts and figures stitch the story together. The result is a textured picture that strikes home.

With a new trend toward economic reporting, a skilled practitioner might turn up anywhere. Bill Drozdiak, the *Washington Post* correspondent in Paris, looks like a normal person, an old-fashioned reporter who learned economics out of his back pocket. In fact, he has an advanced degree from the Collège d'Europe in Brussels and other degrees in international economics. He takes pride in the fact that you'd never know it from his copy. The idea is to make it smooth and simple, with as little fancy footwork as possible.

Covering the farm war with France, Drozdiak had it easy. The Americans' weapon of choice was a heavy tax on white wine. Who could miss? From Meursault, he wrote: "The gentle slopes of the Côte d'Or that tumble south from this austere Burgundy village form such a sacred part of French culture that the 19th century writer Alexandre Dumas said its white wine should be drunk 'on one's knees, with head covered.'" From there, he could wedge in the details about trade, tariffs and the European single market.

Drozdiak agrees that anyone can report economics well, as many general reporters do, but that it helps to know what you're talking about. Specialists know when a source is showing off, speaking in tongues or adding extraneous background that can be ignored. Less experienced reporters tend to throw in too much, in fear of leaving out something crucial. Or they simply throw quotes around long-winded explanations and hope for the best.

In fact, most of the endless reports on structural unemployment and such from the Organization of Economic Cooperation and Development can be tossed in the garbage. They are useful as clues toward trends which must then be illustrated by concrete example. Horwitz, for instance, might have caught the train to Hartlepool because of an OECD handout. But I wouldn't put any money on it.

It is the same with the showy, and costly, Group of Seven summits. They are almost never a story in themselves. Instead, they often point to stories that might be developed: Why did the Germans once again refuse to cut their interest rates? How much has reunification socked it to the German consumer? Summits, Revzin figures, are like those Riyadh briefings during the Gulf War. Despite the presence of the swarm, the story is not in that room.

The big picture has its importance. Economic specialists find
it is worth the time occasionally to canvass experts with good records to try to guess what it is. But the writer has to know enough
about the small pictures to make sense of the big one. He has to
relate punditry and prophecy to real life, or the reader skips on.

Readers who know economics can usually tell when reporters
do not. The problem lies in between the extremes. Most people have
a notion about how things work. A well-crafted newspaper story or
broadcast report can shed some useful light. Too often, newspeople
simply parrot words they don't understand. An economics writer
friend watched a blow-dried anchorman at a local Cleveland station
receive a late bulletin while reading the news. He glanced at it,
looked up with a broad smile, and announced: "Good news. The
prime rate is going up!"

If American journalists are sometimes confused about international economics, so are a lot American politicians who make decisions about it. People often forget that, like the United States,
every country acts in its own best interests. You have to wonder
when a U.S. Treasury secretary emerges from the Bundesbank in
Frankfurt shaking his head in disbelief that the Germans won't cut
their interest rates in time to help his boss get reelected. Or when
a New York op-ed writer says the French are being stubborn in farm
talks while the Americans have made a heroic, self-sacrificing offer.
Japan unfairly protects its rice farmers, the complaint goes, but no
one mentions American peanut growers, probably the smallest and
best-protected farm lobby on earth.

Since the oil crisis of the 1970s, all major economies have in-
teracted closely. They have been linked tightly by the global flow of
money since recycled petrodollars flooded international banks after
the first oil price shock. Big investors are influenced by a large U.S.
deficit or high German interest rates, and this affects money movement. Global marketing ties together economics at a human level,
and this link is expanding rapidly.

But the world's economies are not exactly intertwined. Decisions made in Washington affect the United States and only periph-
erally Europe, Asia and beyond. And this works in reverse. The
German interest rate policy affects Germany first, then its European
partners and then, as a by-product, the United States and the rest

of the world. The economies of the English-speaking countries slumped about the same time, in the late 1980s. When things began to improve in 1992, the slump started unevenly in Europe. Japan suffered for its own cyclical reasons. It was important for people in each country to keep up with developments in the others. But the necessary plans of attack were different in each.

Faced with having to make sense of these complications, editors are sending some correspondents back to school. A number of fellowships are designed to teach advanced basics to reporters who plan to specialize in economic beats. This has helped, but formidable obstacles remain.

Good economics reporters, to start with, must be good reporters. A misread balance sheet or lapse in arithmetic can be devastating. Shaking out information takes extra skill. Sources who might prattle on for hours about political problems suddenly clam up when big money is involved. Negotiations depend heavily on secrecy and smokescreens. Communiqués after meetings are only the ice floe's tip. The real clues come from tapping the participants. When a finance minister says something will go up, a reporter has to know what else will come down. He has to know as much about Keynesian doctrine or the concept of Mill as the sources who throw around the terms in an effort to mask a bad call.

The job takes Jobesque patience, waiting hours in unheated halls for someone to come out and raise an eyebrow in answer to questions. Nights are spent on soporific company reports and legal documents. And the rewarding moments are more cerebral than those in other foreign reporting. Without the adrenaline rush of high adventure and shellfire, the economic reporter must be satisified with the outraged howl of a nailed cheater.

The simplest stories can take hours of work. Often official spokespersons read from briefing sheets they don't understand. If an important reference figure is missing, they can't supply it. In a lot of societies, close enough is an acceptable category.

Once Bob Sullivan, then with UPI in Brazil, spent an entire day trying to pin down a single figure for a one-line dispatch to his agency's special commodities service. It helped that Sullivan is a maniac for accurate detail. He read in four major Brazilian papers that sugar prices in local markets would be raised 12 percent to 5.50 cruzeiros a kilo by following Monday. But none gave the old price, and he had forgotten how to work it out mathematically. He knew 12 percent of 5.50 was not the answer. Sullivan called a supermarket and was told the price was 4 cruzeiros; that made no sense. Then he asked the Economy Ministry spokeswoman about the report. It had to be correct, she said. It was in the prestigious *Jornal do Brasil.* He pointed out that the difference between 4 and 5.50 was more than 12 percent. She said someone would call back, and someone actually did.

The woman's boss confirmed the report. Asked about the old price, he started out, "Let's see, twelve percent of five-fifty. . ." After some discussion, he said the ministry did not fix prices—Sullivan would have to call the special interministerial commission on consumer prices. He did, and a spokesman told him that of course the story was true. It was in all the papers, wasn't it? Sullivan pleaded with him to recheck the official announcement. The man called back to say the commission knew nothing about it. In fact, the people who set policy would not be meeting for another month.

Sullivan called back the ministry and one of the newspapers. From both, he learned that the economic minister had mentioned a 12 percent increase. But, asking yet another ministry official, he learned that the new price was for refinery owners, to be applied to wholesalers only. He then went to the economics desk of the *Jornal do Brasil* where, after a brief argument, he got an admission that someone had screwed up. A group of local reporters had misinterpreted the minister's remark and, in gang fashion, worked out what the new retail price would be. Their math was bad. Just to make sure, Sullivan went to a nearby supermarket. He was told that if the price was increased, it could never be applied by Monday, since the old price was printed on the bags and it would take two weeks to a month for old stock to be sold out.

The next morning, Sullivan opened one popular paper which had not carried the erroneous report. Its main headline read, "New Price Increase to Housewives for Sugar, 5.50 by Monday."

To economics correspondents, all figures are at least slightly suspect, and they can mislead the most experienced specialists. Any smart statistician can juggle numbers to show just about anything to the casual observer. A minister hustling international loans will emphasize different figures from those he might cite to local papers as election time approaches. Companies do their own shuffling. In the United States, high earnings at the end of the year run up a company's value on the stock exchange. In Europe, however, companies prefer to disguise their earnings from union leaders and tax collectors.

Some governments simply lie. Others could not give accurate figures if they wanted to. Sophisticated data collection is too much of a luxury in poor countries. Because each government reports economic statistics differently, international comparisons are often meaningless. For example, two countries with exactly the same unemployment situation may differ five percentage points in their official jobless rate.

In much of the world, knowing how to go after a business story is not enough. Financial investigative reporting in Europe is in its earliest stages. With nothing similar to the Securities and Exchange Commission or Freedom of Information Acts, local journalists do almost no investigating. American and some British papers try sometimes, but they are hindered by the lack of tools to pry out information. Mostly, reporters stick to stories with an American connection so the SEC can help them get started. Two blockbusters, the BCCI scandal and the Robert Maxwell collapse, both had this entry point.

This is the growth area in economic reporting. As money flies around the world, from cautious dictators and drug barons, someone will have to track it. Most likely, it will be American correspondents, using increased resources for international investigations.

For the general readers, the large papers and newsmagazines offer fairly complete coverage of the big picture and a lot of fragments of smaller pictures. But there are alternatives. The *Financial Times,* as its name suggests, covers economics with British thoroughness. It is also a good general paper, with solidly reported news stories and a broad sweep of commentary.

The *Economist* is treasured by a new class of American internationalists who like to see it lying in plain sight on their desks. Its news columns range wide, from the week's major stories in obscure parts of Asia to a provocative American Survey. It is also a journal of opinion, sometimes fiercely held opinion. Readers might forget that although the tone suggests correctness of view and ironclad accuracy of fact, that may not necessarily be the case. All journalists, even British ones whose self-assurance might suggest otherwise, are susceptible to error.

# Chapter 16

# Human Rights Reporting

Around Christmas of 1981, elite troops of El Salvador's armed forces walked into the village of El Mozote and opened fire. They cut down old men and infants, mothers, husbands and teenagers. When they had finished, El Mozote was torched. Their battalion, named Atlacatl after a Pipil Indian chief, was the first to be trained by American advisers. U.S. attachés were proud of the dashing commander. Looking for guerrillas or sympathizers, these showcase soldiers destroyed the village to save it.

For a nation singed by the Vietnam War, this should have had a familiar ring. America's Southeast Asian debacle had little to do with firepower. The United States was humbled because we told ourselves we were upholding democrats—moral equivalents of our founding fathers—when the people who were suffering knew otherwise. Death squads were already sullying the image of El Salvador's right-wing leaders. The massacre at El Mozote showed that whatever we might win, it would not include hearts and minds.

Soon after the assault, word filtered back to San Salvador that something dreadful had happened in the province of Morazán, a guerrilla stronghold. Ray Bonner of the *New York Times,* once a U.S. Marine and then a Nader's Raider public service lawyer, made his way to the scene. Before going, he let word slip to the competition, Alma Guillermoprieto of the *Washington Post,* a Mexican American who took up reporting when she missed the final cut as a Twyla Tharp dancer. She also got there, on a burro.

Separately, the two reporters found the remains of people buried in the ashes of their homes. Villagers explained what had happened. Rufina Amaya, hiding behind a tree, had watched them kill her blind husband and her four children; the youngest was eight months old. Survivors made up a list of 733 victims. The Salvadoran Human Rights Commission counted 926.

For Bonner and Guillermoprieto, it was reporting in the old tradition, a close-up look at what is known abstractly as "human rights abuses." One family's details were checked against another's. When truth is so overpowering, it emerges intact. But the timing was embarrassing for the Reagan administration. To get more money out of Congress, the State Department had to certify that El Salvador was making progress in human rights.

The assistant secretary of state for inter-American affairs was Thomas O. Enders, who had worked hard to cover up secret U.S. bombing in Cambodia. A week after the El Mozote dispatches, he said that nothing supported the reporters' claims. He based this assertion on an investigation by two U.S. Embassy officials who had never made it to the village and who had not ruled out a massacre. Massive aid continued to the Salvadoran armed forces, which tortured and killed thousands of victims during the 1980s.

Bonner was targeted, and not only by the government. In a thirty-six-inch editorial entitled "The Media's War," the *Wall Street Journal* observed: "Much of the American media [in El Salvador], it would seem, was dominated by a style of reporting that grew out of Vietnam—in which Communist sources were given greater credence than either the U.S. government or the government it was supporting." On the "MacNeil-Lehrer Newshour," a *Journal* editorialist said Bonner had "an ideological orientation."

U.S. officials sought ways to undermine Bonner's credibility. Attacks from the right meant that he was embraced, to his discomfiture, by the left. He found his editors at the *Times* wary of his factual reporting from El Salvador. In Nicaragua, he wrote five stories, and three of them did not make the paper. Eventually, he left the *Times*. Among his friends, he blames mortal wounds inflicted by the dispatch from El Mozote.

Confirmation came nearly eleven years afterward, in 1992. Pressed by human rights groups, the government allowed a team of forensic archaeologists to inspect El Mozote. It found government shell casings and other clear evidence of a massacre.

But that was later. After El Mozote, the reporters who continued to track down human rights abuses had a tough time of it. Documentation was hard to assemble. Culprits had friends in court: officials, lobbyists and public relations firms, all eager to shoot the messenger. As in Vietnam, correspondents found something different from the picture sketched in Washington. Commentators back home, equipped with no facts but committed to a point of view, drowned them out.

In Central America, yet another authoritarian regime got away with murder, committing the same sort of atrocities that qualify as cause for war when it suits policy. More, the United States stained its honor and damaged national institutions.

In a *New York Times* column after the truth was established, Anthony Lewis drew the conclusion: "The *Journal* editorial had a significant effect. Other newspapers worried about looking soft on communism and toned down their reporting from El Salvador. . . . The press could learn again how essential it is to be skeptical of convenient government denials."

In human rights reporting, the press could learn again how essential it is to be skeptical of everything. How authorities treat their people is a crucial factor in any conflict. Among a correspondent's first bitter lessons, however, is that even reasonable people will exploit human rights issues if it suits a larger purpose. Some ignore atrocities, and others invent them.

The Romanian revolution against Nicolae Ceausescu began in Timisoara, a restive city of ethnic Hungarians. A local priest spoke out, rallying thousands, and Ceausescu's hated Securitate tried to impose silence in the usual manner. Each morning, reporters from Belgrade drove to the sealed Yugoslav-Romanian border in hopes of getting across. Each night, they returned with horror stories that had escaped from Timisoara.

Suddenly, the border opened. Ceausescu fell, and Securitate storm troopers dug in to fight for their lives. Insurgents at makeshift roadblocks shot at anyone who provoked their suspicion. Reporters were free to take their chances. When the first batch reached Timisoara, it found a new set of local authorities eager to talk.

Ceausescu's men were monsters, they said, and they offered to show evidence. For instance, there was the mass grave.

The next day, a news agency dispatch on the front page of the *New York Times* told of thousands of bodies heaped into a mass grave. Similar stories, from a handful of reporters, appeared in newspapers all over the world. Television crews and press photographers sent back gruesome pictures. Authorities had shown a few bodies. The rest, they said, were lying under the bulldozed earth. The version stood unchallenged until a second wave of reporters took a closer look.

The corpses on display were months old. One had long stitches in the chest from a hasty autopsy. An infant had been placed atop a woman, a calculated *mise-en-scène* to elicit shock. In fact, residents said, the mass grave was an old paupers' cemetery, far too small to accommodate the numbers in question. The story was faked to whip up feelings against the fallen regime.

Some media critics seized upon this incident as an open-and-shut case: "the press" lies. Others, more charitably, allowed that it was mere incompetence. In fact, the Timisoara story is a stinging reminder that a complex world cannot be covered simply. Even careful reporters trying to do their best can make mistakes.

Dusan Stojanovic, an experienced hand in the AP's Belgrade bureau who had proven his skill time and again, was among the first reporters racing to Bucharest. At night in Timisoara, he saw the purported mass grave on local television. With his colleagues, he hurried over to check it out. "It was dark, and we could hardly see," he recalled. "They said they had dug up only a few bodies but thousands more were still buried. People were shooting in Romania. Everything was confused, happening fast. It made sense. Look, I'm no forensic expert. This was 1989. I hadn't seen many bodies in Yugoslavia." He added, with a bitter laugh, "If this happened now, I'd know about bodies."

Tanjug, the Yugoslav news agency, had also reported the story. Agence France-Presse picked it up. Photographs and videotape showed the macabre bodies. Other reporters wrote the same thing. Few stayed behind to investigate fully because the big story was Ceausescu's fall in Bucharest.

When the story calmed a bit, correspondents went back to check. Rone Tempest of the *Los Angeles Times* suspected something was wrong. "I'd seen enough bodies in India," he said. "Those people could not have been killed recently." When reporters insisted on evidence to support the high numbers claimed, local authorities waffled. Reality was bad enough, but the good guys, the ones who had risen against Ceausescu's cynical lies and manipulation, started out by using his old handbook. If Stojanovic had slipped up, anyone could. Yet again, here was a case for suspended belief.

Ideally, people who care about the world should be able to keep track of human rights abuses in some consistent way. To whatever degree it is respected, concern for people's freedoms is a tenet of every U.S. administration. The word "moral" comes up often to justify diplomatic pressure, sanctions or the occasional invasion. By and large, decent people want their leaders to do the right thing, to reward democrats and lean on dictators. As the cases in El Salvador and Romania show, however, our news-gathering system is of limited help.

The genre of human rights reporting had a heyday in the 1970s, and it is still a powerful force. Done well, it can shame governments into backing off. It can enflame U.S. public opinion, prompting legislators to take action. It counterbalances favorable stories planted by image makers hired to win friends for despots. But it is never easy for the correspondent, and it can be hard for the reader to follow.

I discovered this new field at lunch one day in 1975 in a Buenos Aires restaurant. The "legal attaché" of the American Embassy, an FBI agent, mentioned that his previous luncheon companion had offered to give him a pair of kids. The man was leading a secret police unit which had kidnapped and tortured to death a Uruguayan couple. He did not know what to do with the children.

The agent was referring to the day's big story. Four Uruguayans had been seized in predawn raids, and their mutilated bodies turned up in a car in downtown Buenos Aires. The children's father was a political leader who had sought refuge in Argentina. He was about to testify in U.S. congressional hearings on human rights in Uruguay. Another was the former speaker of Uruguay's lower house, dissolved in a military takeover. When armed men burst in to kidnap them, neighbors called the police. No one responded. Later, investigating officers refused to lift fingerprints. We could only guess why.

My source explained that all four had been killed by security agents as a favor to the Uruguayans who kept tabs on Argentine leftists in Montevideo. It was a routine professional courtesy.

The strawberries came, and my source kept talking. His job was to know things he couldn't tell many people. Day after day, he consorted with official killers, learning what he could and then passing the information on to Washington. There, it remained in the files. No one wanted to make waves with the anti-Communist military rulers who had packed off the democratically elected but clearly overwrought president, Isabel Perón. Finally, the FBI man's conscience pushed him to unload to a friendly reporter.

The "mysterious right-wing terrorist groups" we wrote about, he said, were the regular state security agencies and military intelligence services. Each picked up suspects at will and asked questions. A favorite inducement was pouring gasoline in the ear, which caused such excruciating pain that victims would say anything before the eardrum ruptured, and they died. With each kidnapping, the death squads seized address books and letters to widen their circle.

My source explained why bodies had begun appearing on a Uruguayan beach. A military helicopter lift took victims out to sea for dumping. Each agency booked fifteen-minute periods. Agents tried to eject their victims while still alive so they would suck in water and sink to the bottom. This was not always possible. And, during a few days, pilots picked the wrong spot, and currents carried the bodies north instead of southward to Antarctica.

Despite their reputation as moderates determined to protect human rights, he said, Argentina's junta members allowed lower ranking officers a free hand to win the "dirty war" in any way that worked. Kidnapping and torture were not excesses by zealots. They were the tacit official policy.

I had known my informant for years, and friends had known him much longer. He was congenitally honest. From his details, and his tone, he had to be telling the truth. To be certain, I found a senior air force officer who I suspected might confirm the broad outlines. He did.

This was a scoop, and I did not know what to do with it. Even in early 1976, during the post-Watergate flush when reporters were believed, I could not accuse the Argentine government of mass murder without offering a source. The tried-and-true "Western diplomats" was too vague, and "U.S. diplomats" was too specific. Both were incorrect. The man was a cop. "Western law officer" would amount to naming him, a possible death sentence. (He has since died of natural causes.) And on the subject of potential death sentences, I could not help but consider my own.

Picking my words carefully, I wrote a general lead that said security forces had cracked down heavily on suspected leftists. Then I zeroed in: "Responsible sources who asked not to be identified in any way said military helicopters were being used to dispose of suspects—still alive or dead from torture—by dumping them out at sea. The sources said lower grade officers, acting without specific orders, were responsible. Official spokesmen deny any such activity."

Anyone who knew the business understood what I had written. No reporter could make such assertions if not convinced they were true. To a casual reader, however, such sidestepping sounds like uncertainty. There would have to be more. Soon afterward, my colleague from the *Washington Post* had other accounts. Then a curious process began. Amnesty International in London issued a statement about official Argentine terrorism, based largely on our vague reports. That meant we could write hard leads, attributed to Amnesty International, and then throw in whatever else remained in our notebooks. Before long, the point was made.

As soon as the repercussions reached Buenos Aires, the official killers sought to improve their image. Rather than moderating their methods, they simply added reporters to their lists. The *New York Times* correspondent decided to look closely at the death squads. After two discreet inquiries on a Saturday, he received a Sunday morning phone call, polite and anonymous: "Señor, we do not think it wise for you to pursue this story." Neither did his editors.

A main problem with human rights reporting is that it escapes all logic. Editors disagree on the basic premise. Some feel the need to expose violations wherever they occur. Others believe that harsh treatment is endemic in developing countries, like bribery and inefficiency, and that focusing on it amounts to belaboring the obvious. For reasons which few can explain, the rights of some humans far outweigh those of others. Overall, a country's relative performance on human rights depends less on reality than on the importance attached to it and on how many reporters are looking into it.

Until the Soviet Union collapsed, an exit visa delayed in Moscow was a bigger story than the systematic execution of thousands in some remote part of Africa. When Chinese tanks crushed a student uprising around Tiananmen Square, most of the world watched. Years later, the oppression continues almost unnoticed.

During the 1970s, the Philippines under President Ferdinand Marcos was wide open to reporters, and they wrote about whatever abuses they found. Across the water in East Timor, Indonesia sealed the borders to repress a separatist movement and hide a famine. Perhaps one hundred thousand people died from starvation and military assault before word filtered out.

The same imbalances continue. Turkey, a member of NATO with pretensions to the European Community, tortures with impunity. North Korea escapes specific charges by banning all reporters. In parts of the Middle East, where visas are granted as favors, editors are reluctant to squander their access by harping on human rights. In these circumstances, any comparative judgment— whether one regime is better or worse than another—is flatly impossible.

Ethnic elements weigh in, as can be seen by comparing Argentina with Guatemala. By 1979, after four years, Argentina's "dirty war" against left-wing subversion was the most celebrated human rights cause of its time. Cameras lingered on the Mothers of the Plaza de Mayo, who marched silently each week to protest mysterious kidnappings and murders. Altogether, *los desaparecidos,* the disappeared, numbered somewhere between eight thousand and ten thousand. This is a staggering figure for a nation of thirty million.

But in the late 1970s and early 1980s, tens of thousands of Guatemalan peasants were strafed, bombed or burned by the napalm which razed whole sweeps of countryside. Intellectuals, union leaders and students were hunted down and slain on the suspicion of leftist leanings. A conservative guess at the death toll is seventy thousand out of a total of eight million. This institutionalized slaughter was reported only sporadically, and it caused little stir. Argentines, of European stock, rate higher than Indians.

Even in the same country, the disparities are wide. At about 2 A.M. on November 16, 1989, intruders roused six Jesuit priest-professors from their beds at the Central American University in San Salvador. They lined up the Jesuits, face down on the grass outside. Methodically, they smashed each skull with assault rifle fire. Finally, they shot the priests' housekeeper and her teenage daughter. The incident, reported throughout the world, brought fierce pressure on the armed forces. For once, there would be trials.

Two days after the priests were slain, eight young men were lined up against a peach-colored wall in a San Salvador neighborhood and cut down with M-16s. The area was mostly evacuated because of heavy fighting. But the youths, most of them players on a neighbor soccer team, had stayed behind to protect their homes from looting. Soldiers shot them without a pause. Doug Mine, who covered El Salvador for the AP, spent ten days ferreting out the facts. His dispatch moved on the AP wire. It made no waves. No one was held to account.

"These guys were just average poor Josés, a couple worked in a soft-drink factory, one was a cook, most were unemployed," Mine wrote me later. "Nobody, beyond their families, much cared that they were killed."

By then, Mine knew what he was up against. He went to Argentina at the tail end of the dirty war, and he watched its aftermath. It hit him so hard that he dropped out for a year to examine human rights abuses in a novel. Then he went to El Salvador to cover another dirty war in full swing.

Mine wrestled with the familiar obstacles. Human rights reporting is almost always political reporting. People are tortured and killed for their ideology, race or religion, all factors of power distribution in an authoritarian state. In denouncing abuses, local human rights groups try to portray the state and its security apparatus as the oppressors, in any way they can. Their information is often accurate. But as sources, they are suspect.

"In ten years, I've not found a local human rights organization that did not mix, to some degree, its humanitarian agenda with a political one," Mine said. International organizations work hard to promote respect for individual liberties, he added, but "it would be impossible for them not to be manipulated occasionally because most information put out by governments or local organizations on the subject of human rights is intended not to inform but to manipulate."

Another problem is the devalued terminology. The phrase "human rights" is hopelessly vague. At one academic seminar on the subject, a speaker condemned summary execution by the thousands in Latin America. Another complained with equal passion that Soviet Jews could not get matzohs on Passover. "Torture" means little on its own. Under an extended definition, most urban police forces in any Western country could qualify. But not many use dental drills for their interrogations. "Genocide," as horrible a word as exists in any language, is thrown around with such currency that when it actually applies in some case it triggers little revulsion.

Statistics by themselves can be too numbing to absorb. Few people can relate to them. Not many Americans took notice of Argentina's abuses until Jacobo Timmerman wrote of his own experiences in a book that was excerpted in the *New Yorker*.

When Biharis and Bengalis fought an ethnic war in East Pakistan, before it separated as Bangladesh, Pakistani officers took some reporters around to see the butchery. My colleagues and I calculated that half a million people had been slaughtered in six weeks—hacked to death, shot, stuffed down wells. Who could relate to such a number? To reflect the horror, I chose an image to start out my dispatch: "Vultures too fat to fly perch along the Ganges . . ."

The new predominance of television has also complicated human rights reporting. When the camera is on, it is a compelling medium. No written words can convey as much as the sound of screams from the next room. But the camera is seldom there. Only rarely can a concealed lens catch sights that guards and escorts want to keep hidden. To a people used to seeing and hearing rather than reading, written reporting omits reality.

The most effective human rights reporting is, as it always was, a careful recounting of the specific facts, with as much detail as possible about the known culprits, set in a wider political frame. Doug Mine put it well:

> Were I asked to counsel a young journalist regarding coverage of human rights, I would recommend that he or she try not to view repression, oppression, abuse or persecution as an issue. Statistics, inaccurate though they may be in this field, are important. But the principal objective is to present a slice of human drama, to describe concrete instances of suffering and anguish that may awaken in a reader a degree of empathy or sympathy or indignation that in turn might provoke a further response. That response, whatever it may be, just might make it more likely that fewer people will be tormented and slain than would have been the case if the story had never been written. And even if there is no response, at least the public will not be able to allege they were unaware of what was going on. Go find victims and their families, go to their homes, earn their trust, share their lives if only for a short time and let them tell what it was like. Only then will the numbers begin to take on meaning.

Chapter 17

# Whatever Happened to Development Journalism?

After things went irretrievably wrong in Somalia, the three networks sent nearly two hundred people among them, counting two anchormen and correspondents from halfway around the world. Meantime, in neighboring Kenya, the staging base for Somalia, things were going uncommonly right. The former English colony, a reputed bright spot on a darkening continent, scheduled its first open elections in twenty-five years. The networks ignored them. And no one was surprised.

A lot was at stake. For years, people agitated to get rid of President Daniel arap Moi, who inherited the job from the old lion, Jomo Kenyatta. Moi amassed a fortune, somewhere in the billions of dollars. He jailed detractors, and some were tortured. Students were stifled, as in China. The opposition, he said, he would crush "like rats." Finally, donors suspended aid until Moi faced the voters. He agreed. Here was a potential example for real democracy in Africa.

Although he disrupted opposition campaigns, stirred up tribes and cheated on election day, international observers agreed that Moi had won in voting that was fair enough. Five candidates split the opposing vote. Democracy was limping back to Kenya. But a month after observers went home, Moi suspended the multiparty parliament after its first day. This was only Africa. Who would notice?

From 1960 to the 1980s, forty independent African countries joined the world community. In 1989, U.S. news organizations paid less attention to all of them put together than to the trial of Zsa Zsa Gabor for slugging a Beverly Hills cop. Or to a few California gray whales trapped in Alaskan ice. And that was when we were watching more closely.

It is not just Africa. Changing winds brought independence to new nations in the South Pacific, as well as to odd bits in the Caribbean and on the South American coast. Malaysia and Singapore emerged in Southeast Asia. The Indian subcontinent, Indonesia and Indochina have been free only since World War II. They joined such "developing" states as Ethiopia and Thailand, more or less free since antiquity, in something called the Third World.

Each new nation had a different sort of start. Some did well, but many went to the other extreme. In the Congo (now Zaire), an overwrought youth at a parade yanked away King Baudouin's sword before the Belgian monarch could hand it over with ceremony. Within months, the new prime minister was beaten to death by rivals, the rich copper-mining province seceded, the diamond region also seceded, tribes went to war, and the United Nations sent combat troops. Within a few years, rebels torched parts of the Congo, murdering and raping Europeans, until white mercenaries and Belgian paracommandos beat them back. And then the CIA helped Joseph-Désiré Mobutu (Sese Seko) seize power.

Every state had serious problems, mixtures of colonial legacies, ethnic rivalries and pressures among people angling for their piece of the spoils. In most, the elites who took power at independence resisted passing it on to anyone else. This meant either coups d'état or frustrated dissidents. And nearly all were left to develop in the shadows, unnoticed by the West—or the North—which focused its spare attention on Vietnam.

Editors could not keep up. An AP supervisor picked up a United Nations dispatch mentioning the Central African Republic, and he barked: "Goddamn it. Don't just say 'central African republic.' Say *which* central African republic."

The few correspondents working in the developing world wrote about wherever they happened to be. Popular bases, such as India and Kenya, were well-covered. When a crisis demanded attention, reporters caught a plane. As time permitted, each cruised a vast territory and wrote "situationers" which wrapped up all the developments since the last trip. Whatever upbeat things they also wrote, they always dug at problems. Reporting, by nature, looks at what is not going according to plan. In between visits, resident news agency stringers covered what could not be ignored.

In the mid-1970s, officials from developing nations got together to complain how they were being covered—or not covered—by the "Western press." They had a point. Overwhelmed by a confusing mass of new names, along with long lists of leaders who often fought one another for power, editors threw up their hands. Even when correspondents made their infrequent visits, their stories often died on the spike.

News from the developing world was, by and large, ill-informed, superficial and sporadic. It focused on the coups and earthquakes. The most violent and chaotic nations captured the headlines. Peaceful ones went through birth and their early years with scarcely a mention. At the same time, there were sensitive, penetrating dispatches from correspondents who worked hard to get things right. Some of today's star journalists did their early work in Africa and Asia, producing balanced copy giving both sides. That leaders did not always like what they read was another matter.

By 1976, this was a virulent international issue. Universities brought together officials, journalists and academics. Intergovernmental committees debated courses of action. Think tanks opined. The players met repeatedly to find common ground. At the biennial general conference of the U.N. Educational, Scientific and Cultural Organization (UNESCO) in Nairobi, the Soviet Union pushed for a resolution that would have sanctified the state control of media.

Stung by the criticism and worried about the implications, American editors suddenly noticed the Third World. Because scrutiny increased, however, complaints grew more strident. The theory was that if reporters wrote at greater length and more often, with emphasis on development, discord would vanish. If Third World journalists and officials exchanged views with Western colleagues, they would merge in a new genre of "developmental journalism." It did not work out that way.

Western news organizations tried at first. In 1975, a news agency editor told me: "If a man writes about Somalia being backward in some respects, we want to be sure he also writes about the successful campaign against illiteracy. It is unfair to point out that the capital has only one stoplight unless we explain that it has no cars, either, and what that means to society." He realized only later that literacy campaigns would not lead Somalia to thriving and peaceful development.

But the conflict was not about misunderstanding. It was a deep philosophical difference over the role of the press in society. Fragile governments wanted cheerleaders to help them attract foreign aid and win over their people to various social experiments. Correspondents felt obliged to work as they did everywhere else in the world, to call things as they saw them.

In 1977, an Indonesian information official told Lew Simons of the *Washington Post:* "These critical reports you've all been making lately hamper our speed of development. They draw the attention of the people away from development to other issues, which creates frustration.... If correspondents employ the Western tradition of hitting issues face-on, they will not achieve their mission. They must follow the slower, more indirect Indonesian way, or else our government will ban foreign journalists and will ignore their reports."

No wonder he was steamed. One of Simons' dispatches began: "Shortly after daybreak one recent morning a herd of gnashing bulldozers rumbled into a quiet neighborhood on the edge of the city and began destroying the small red-tile-roofed houses. The 20 families who lived in the settlement stood quietly by and watched their homes churned into the thick, brown mud. They had been told only the day before that although they held legal deeds to the property, the land had been taken over by a development company that has plans to build a golf course and a luxury housing project."

The company, Simons explained, was owned by a brother of President Suharto and other powerful government figures. The displaced families were assigned to hastily built barracks. One distraught man committed suicide. Another was hospitalized with heart failure.

"A few lines about the incident appeared in one Jakarta newspaper, but no names of the company's officers were printed," Simons wrote. "This kind of incident and others of a far broader magnitude and with far graver consequences occur with regularity in Indonesia. 'The people of this country expect their leaders to enrich themselves and members of their families,' said a Western diplomat. Beneath the unruffled surface, frustration and bitterness are slowly mounting to a boil."

Indonesia expelled a few correspondents and denied visas to others. In some cases, hard reporting continued from the outside. Reporters who got in wrote cautiously, but few did any cheerleading, and the level of hostility grew. By controlling access, Indonesia has kept reporters away from sensitive areas like East Timor. But it has also paid, as editorialists denounced the government as colonialist and brutal.

In nearby Singapore, Prime Minister Lee Kuan Yew ensured that local newspapers shaped whatever image suited his purpose. He tried to enlist foreign correspondents to fall in line and bristled when they did not. In the 1970s, Lee came up with the phrase "rugged society" to suggest tough pioneer nation builders. In the *Washington Post,* Jay Mathews poked a pin in the bubble: "In this city-state built by monumental risk-takers, children are no longer allowed to skateboard in the streets, and Boy Scouts interested in night hikes must settle for walking blindfolded at 4 P.M. Industrious Singapore, once referred to as the 'rugged society,' seems to be going a bit soft."

At the least, the confrontation made editors aware of sensibilities they had ignored. Most asked their correspondents to try to avoid biases and to look at the development process through the eyes of the people about whom they were reporting. But time showed that the political gap was all but unbridgeable.

UNESCO fired the debate, pushed by Director General Amadou Mahtar M'Bow. A Senegalese teacher who enjoyed his power, M'Bow had the perfect issue. By targeting the "Western press," he united almost all of the developing states, the nonaligned nations and the whole Soviet bloc. Some had legitimate complaints. Others wanted weapons to use against obstreperous journalists. Moscow could champion the Third World while winning U.N. support for state control of the domestic press, television and foreign correspondents.

Shadowy committees drafted media policies to help countries impose controls over all reporters working within their borders. Others pushed a plan to license journalists, allowing officials the right to determine who qualified. At the 1978 general conference, UNESCO declared a New World Information and Communications Order (NWICO, for the masochists) to correct imbalances in the "free flow of information."

With help from UNESCO and international news agencies, small states built up their own national news services. Some offered a substantial report delivered by teleprinter. Others produced a weekly mimeographed bulletin.

Meanwhile, Yugoslavia and Cuba joined with India and others to attempt a nonaligned news pool. The idea was to circumvent a system by which the international agencies covered news in one country and sent it to the others. Each state would cover its own news for the rest. At the 1976 summit meeting, fifty-eight nonaligned nations endorsed the pool.

Prime Minister Indira Gandhi of India set the tone: "The media of powerful countries want to depict the governments of their erstwhile colonies as inept and corrupt and their people as yearning for the good old days. Leaders who uphold their national interests and resist the blandishments of multinational corporations and agencies are denigrated and their images falsified in every conceivable way. . . . We want to hear Africans on events in Africa. You should similarly be able to get an Indian explanation of events in India."

The initiative soon sank of its own weight. Western news executives accepted the principle, and a few tried to help get the pool going. But Third World editors found it did not work. The truth, they knew well, was that many leaders *were* inept and corrupt. They did not want to hear Africans on events in Africa if it meant Idi Amin Dada explaining what had happened when Israeli commandos landed in Uganda to take back hostages. If Western agencies missed things, they did not make a policy of denigrating anyone for political reasons. National agencies often did.

The pool demonstrated what was plain from the start. Authoritarian governments did not want more coverage, they wanted favorable coverage. Each censored heavily. When Argentine generals deposed President Isabel Perón in 1976, the official agency, Telam, carried only sports scores from the provinces. Also, there was no universal bond. Editors in Thailand did not want long, lifeless features on fishmeal plants in Tunisia. Like journalists everywhere else, they wanted news.

Western editors who had hoped to replace local stringers with national agencies quickly abandoned the idea. An item about an American arrested on a drug charge might come in over the wire as: "T. Tomson of America . . ." A correspondent, who needed to know it was Theodore T. Thompson, a 29-year-old candy maker from Moose Jaw, Minnesota, tended to distrust the few details that followed.

The debate, meanwhile, plunged into parody. Rhetoric so clouded issues that people could not see the common ground. At a conference in New York, a veteran Asian editor swept an arm dramatically and declaimed: "If any American correspondent wrote about something so boring as the Mekong Project in Thailand, he would be sacked. . . . Editors don't care about such quiet development." By coincidence, the *New York Times* carried a full column on the Mekong Project the next morning.

I gave up on the whole business after debating some academic at another conference. He quoted a short passage criticizing American journalists and attributed it to a spokesman for their kind. He enlisted this unidentified writer, whose name he had forgotten, to refute my argument. The passage sounded familiar, and it took a minute to realize why. He was quoting me. In *Coups and Earthquakes* I had been frank about our failings in what was meant as a balanced presentation of both sides. This guy had me so far out of context he was on another planet.

In the 1980s, the whole issue dissipated as quickly as it had emerged. Working journalists from both sides mostly agreed on what could be fixed and what couldn't. Unlike some of their political leaders, most Third World newspeople have the same commitment to reality as their colleagues elsewhere.

The Pan African News Agency, meant to be a regional model for exchange, withered away at its base in Dakar. James Brooke of the *New York Times* visited PANA after Algeria's worst riots in twenty-five years. For days, editors had waited for the first dispatch. Finally, the telex sputtered, and Algiers came on line. It was a government communiqué. "We can't sell silence," Auguste Mpassi-Muba, the Congolese director, told Brooke. "The one-party states always want to control information."

Many of the American news executives who fought so hard during the first years simply dropped the issue and stopped talking back. They found that State Department officials, who were diplomats and not newspeople, were compromising on principles that could not be negotiated. In such cases, they refused to comply. Then the new Reagan administration pulled the United States out of UNESCO. Britain followed. Frederico Mayor, a Spaniard, took over as director general and set the organization on an opposite course. UNESCO championed a free press as a tool in development.

Third World governments found that editors responded to their press controls by ignoring them. Reporters who could not get a visa to one country went to another. When it came time to parcel out foreign aid, members of Congress leaned toward places they had read something about. News emerging from closed countries is mostly bad news; disgruntled exiles and human rights lobbyists are the only available sources. More tolerant countries saw that reporters actually did write about literacy campaigns and moves toward democracy.

In 1991, new evidence showed that developing societies were not being brainwashed by news from the West. The International Institute of Communications in London watched television on the same night in countries all over the world. "Any worry we had about all or most news flowing from industrialized nations to the Third World is overblown," wrote Everette Dennis, of the Freedom Forum Media Studies Center, analyzing the results. "Television news the world over is quite provincial—mostly local coverage with little connection to the rest of the world. News, in fact, doesn't flow very well at all."

Those people who still recognized the ungainly acronym NWICO carried the debate on into the 1990s. But then the Soviet empire burst into a galaxy of states. Most of the Second World slipped into the Third. Russia, turning westward, was no champion of international press controls. Instead of condemning Western news organizations, officials in many developing countries were trying to learn from them.

If the debate has cooled, much of the problem remains. As more new countries seek coverage and as space diminishes for all world news, frustration is bitter. Decades after the first wave of new nations entered the picture, some newspeople still carry the same misconceptions and biases. Light glares on some stories. On others of equal importance, not a candle flickers.

Altogether, there is not much. In 1991, Compass News Features shut down after seven years of providing specialized dispatches from developing countries. Gerard Loughran, a former UPI editor, helped set it up with funding from the Aga Khan. Compass closed, its managers announced, because of "continuing resistance in the Western world to Third World news."

The *Tyndall Report,* from New York–based researchers, estimated that only 5.6 percent of international news on the main three U.S. networks from 1988 to 1990 was about Africa; without South Africa, Ethiopia and Libya, the figure was less than 1 percent. Without those three countries, Africa got less coverage in 1989 than the trade of hockey star Wayne Gretzky. These numbers were cited in a paper by Sanford Ungar and David Gergen, who offered some suggestions for improving coverage: increase exchanges between African and American journalists, step up minority hiring in American newsrooms, strengthen African journalistic traditions, ease access for correspondents, establish prizes for Africa coverage and provide supplemental information.

These ideas need wherewithal that is now committed elsewhere. Altogether, about two hundred international organizations help journalists improve their work. Nearly all focus on the former Soviet sphere. The World Press Freedom Committee, organized in the United States to counter threats in the 1970s, now directs its efforts toward Central and Eastern Europe. The Center for Foreign Journalists, near Washington, finds U.S. editors and reporters to train Third World journalists. But it is funded heavily by the U.S. government. Independent money, which reinforces the message that the media and the state should be separate, is tough to find.

The genre of developmental journalism, originally seen as a sort of remedial second-tier style to appease authoritarians, has emerged as a valuable specialty. In the hands of skilled practitioners, it tells people in industrial societies about ways of life they might not otherwise fathom. Neither "positive" or "negative," it simply reports what is.

Often, a solid piece of development reporting is not something a head of state wants to see. Kenneth Noble of the *New York Times* went to Kikwit, in Zaire, in 1991 to chronicle what had become of a modern and bustling little agricultural crossroads that the Belgians left in 1960s. He wrote:

> The wheel of history, it almost seems, has come full circle here. Nearly a century ago, when the first Europeans ventured into Zaire's vast interior, Kikwit was a small village whose people and institutions existed in a quiet, self-contained world wholly uninterrupted by the frenetic rhythms of modernity. The village gradually disappeared as a social and cultural force as Belgium, Zaire's colonial ruler, exploited the region's mineral and agricultural wealth, transforming Kikwit into a provincial trading center. A paved highway was built to speed diesel trucks hauling cassava and corn to other regions. While the Belgians were often consummately patronizing to their African subjects, they installed an efficient colonial administration. In time, they introduced health care, water projects, education, telephones and power lines, helping to turn this once isolated village into one of the most affluent and best-tended cities in the core of equatorial Africa.

Kikwit, Noble found, had gone back to the bush. Of the twenty-one stores in a Bandundu Province food chain, one was left, and it was closing. The road from Kinshasa had broken apart, isolating the city of four hundred thousand; main streets had crumbled into dirty sand and disappeared. Squatters overwhelmed old colonial villas, littering the gardens with indescribable filth. Families camped on sidewalks and in cemeteries. Rats and flies, in swarms, added to critical health problems. At night, the sky was lit with only two street lights, one for each remaining nightclub.

"Civilization is coming to an end here," said Rene Kinsweke, manager of the disappearing food chain. "We're back where we started." And Anthony Jones, a former Peace Corps volunteer who worked at a trucking company, one of the last few businesses still functioning, added: "The saddest thing is that most of Zaire seems destined to follow the same fate unless things change soon."

Things were not about to change. Mobutu, still propped up by the United States because he offered "stability," kept a tight course toward the rocks. Every two weeks, he flew his barber over from New York, first class, a trifling expense for a dictator who had stolen billions. That jubilant theft of King Baudouin's sword in 1960 was a telling omen. The evils of colonialism were one thing. But, nearly two generations later, it was clear to the most sympathetic reporters in Zaire and elsewhere that "developing country" was too often a ludicrous euphemism.

But Farid Hossain, the AP correspondent in Bangladesh, wrote a different sort of story from his home village of Kazirpagla, near Dhaka. It was his first trip back in ten years.

"A few years ago, traveling the 20 miles from Dhaka took half a day—a two-mile hike through rice fields to catch the old motor launch, then six hours of chugging upriver. Now it is a 90-minute ride—that long only because one river must be crossed by ferry—and the road that connects Kazirpagla to the capital has moved the farming village forward by a century. . . . 'I call the road an Aladdin's lamp,' said Mohammed Yunus. 'This has brought affluence to my family.' "

The story profiles a transformed village, but it is also about the hundred-mile "World Road" which is linking Dhaka to the south-western port of Khulna, bringing some desperately needed prosperity to an isolated part of an often forgotten country.

In the *Washington Post,* Keith Richburg addressed a question at the heart of development: Why has East Asia in recent decades become a model of economic success while Africa has seen increasing poverty and hunger? He filled half a newspaper page in answering his question. Writing from Nairobi in 1992, Richburg compared his two years in Africa with the four he had spent in Southeast Asia. He started with a quote from Ugandan president Yoweri Museveni, who said Asians "may tend to more discipline than people who take life for granted." But he explored colonialism, ethnic factors, cultural differences, resources, economic systems and leadership. Anyone who survived to the end of the article had a lasting basis for understanding the dilemmas.

The hardest part of developmental journalism is gauging forward movement. Or backward movement. At first, the tendency was to blame the government in power for poverty and instability. When a leader followed Western advice and the economic indicators moved upward, that was a success story. Since general progress was measured by the standards of industrial nations, success was always relative. Then, sensitized by complaints, more reporters looked at base causes—legacies of colonialism, land quality, natural barriers to economic growth—to explain stagnation.

After decades of experience, development specialists settled on a simple conclusion. A crook is a crook, in the First World or the Third. Leaders who do their best for their people, however limited their means, are good leaders. Success or failure does not depend on scale.

Part of the problem can never be solved. A story which seems naive and superficial to an African intellectual might be just what is needed to interest readers who know little context or background. Blaine Harden of the *Washington Post* once began a story on Zambia by describing a high-rise building in which the elevator was raised and lowered by men pulling on the cables; it was broken, and in any case, power was in short supply. After drawing in people who might have skipped on, he also wrote about what was going right.

In the mid-1970s, William German, now executive editor of the *San Francisco Chronicle,* offered me some advice which still applies: "Don't just tell me what happened on a street in Chad. First tell me what the street looks like." Of course, that is only part of it. Chad rarely gets in the paper, in any form.

Chapter 18

# Getting Back
# the News

Who stole the news? Grinches at the top have pushed aside serious reporting for stuff they think will make more money. They have sent fear through an industry built on courage. But that is only part of the picture. We all have a piece of the blame. The news has not really been stolen. It has been mugged, muffled and muzzled, kicked into corners and left to atrophy, pumped out of shape or ignored altogether. Sometimes it obscures everything else around it. Or it is dismembered and stuffed into ignoble little parcels labeled "The World in Brief."

We can get the news back, with little fuss and no more money than we are already spending, but we have to decide to do it. Readers must say what they want. Correspondents must provide it. And then, if editors open the gates, the rest will follow. Grinches, making money with a clear conscience, can smile again. When official or amateur manipulators attempt to meddle, we will all, in chorus, invite them to go screw. It is that simple.

No one will open a bureau in Utopia. We cannot change the underlying problems, which are based on human foibles. As T. S. Eliot warns, "Human kind cannot bear very much reality." But Ross Perot can tell you about perking up latent interest in people thought to be lost somewhere in their couches. All parts of the system can do better by degree, and that will help.

At newspapers and broadcast stations, better world coverage would actually save money. Each must maintain its own reporters to fill the columns and segments devoted to secondary local news. But foreign correspondents are already out there. Their output arrives in torrents, like so much electronic junk mail, and gets thrown away unread. Careful editing would leave room for news that matters, local or foreign.

The best newspaper editors already approach this standard, proving that it can work, in New York, Los Angeles, Washington and Chicago, in Dallas, Philadelphia, Miami, Atlanta, Detroit, Houston and San Francisco, in St. Petersburg and Anniston, Alabama, and a lot of other places. These editors could do better, but their principle is sound: Anything that gets in the paper, from down the block or from Venus, must justify its space. Before readers see it, editors have worked it over.

Similarly, the best news directors at stations around the country think hard about air time. Local news must be a first priority; that is where they compete. Networks are supposed to supply the world news. But they know the networks are not enough. They use their budgets to focus attention on the biggest stories which they might do well on their own. Their principle, too, is that any story must earn its air, nearby or far away.

For the networks, doing better requires only a shift in focus. Analysts who pronounce the death of over-the-air network news are a trifle premature. The big three far outshadow CNN in audience. Often, they do a better job. Round-the-clock coverage is helpful, but solid content, whoever provides it, is more important. Networks can use more from good correspondents already in place. By trimming needless live coverage and anchor road shows, they would have money within existing budgets to send crews to vital stories they now ignore. Air time is already there; it takes only a decision to allocate it differently.

Billions of dollars are involved, but the "media" are cottage industries. Making them better depends on each individual who fashions their products and on each customer who buys the products, one piece at a time. We all stole the merchandise. We all can give it back.


Editors come first because they watch the door. It doesn't matter what correspondents produce or consumers want if the editors cannot put those two groups together. Coverage would improve overnight if sensible professionals who understood the shape of the world stepped in to straighten out the channels. The talent is out there. Good editors cost the same as bad ones.

Every news organization, from a television network to a small daily, needs two levels of committed editors. At the top, someone must decide to reflect reality from abroad. Further down, someone must carry out this decision. The rest of the system cannot help but follow. Correspondents would rise happily to the occasion.

The news agencies will respond. They are general suppliers, equipped to fill any order. Their customers talk all at once, and a few outshout the others. They have to guess at what is needed and play safe with a low common denominator. If more quality is demanded, it can be provided.

Editors who keep correspondents abroad deserve everyone's gratitude, especially those not forced do it because of the competition, and others might follow their example. There is already plenty of capacity as a base to build upon.

Every situation differs. Relying on their own feel and surveys, editors must decide what their market wants. If it is potato chip soufflé recipes and school board scandals, they are bound to provide it; they run a business. But whole pages? They can also find space for what others want, what everyone needs and what the public trust expects of them: serious treatment of news. More and more, other readers will acquire the taste.

Common wisdom is that local news sells and foreign news does not. Surveys and experience throw this notion into serious doubt, but let us assume that it is true. Then what? Too many editors overfill their news holes with overwritten or pointless local copy. Then they spray world news into the cracks, like liquid insulation. People make no sense of it. In focus groups, they say they skip over it. And the world slips further out of sight.

At a medium-sized southwestern paper, I once asked the news editor how much space he had for foreign news. It's not the size of the news hole that counts, he replied, it's what you put in it. In his case, size also counted. The executive editor had shoved aside substance for long, often soppy, local features. His best copy editor quit in disgust. The news editor had to treasure every free inch, ensuring each dispatch had a clear point, a so-what paragraph to explain its meaning and enough flavor to leave a mark on readers. If he could have worked on a larger canvas, his city would have been better served.

Attitudes pass unwittingly to the public. Once I spoke to a group of Arizona editors, and one of them asked: "What makes you think that miners in San Manuel give a damn about Zambia?" He pulled Zambia out of the air as one of those funny-sounding places about which he clearly did not give a damn. Zambia, I said, produced copper. Trouble there shook the world price. Little is more crucial to copper miners in San Manuel.

This touches on responsibility. A dogfight in Brooklyn is not more important than a revolution in China. It never was. But embattled mandarins might once have been of only academic interest to Americans protected on both sides by oceans. No longer. Like it or not, the United States is riding shotgun for the free world. The bushes are alive with bandits. Economically, the world is up for grabs. New businesses down the block are willing to try anything for a foot in the door. In such a state, who tells the people what they need to know? The schools? The government?

Editors can make their readers and their viewers understand this. But even if they could not, they would owe serious coverage to that body of citizens that does not have to be convinced. Here is a simple sixty-second exercise for gatekeepers at every level: Each morning, while shaving or applying makeup, look in the mirror for a full minute and ask yourself for an update on your mission in journalism. Then go on to work.

We correspondents have no less responsibility. For all the apparatus above us—the corporate structure, the commentators who interpret raw data, the cheerleaders who write house ads—we are where the rubber meets the road. However loud it may boast or whatever its stars may earn, no organization is better than its lowest paid stringer in Amnesiastan. In fact, if any of its reporters foul up, all of "the media" pay.

We are harder to control. Mostly, we answer to our own consciences. Editors place a general trust in us, and we have to make good on the details; they are too far away to check up. Like the editors, we would benefit from that morning minute at the mirror. Better, ten minutes. We must each try to dig deeper and think more clearly. If we don't, we have to depend on our bosses to replace us. People seldom turn themselves in for incompetence.

Gross misfeasance is not the issue. Most correspondents are too singleminded for that. It comes with the calling. One time, a colleague and I interviewed mothers of torture victims in Buenos Aires. In the cathedral, an old woman held us spellbound. She was so compelling that we forgot to ask her name, and the desk would demand it. The interview was lost. "Why shouldn't we just make up a name, Maria López Martínez, or something?" my friend asked. "No one ever comes looking. We don't give an address. It doesn't matter. She's just a wonderful old woman speaking for others in her place." We both laughed. You don't do that.

But I've known the odd reporter who would make up not only the name but also the quote. The rationalization is that this is a literary device which reflects the true situation. It is also dishonest, lazy and a further erosion of standards already under enough pressure. We make up a professional collective, like it or not, and amateurs endanger our credibility. Years later, people remember the jerks at those Riyadh briefings, not Richard Pyle, who persistently and coherently forced briefers to say something. One reporter who called on a colonel ran into Geraldo Rivera, scowling, on his way out. Geraldo, the colonel said, wanted to do a piece on lesbian voodoo rites among female soldiers. Like the rest, he was "media personnel."

So what to do? Certainly nothing formal. The point of a free press is that it is self-cleansing. That it does not always clean itself is beside the point. There is no better alternative. Peer councils would have neither authority nor respect. If there is need, we come together. When we identify a wrongdoer in our ranks, we get him one way or another. You'll have to trust us.

Our main challenge is to keep in mind who is counting on us. Too often, we write for one another. "Most foreign reporting is flat unless the correspondent remembers the breakfast table back home," observed Kevin Buckley, a former *Newsweek* reporter who is now executive editor of *Playboy*. He was right. Reporting is about people, and it is for people. We must take readers or viewers along, step by step, through complex situations. We have to help them across cultural bridges. Events and emotion in one society must be shown in terms that relate to people in another.

Simple devices can make this connection. In Guatemala, death squads in the Mayan backcountry influence the price of coffee. Jim Sterba of the *Wall Street Journal* drew readers into rural India with one of his signature intros: He named the U.S. cities for which Indian laborers make manhole covers. When Polish workers rose in Solidarity against Communists, I felt their mood on the road with truckers. Their traveling music was Willie Nelson.

*Harper's* magazine, to show the gulf between the First World and the Third, reproduced the pay slip of a woman named Sadiah who works at a Nike shoe factory in Indonesia. In 1992, her net monthly earnings for ten-and-a-half-hour shifts, six days a week, were $37.46. That is half the retail price of the shoes she makes. At that rate, it would take her 44,492 years to earn what Michael Jordan made for endorsing her product.

With no direct link, human detail can be enough. Everyone can relate to people half a world away if they recognize familiar sentiments. When a little boy toppled down a well in Italy, he brought Americans to edge of their chairs almost as quickly as a little girl in Texas. It works both ways. The film *Home Alone* was a hit everywhere. To evoke interest in an African famine, effective reporters go beyond numbing numbers to write about Abdi Ibrahim Mohammed, age five.

We can look harder at what is working, how other societies have solved problems that overwhelm the United States. Often, blinded by their own lights, Americans miss the obvious elsewhere. Correspondents have to pierce those ethnocentric mental barriers. During 1992, a dentist in San Francisco worried that I would not be around for him to finish a simple job on my teeth. I assured him there were dentists in France. He looked doubtful.

A shift in approach has been dawning on us for some time. In 1968, Seymour Topping came home to be foreign editor of the *New York Times*. He wrote to his correspondents: "We can be less preoccupied with the daily official rhetoric of the capitals. We should report more about how the people live, what they and their societies look like, how their institutions and systems operate. Our report should reflect more fully the social, cultural, intellectual, scientific and technological revolutions which, more than the political, are transforming the world society. And to comprehend, our readers must have more sophisticated interpretive writing."

A new breed of journalist has to dig deeper into societies to show how their failings affect the wider world. We have skirted corruption, for example, in a patronizing belief that it is simply part of life in other places. But if Honduran generals traffic drugs into the United States, in full view of U.S. officials who want their support, this is a story. If American backing allows a President Mobutu of Zaire to terrorize his people and steal billions, we should say so.

In the early 1990s, the AIDS virus blitzed India, spreading from prostitutes to young bachelors and men in cities who had left families in villages. Authorities did little, declaring that AIDS was no problem because Indians were not promiscuous. Elsewhere in Asia, the epidemic expanded fast. U.N. field experts tried to intervene but were limited by scant resources and official restraints. By the time reporters caught on, it was too late for millions. Stories like these should break earlier.

We have to keep track of events to be sure leaders keep their stories straight. The White House, in 1990, committed half a million troops to defend a medieval kingdom where women could not drive, let alone vote, and thieves' hands were amputated. Soldiers were told they were there to protect democracy. The president said the message was that America would not tolerate aggression. The secretary of state said it was about jobs. And everyone knew it was really about oil. If it was about democracy, how did we affect Kuwait and Saudi Arabia? If it was about aggression, where were we during the next abuse? And if it was about jobs, what was the result?

Throughout the 1992 campaign, George Bush boasted that children could now sleep safely. We might have chimed in: The Soviet arsenal is fragmented, with lots of fingers on triggers. China is buying much of it. Black marketeers are after nuclear components. Japan has plutonium. The Balkans are boiling. The Kremlin was a threat, but it policed its satellites and clients. How out of touch are we?

Governments do not level with citizens about domestic affairs. When the scene shifts abroad, governments cannot level with citizens. Each administration has a foreign policy to sell. But more, Washington's ability to see the world is sharply limited. Correspondents have got to report the news, more effectively than ever. And we've all got to stop stealing it.

All who purvey the news might do well to deglamorize the system and step back from the spotlight a few paces. After CNN did its laudable job in Baghdad, the producer responsible for much of it, Robert Wiener, wrote a behind-the-scenes book. A *Washington Post* reporter, reviewing it, paid tribute to the job done, but he noted:

"Barely a sentence passes in this book without some kind of inter-jection by Wiener to remind the reader that he was there. . . . Ulti-mately, 'Live from Baghdad' exposes the lack of journalistic depth to Ted Turner's lieutenants working at 'ground zero' in the field."

I could see what had gotten to the reviewer. In my copy, I'd underlined a passage that explained how awestruck an American diplomat was to be on television. "It was only natural that he felt flattered," Wiener wrote. "Being on a first-name basis with network anchors can be heady stuff for civilians. Hell, it could even be heady for some journalists." Civilians?

On differing levels, this sort of hubris taints the business. Re-porters, anchors and editors in the window may be good at their work, but so are a lot of other professionals and craftspeople. The spotlight, if it happens to be around, adds nothing but distraction. There's nothing attractive about the nickname correspondents use among themselves, hacks, but it ought to keep us in our place.

But readers and viewers face the biggest challenge. If the sup-pliers have not done better, it is because consumers have not de-manded it. Who would dream of having a tonsil out, or a toilet fixed, without asking about the person doing it? If surgeons or plumbers foul up, they are sued. But who asks about the people who presume to be covering the world? Customers howl when a merchant does them wrong. Why do newspeople get off so easily?

Get involved. Learn about local newspapers and broadcasters. Try out larger papers from somewhere else. Or magazines that promise something different. Switch on NPR and BBC, if you can find it. Shop around for the best network news, and then let all three know why you made your final choice. Watch CNN but don't believe the hype. Make your own decisions and then write Atlanta. Write letters to individuals. Get your friends and clubs to do the same. Complain. Lobby. Explain.

When something impresses you, say so. Most likely, a gleeful editor will clutch your letter and race up to the publisher's office with it. You think I'm joking. Subscribe to newspapers and give them a chance. If they disappoint you, drop them and tell the editor why. An irate call to a bored and overworked circulation clerk makes no impact. That is like walking out on a French waiter, who then has one less table to worry about. Write to the boss.

Letters to a specific editor make an impact; editors' names are on the masthead. "Personal" on the envelope helps move it along. The more thoughtful and specific the argument, the deeper it will penetrate. Station managers and network executives are used to numbers, percentages, focus group reports, so any serious communication from real human beings cannot help but make an impact. They are harder to reach than newspaper editors. But each of them lives and dies on the ability to read public mood.

Interested groups can write collective letters, or organize letter-writing campaigns so different points of view get across. In communities, editors can be invited to speak to organizations. During the questions that follow, they learn from their audience. Consumer advocates know how little it can take to convince corporate executives to alter course. It is often easy in the news business. Pressure tactics are less effective, and crank letters go in the garbage. What works is anything that sounds to the gatekeepers like the legitimate voice of the people they are already trying their best to reach.

If there is no change, consumers can do what they do when there aren't enough nuts in the Hershey bar. Readers who don't like one paper can subscribe to another. Television viewers only have to switch the channel. If there is a groundswell, it will be felt.

It takes some effort to make the most of the good reporting already out there. But there is plenty. Get to know bylines of correspondents and columnists. Note what they say in February and check it against July. Or the following February. You will find the ones who get things right.

When you read a newspaper, examine the sources. Who is named and why? If someone is not named, is there a good reason? Do facts back up the assertions? Soon enough, you'll be able to separate good reporting with protected sources from shortcut reporting where the correspondent did too little legwork.

When you watch television, notice the correspondent's dateline. If it is narration from a studio in London and Tokyo, shake out the grain of salt. Try to identify the source of the videotape. Networks are seldom much help in this. Blurring over the line helps cover up rounded corners. And remember the word "exclusive" is not very useful and not always honest. It's a hucksters' word.

Finally, there are those two tools, as useful as fire and the wheel: suspended belief and triangulation. Don't believe anyone's copy without conditions. Register it. React if it says a nuclear warhead is headed to a neighborhood near you. But check it. Reporters always seek a second source. So should readers. Triangulation is the extension of this process. Find another source but also look for pictures and more background. By looking a little harder, you'll find out why you should be interested.

Readers, correspondents and editors all have the same goal. We need a daily running record of human events, backed up by fuller briefings for people who want more. Whether they watch, listen or read, Americans have to depend on news organizations for guidance on what is really important. We need solid news judgment, not a carnival barker's flair for what appeals. We must repair the swarm's radar and split the pack so that reporters can cover more than one story at a time. The point is not whether to give people what they want or what they need. It is helping them see why what they need is also what they want.

In the end, doing better depends on the people in boardrooms who chart policy. Some are convinced that well-presented foreign news will feed a new demand. But too many others, in the belief that world news is a luxury for a minority, are reluctant to provide something people may never want. They raise the inevitable question: Why should Americans care about foreign news?

The simple answer seems to be fading from fashion. People have to be informed, and news executives assume a traditional responsibility to inform them. By not telling readers, viewers, and listeners what they need to know, they betray a public trust. According to a new view expressed once by a network executive who also sold lightbulbs, however, companies have an equal duty to make money for their stockholders, whatever the product.

But there is a more complex answer. Every story has some impact, however indirect. A coup that paralyzes Haiti could be a problem if it happens in early spring; Haiti is where all the baseballs are made. Sometimes you needn't stretch so far. A quarrel over well fields under remote marshes could mean that soon your brother will come home in a body bag.

In explaining why the world is too fearsome to follow, Don Kellermann of Times-Mirror Survey, put it: "I can worry about my own grandchildren, but how can I worry about every grandchild in the world? It is too much to absorb." But with a different angle on the same example, Bill Ahearn, the AP's executive editor, explained why he was aiming so much of his budget at international coverage: "Much of what we report concerns our children's lives—this is not a country, it's a world. I think about my five-year-old, my two-year-old."

Ahearn is right. A BBC executive, asked why the admirable Beeb worked so hard at news, replied with emblematic understatement: "A world that is well-informed is a world that is rather safer." No nation can defend itself against an enemy it does not understand. This applies to a hostile nation, a predatory economic bloc or a climate that is quietly frying you toward extinction. "Patriotism," observed Stephen Cohen in the *Nation,* "is never having to say you didn't know."

James Hoge, editor of *Foreign Affairs,* noted, "We have yet to discover a period of human history when there was a stable world order without a strong lead player." Americans cannot withdraw from that role even if they want to. Individually, Americans worry most about the economy. But without concerted international action, Hoge said, steps to address the American economy amount to raindrops in the ocean. Issues that matter—the environment, drugs, trade—are global issues.

It is the simplest of concepts. We take notice of threats, human and natural, so that we can act while there is still time. Our lives, or at least our grandchilden's lives, depend on it.

And self-interest is only part of it. Why should anyone care about anything? In any given year, with no more money than the government now spends, Americans can save at least a million lives. In 1991, by paying attention, we could have spared the world a war. In 1992, we could have saved whole societies. The real question is, What kind of people are we? Are we really too busy to notice what is happening within our line of sight, possibly heading our way?

Back in the 1960s, New York City shocked itself with the case of Kitty Genovese, a woman who was raped in full view of neighbors who did nothing to help. She lay there, pleading for help, until she died. No one wanted to get involved. Later, there was great handwringing; what had become of humanity? If you take the case to the *n*th power, that's the answer to why Americans should care about foreign news.

Serious change will come if the people who are surveyed and focus-grouped and measured by feel ever manage to let enough news executives know that they want something better. Knickerbocker's madmen are ready to respond if anyone wants to listen. In 1989, I wrote an essay for the Freedom Forum Media Studies Center. The "amens" in my mail were overwhelming evidence of what was on my colleagues' minds. The essay started out along these lines:

Little in America today can electrify the human soul like those dog-eared lists, fat as Omaha phonebooks, on pedestals at the entrance to the Vietnam Veterans Memorial. Their 793 pages of war dead name 145 Zs alone, 8 Zuñigas and 19 Zimmermans. There are 5 McNamaras and 33 Kennedys.

As you walk past those names, each etched into black granite, the rows start out ankle-high. They soon reach your waist. Before you know it, you are in over your head. Then the wall of names recedes, and you look up the Mall. Beyond the obelisk honoring the first American president, the man who shaped our basic values, you see the Capitol dome, under which those values are to be kept freshly defined.

The memorial is a stunning monument to America's will to do the right thing in a world badly in need of someone's help. Even more, it marks Americans' stubborn refusal to pay enough attention to determine what the right thing is.

# INDEX

070.4332 R813w        940615
Rosenblum, Mort
Who Stole the News?

070.4332 R813w        940615
Rosenblum, Mort
Who Stole the News?

| DATE DUE | BORROWER'S NAME |
|---|---|
| MAR 15 1995 | *(signature)* |
| | |
| | |
| | |